RETRIEVING
HISTORY

EVANGELICAL RESSOURCEMENT
ANCIENT SOURCES FOR THE CHURCH'S FUTURE

D. H. Williams, series editor

The Evangelical *Ressourcement* series is designed to address the ways in which Christians may draw upon the thought and life of the early church to respond to the challenges facing today's church.

RETRIEVING HISTORY

Memory *and* Identity Formation *in the* Early Church

STEFANA DAN LAING

Baker Academic
a division of Baker Publishing Group
Grand Rapids, Michigan

Published by Baker Academic
a division of Baker Publishing Group
P.O. Box 6287, Grand Rapids, MI 49516-6287
www.bakeracademic.com

Printed in the United States of America

Library of Congress Cataloging-in-Publication Data
Names: Laing, Stefana Dan, 1971– author.
Title: Retrieving history : memory and identity formation in the early church / Stefana Dan Laing.
Description: Grand Rapids : Baker Academic, 2017. | Includes bibliographical references and index.
Identifiers: LCCN 2016059364 | ISBN 9780801096433 (pbk.)
Subjects: LCSH: Memory—Religious aspects—Christianity. | Church history—Authorship. |
    Church history—Historiography. | Identity (Psychology)—Religious aspects—Christianity. |
    Identification (Religion)
Classification: LCC BV4597.565 .L35 2017 | DDC 270.1072—dc23
LC record available at https://lccn.loc.gov/2016059364

17 18 19 20 21 22 23   7 6 5 4 3 2 1

In keeping with biblical principles of creation stewardship, Baker Publishing Group advocates the responsible use of our natural resources. As a member of the Green Press Initiative, our company uses recycled paper when possible. The text paper of this book is composed in part of post-consumer waste.

To Fulga Pascu Dan and Emanuel Titus Dan[†],
fellow pilgrims and citizens of the Heavenly City,
my first and best teachers,
who sped me along the path of historical studies
and always urged me to use my discipline
in the service of the church.

CONTENTS

SERIES PREFACE

THE EVANGELICAL RESSOURCEMENT: Ancient Sources for the Church's Future series is designed to address the ways in which Christians may draw upon the thought and life of the early church to respond to the challenges facing today's church. The term *ressourcement* was coined by French Roman Catholic writers in the mid-twentieth century as descriptive of theological renewal that declared Christians must return to the sources (*ad fontes*) of the ancient Christian tradition. The operative assumption was that the church is apostolic (formed and directed by the Old and New Testaments) and also patristic (indebted to the intellectual and spiritual legacy of the fathers of the church). Much of our understanding of the Bible and theological orthodoxy, directly or indirectly, has come through the interpretive portals of the early church, which is an integral part of the Protestant identity, no less than it is for Roman Catholicism or Eastern Orthodoxy.

Using the methods and tools of patristic scholarship, each series volume is devoted to a particular theme related to biblical and theological interpretation. Similar to the past practices of *ressourcement*, this series is not seeking to appropriate the contributions of the early church in an idealized sense but through a critical utilization of the fathers as the church's primary witnesses and architects for faithfully explicating the Christian faith. Series readers will see how (1) both Scripture and the early tradition were necessary for the process of orthodox teaching, (2) there is a reciprocal relationship between theology and the life of the church, (3) the liberty of the Spirit in a believer's life must be balanced with the continuity of the church in history, and

(4) the Protestant Reformation must be integrated within the larger and older picture of what it means to be catholic. In effect, it is the intention of this series to reveal how historical Protestantism was inspired and shaped by the patristic church.

As Protestantism confronts the postdenominational and, in many ways, post-Christian world of the twenty-first century, it is vital that its future identity not be constructed apart from the fullness of its historical foundations. Seminal to these foundations is the inheritance of the early church, "that true, genuine Christianity, directing us to the strongest evidence of the Christian doctrine" (John Wesley). Therein Christians will find not a loss of their distinctiveness as Protestants but, as the sixteenth-century Reformers found, the resources necessary for presenting a uniquely Christian vision of the world and its message of redemption.

PREFACE

THE YEAR 2014 marked the twenty-fifth anniversary of the government repression of protesters in China's Tiananmen Square. It also marked twenty-five years since the fall of the Berlin Wall and the Iron Curtain in Eastern Europe. As a commemoration, journalist and NPR China correspondent Louisa Lim released a volume in 2015 titled *The People's Republic of Amnesia: Tiananmen Revisited*.[1] For the Chinese people, the events of June 4, 1989, are a dim memory if a memory at all, since the government has chosen to suppress and expunge that event from the collective memory. No public commemorations of the event are allowed at the square, which has been repaved to cover traces of blood. Security is tight on anniversary days to prevent any public demonstrations. Government censorship of the internet ensures that information regarding the events remains scant and unavailable. Since a memory of the power of collective solidarity has been erased from the media and history books, millions of Chinese young people are growing up without any knowledge of the events of June 4, 1989. This has led to politically apathetic young people and a content but vigilant Communist Party propagating an "amnesiac drug of shallow nationalism."[2]

By contrast, Romania, which experienced the bloodiest revolution of all the Communist bloc countries, has sought to keep alive the memories of the 1989 revolution. In and around the central square in

1. Louisa Lim, *The People's Republic of Amnesia: Tiananmen Revisited* (Oxford: Oxford University Press, 2015). Lim formerly reported for the BBC.
2. Andrew J. Nathan, endorsement for Lim, *People's Republic of Amnesia*, available at http://www.oupcanada.com/catalog/9780190227913.html.

my father's hometown of Cluj-Napoca, travelers can see inscriptions and monuments commemorating the unarmed civilians who were brutally slain by government forces. An especially moving sculpture of seven huge asymmetrical bronze columns stands in one corner of Union Plaza (Piața Unirii). It is called Stâlpii Împușcați, literally translated as "Shot Pillars." The sculpture represents those who were killed in the square on December 21, 1989. In addition to this public memorial, in 2014 on the twenty-fifth anniversary, a volume of photographs documenting the events was released with the same title as the sculpture, commemorating "A quarter century with the Martyrs of the December 1989 Revolution in Cluj-Napoca."[3] My uncle Nelu explained to me that the sculpture represents those slain as present rather than absent. The dead are not gone, he explained; they are still present among us. For those who remain, the "martyrs'" example of courage is publicly visible, inspiring viewers to boldness in the face of repression, and confronting the socially and politically apathetic to action and hope. In fact, several groups present at the memorial displayed a banner that read, "History will not forgive us if we forget it." The eventual overthrow of the Communist Party and dismantling of its structures were a tribute to those who had risked their lives in the square that winter day. Despite its admission into the European Union in 2007, Romania has not fully recovered politically, socially, or economically. Nonetheless the people have a collective narrative of overcoming, examples of courage and sacrifice, and memories to remind them that a tyrannical atheistic regime cannot keep the faithful subjugated forever. It is God who raises up and topples regimes.

Not surprisingly, China's reaction to the Romanian revolution was to watch in dismay as the people prevailed while chanting Christian slogans on their knees and out in the open, after four decades of atheistic dominance. "God exists!" they shouted. The Chinese continue to be perturbed, no doubt, by pro-democratic demonstrators around the world (even in neighboring Hong Kong and Taiwan) who will not allow the suppression of China's collective memory. They understand that the loss of collective memory is closely followed by loss of identity as a people striving for freedom and democracy.

3. Radu Feldiorean and Ioan Cioba, *Stâlpii Împușcați* (Eikon, 2014). This volume showcases the photographs of Razvan Rotta, documenting the events of December 21, 1989. Accessed at http://www.clujazi.ro/galerie-foto-cluj-napoca-25-de-ani-de-la-revolutia-din-1989/. For an interesting piece on political and ethnic statuary in Cluj-Napoca, see Paul Stirton, "Public Sculpture in Cluj/Kolosvár: Identity, Space and Politics," in *Heritage, Ideology, and Identity in Central and Eastern Europe: Contested Pasts, Contested Presents*, ed. Matthew Rampley (Martlesham, Suffolk: Boydell, 2012), 41–66.

The Importance of This Material

One more alarming example of the attempt to destroy collective memory is evident in the recent operations of ISIS. In the summer of 2014, ISIS devastated ancient Christian communities in Mosul, Iraq (ancient Nineveh), intentionally destroying Judeo-Christian religious archaeological sites and churches, as well as important archaeological ruins in the city of Palmyra in Syria the following year. These radicals are attempting to wipe out history, obliterating any indication of the presence of Christianity in the Middle East (admittedly their fanatical destructiveness is not limited to Jewish and Christian sites). They also understand that memory—that is, a sense of one's antiquity and received heritage—and identity are a powerful combination for the continued existence and sustenance of nations and religions.

The chief importance of the ancient texts examined in this work is that they demonstrate that the past affects the present and future, and they show how that process unfolded in a particular period within the church's history. Familiarity—and even more, direct engagement—with the sources both reveals and forms an identity: the encounter can elucidate for Christians our heritage of belief, devotion, and action, to be remembered, celebrated, emulated, and shared. This heritage was bequeathed to us by ancient disciples of Jesus; it constitutes "things we have heard and known and that our fathers have passed down to us," as described in Psalm 78:3 (HCSB). Like Israel, we have a responsibility to pass it further: "We must not hide them from [our] children, but must tell a future generation the praises of the LORD, His might, and the wonderful works He has performed" (78:4 HCSB). As the psalm proceeds, it sets up the polarities of remembering and forgetting, and the spiritual ramifications of each. When the Israelites remembered God and his deeds in the life of their nation, they remembered to keep the torah he established; when Israel forgot God and "the wonderful works He had shown them" (78:11 HCSB), the result was disbelief, apostasy, and outright rebellion.

Why Evangelicals Need This Book

Free Church evangelicalism has entered into a period of identity crisis, whether it is termed that way or not: churches increasingly reflect the culture of the moment, with its emphasis on faddishness, gimmickry, and entertainment, and turn to culture rather than mining their own heritage for stalwart examples of homily, liturgy, discipleship, leadership, evangelism, and so on. In fact, I wonder if the martyrs and other early Christians would recognize today's churches, modeled as they are on the mall, warehouse, stadium, and theater. We must recognize the existing continuity between the ancient church and us—who we *were* shows us who we *are* and challenges us to be who we ought *to be* in the future. While Israel was admonished to "remember" and to stand at the crossroads seeking out the "ancient paths," the church today is merely looking *around* rather than looking *back*. Walking in the "good way" of those ancient paths was supposed to grant "rest for your souls" (Jer. 6:16). Instead, taking their cue from the surrounding Canaanite culture, Israel stumbled, choosing the "side roads, not the highway"; the cause for such a diversion is equally clear: "My people have *forgotten* me; they make offerings to false gods" (Jer. 18:15, emphasis added). Evangelicals can benefit from looking back in order to remember the work of God in building his church through faithful men and women who tried to live out the gospel under a wide range of circumstances. Historical and spiritual amnesia is not a viable option and can even prove disastrous.

Truthfully, there exist both similarities and differences between us and early Christians, and I do not suggest that they were just like us or the reverse. There does exist a clear continuity and "family resemblance," however, between the apostles, martyrs, mothers and fathers of the church, and believers today, so that we can derive immense and immediate benefit and even refreshment from reading the works of early Christians. Further, their works, which were intended for posterity, became our history in that many patristic writers composed historical material with an eye toward the future. In other words, they wrote for the church, and we are their intended recipients. We ought, therefore, to pay our forebears in the faith—the "cloud of witnesses" of Hebrews 11–12—the respect of looking at the material they left for us. Although much of it has been ravaged by time and circumstance, we ought to try our best to understand what they wanted to tell us.

Evangelicals also need to read this material to defuse the suspicion with which they often regard late patristic and early medieval Christianity. Evangelicals tend to accept (outright or implicitly) the idea of a chasm between New Testament Christianity and the Reformation, concluding that true and biblical Christianity was absent from the mainstream church between the apostles and Luther. These sectarian views rob their adherents of the benefit of a broader perspective on their own history as well as their place in a long and rich metanarrative.

Issues of Genre

Whereas patristic introductions typically deal with the fathers' doctrinal works, this book will focus primarily on their historical works.

It shows how diverse genres (spiritual biography, apology, heresiology) overlap with history because an author has taken a historical approach to such things as commemorating those who fell in persecution, depicting examples of discipleship, defending a sound faith or scrutinizing unsound challenges to that faith, and telling the story of the church. So while there is an attempt to distinguish between kinds of historical writing by introducing four historical forms, the fluidity of genre must also be taken into account. For example, some of the martyrological accounts may be characterized chiefly as hagiography, but they also contain apologetic and/or polemical speeches (as in the trials of Pionius and Apollonius). Irenaeus's heresiological work *Against Heresies*, while scathing in its polemic, also contains critical (and sometimes lilting) passages of constructive theology on the doctrines of creation and theological anthropology, expounding upon the pivotal importance of the *imago Dei* in humans. There also appears to be some degree of reciprocity between church history and apologetic literature, which intersect in some interesting ways.

Another Introduction to the Early Church?

A steady stream of recent publications serves as introductions to the church fathers. Recent examples include Paul Foster's volume *Early Christian Thinkers* (IVP Academic, 2010), Bradley Green's *Shapers of Christian Orthodoxy* (IVP Academic, 2010), Bryan Litfin's *Getting to Know the Church Fathers: An Evangelical Introduction* (2nd ed., Baker Academic, 2016), and Michael Haykin's *Rediscovering the Church Fathers: Who They Were and How They Shaped the Church* (Crossway, 2011). Joan Petersen's book *Handmaids of the Lord* (Cistercian, 1996) introduces the lives of some "church mothers," female ascetics from the patristic period, while Hans von Campenhausen's *The Fathers of the Church* (Hendrickson, 2000) combines his two classic and enduring volumes *The Fathers of the Greek Church* (1955) and *The Fathers of the Latin Church* (1960). This present book does not intend to be an introduction to patristics; it assumes that the reader already has some familiarity with the period, although I have taken some measures to introduce key figures who may be unfamiliar to the reader and to provide a bit of context for them. The volumes of the Evangelical *Ressourcement* series are building upon these introductory works, bolstered by a recent healthy uptick of interest in history and what it has to offer (John Fea, *Why Study History?* [Baker Academic, 2013]), as well as more technical and methodological interests (as in Jay Green, *Christian Historiography: Five Rival Versions* [Baylor University Press, 2015]).

This book spans the period (roughly) from the apostles to the Council of Chalcedon (451) and gives attention to some figures who are mainstays among the church fathers, but it does not focus *exclusively* on those in the mainstream. It also includes and introduces figures who are less well known outside the world of patristic scholarship. For example, chapter 4 on martyrology before the Constantinian "Peace" includes well-known martyrs like Polycarp, Perpetua, and the martyrs of Lyons, but also lesser known (but no less important) martyrs, such as Pionius, Carpus, Phileas, and Agape and her companions.[4] Chapter 5 on hagiography after the "Peace" features Athanasius's classic *Life of Antony*, but also treats in detail Gregory of Nyssa's *Life of Macrina* and Gerontius's *Life of Melania*. These Christians' friends and followers composed or preserved accounts of their lives and deaths that amply demonstrate the literary and historiographical features treated in this volume. Chapter 6 on church history includes Eusebius, the best-known writer (and pioneer) in this literary genre, yet we also want to look at the continuation of his legacy via several less well-known historians—Socrates Scholasticus, Sozomen, and Theodoret of Cyrus (also a bishop, apologist, and theologian).

Aim of This Work

My hope is that this book will ignite a powerful desire in readers to listen to the witness(es) of the past, who testified for Christ "in season and out of season" (2 Tim. 4:2). The importance of reading, understanding, and learning from history cannot be overemphasized: the act of remembering is a crucial exercise that ensures the church's survival as an institution in a way consistent with its own identity as the church established and sustained by Christ. History is one way to understand God's will and his providential working in the universe. The record of his dealings with his people (whether Israel or the church) across time inspires confidence in God's sovereignty, reliability, covenant faithfulness, and love. The call of believers into a life of discipleship remains the same across the ages, and valuable examples of lived-out discipleship beckon us through vivid narratives to follow and to persevere in the Christian life. To seek out, read, and engage these ancient texts and ancient Christians is not merely for the sake of intellectual curiosity; it is also critical for the formation and ongoing affirmation of Christian self-identity, even after two millennia.

---

4. More will be said about hagiography in later chapters, esp. chaps. 4–5.

Acknowledgments

I thank Daniel H. Williams at Baylor for the kind invitation to contribute to this series and for his encouragement to continue the project. Hearty thanks are also due to the editors and staff at Baker Academic, for their expert advice, helpful nudging forward, and commitment to seeing the volume through to completion. Additionally, I owe a great debt of gratitude to colleagues and staff at the Southwestern Baptist Theological Seminary's Houston campus (Havard Center for Theological Studies), especially to my colleagues in historical studies, Miles S. Mullin, John Wilsey, and Stephen Presley. Colleagues in the Evangelical Theological Society, specifically members of the Patristic and Medieval History section, were gracious to allow me to present parts of my research for this manuscript and offer their feedback. Norma Carmona and Dawn Claunch read and commented on portions of the manuscript in earlier stages, and James Guittard and James McKinney in the reference department of Roberts Library provided excellent and speedy service.

Above all, appreciation is extended to Sydney, Sophia, and Alasdair, for providing so much joy along the journey of research and writing, and also to my husband, John Laing, who is a true partner to me, always an encourager, supporter, and fellow scholar.

Stefana Dan Laing
June 1, 2016
Feast Day of Justin the Martyr,
remembering that there are martyrs still

Visit www.bakeracademic.com/Retrieving History to access discussion questions for each chapter.

Abbreviations

General

AD	anno Domini, in the year of our Lord
BC	before Christ
ca.	*circa*, about, approximately
chap(s).	chapter(s)
d.	died
esp.	especially
Gk.	Greek
r.	reigned

Bibliographic

AARSR	American Academy of Religion Studies in Religion Series
ACW	Ancient Christian Writers
ANF	*The Ante-Nicene Fathers*. Edited by Alexander Roberts and James Donaldson. 1885–87. 10 vols. Repr., Peabody, MA: Hendrickson, 1994.
EEC	*Encyclopedia of Early Christianity*. Edited by Everett Ferguson. 2nd ed. New York: Garland, 1997.
FC	Fathers of the Church
NICNT	New International Commentary on the New Testament
NovTSup	Supplements to Novum Testamentum
NPNF[1]	*The Nicene and Post-Nicene Fathers*, Series 1. Edited by Philip Schaff. 1886–89. 14 vols. Repr., Peabody, MA: Hendrickson, 1994.
NPNF[2]	*The Nicene and Post-Nicene Fathers*, Series 2. Edited by Philip Schaff and Henry Wace. 1890–1900. 14 vols. Repr., Peabody, MA: Hendrickson, 1996.
SBL	Society of Biblical Literature
SC	Sources chrétiennes

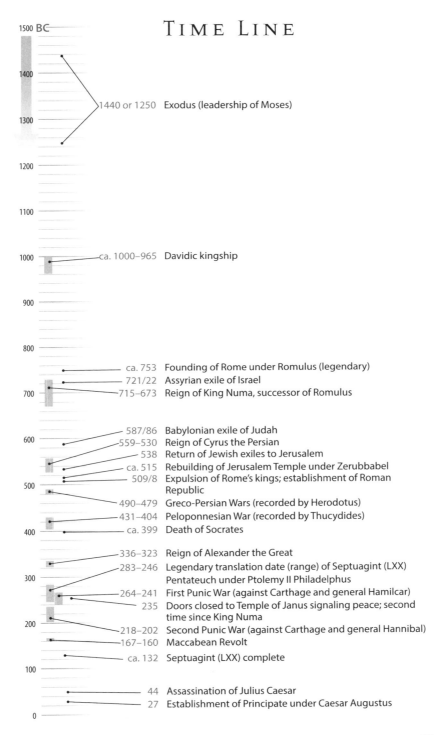

TIME LINE

1500 BC

1400

1440 or 1250   Exodus (leadership of Moses)

1300

1200

1100

1000   ca. 1000–965   Davidic kingship

900

800

ca. 753   Founding of Rome under Romulus (legendary)
721/22   Assyrian exile of Israel
700   715–673   Reign of King Numa, successor of Romulus

587/86   Babylonian exile of Judah
600   559–530   Reign of Cyrus the Persian
538   Return of Jewish exiles to Jerusalem
ca. 515   Rebuilding of Jerusalem Temple under Zerubbabel
509/8   Expulsion of Rome's kings; establishment of Roman
500   Republic
490–479   Greco-Persian Wars (recorded by Herodotus)
431–404   Peloponnesian War (recorded by Thucydides)
400   ca. 399   Death of Socrates

336–323   Reign of Alexander the Great
283–246   Legendary translation date (range) of Septuagint (LXX)
300   Pentateuch under Ptolemy II Philadelphus
264–241   First Punic War (against Carthage and general Hamilcar)
235   Doors closed to Temple of Janus signaling peace; second
        time since King Numa
200   218–202   Second Punic War (against Carthage and general Hannibal)
167–160   Maccabean Revolt
ca. 132   Septuagint (LXX) complete
100

44   Assassination of Julius Caesar
27   Establishment of Principate under Caesar Augustus
0

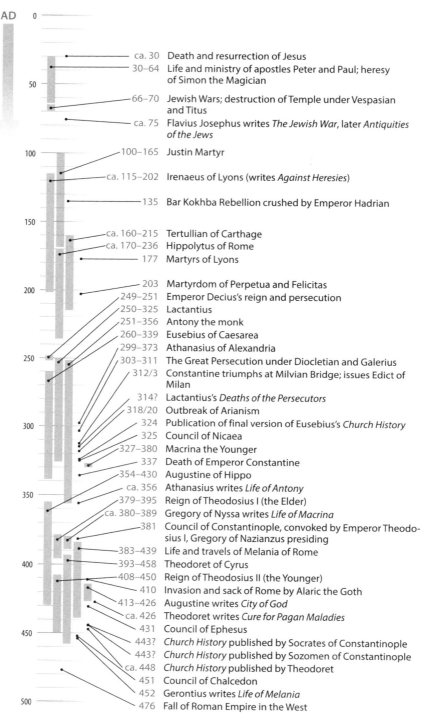

AD 0

50

ca. 30   Death and resurrection of Jesus

30–64   Life and ministry of apostles Peter and Paul; heresy of Simon the Magician

66–70   Jewish Wars; destruction of Temple under Vespasian and Titus

ca. 75   Flavius Josephus writes *The Jewish War*, later *Antiquities of the Jews*

100

100–165   Justin Martyr

ca. 115–202   Irenaeus of Lyons (writes *Against Heresies*)

135   Bar Kokhba Rebellion crushed by Emperor Hadrian

150

ca. 160–215   Tertullian of Carthage

ca. 170–236   Hippolytus of Rome

177   Martyrs of Lyons

200

203   Martyrdom of Perpetua and Felicitas

249–251   Emperor Decius's reign and persecution

250–325   Lactantius

251–356   Antony the monk

260–339   Eusebius of Caesarea

299–373   Athanasius of Alexandria

250

303–311   The Great Persecution under Diocletian and Galerius

312/3   Constantine triumphs at Milvian Bridge; issues Edict of Milan

314?   Lactantius's *Deaths of the Persecutors*

318/20   Outbreak of Arianism

300

324   Publication of final version of Eusebius's *Church History*

325   Council of Nicaea

327–380   Macrina the Younger

337   Death of Emperor Constantine

354–430   Augustine of Hippo

ca. 356   Athanasius writes *Life of Antony*

350

379–395   Reign of Theodosius I (the Elder)

ca. 380–389   Gregory of Nyssa writes *Life of Macrina*

381   Council of Constantinople, convoked by Emperor Theodosius I, Gregory of Nazianzus presiding

383–439   Life and travels of Melania of Rome

400

393–458   Theodoret of Cyrus

408–450   Reign of Theodosius II (the Younger)

410   Invasion and sack of Rome by Alaric the Goth

413–426   Augustine writes *City of God*

ca. 426   Theodoret writes *Cure for Pagan Maladies*

431   Council of Ephesus

450

443?   *Church History* published by Socrates of Constantinople

443?   *Church History* published by Sozomen of Constantinople

ca. 448   *Church History* published by Theodoret

451   Council of Chalcedon

452   Gerontius writes *Life of Melania*

500

476   Fall of Roman Empire in the West

Invitation to the Past

In my career I've found that "thinking outside the box" works better if I know what's "inside the box." In music (as in life) we need to understand our pertinent history, . . . and moving on is so much easier once we know where we've been.

—Dave Grusin, musician (this quote appears on a Starbucks cup in the series "The Way I See It," #182)

Before we can responsibly go into the future, we must go back.

—D. H. Williams, *Retrieving Tradition and Renewing Evangelicalism*, 13

The Past Is Trending

Most people have some interest in their origins, whether geographical, familial, or cultural; indeed many are self-consciously shaped by their past. Some also have an interest in their spiritual origins, allowing these to shape and form their spiritual identities, as well as their theology and worship. The latter is increasingly becoming the case, as a spirit of antiquity or appreciation of "the past" seems to be blowing through evangelicalism, even through such an ultracontemporary permutation

1

of evangelicalism as the Emergent Church movement.[1] It may even be part of a broader cultural movement, as suggested by the above quote from Dave Grusin, popularized by Starbucks. Many Christians are turning back to an earlier era, that of the church fathers, seeking renewal in their worship practices (liturgy) and doctrine. Some are revisiting the past to mine apologetic arguments and strategies for defending the faith against current opposition such as the New Atheism or cults, or just to learn from ancient apologists how to engage a hostile or unbelieving culture; others seek ancient wisdom for living as a Christian in a pluralistic and postmodern society, or for living as a disciple, growing and thriving spiritually in an age of affluence, freedom, godlessness, and pop spirituality.[2] Some appear to be searching for a sense of historical, personal, and theological identity in this age of the nondenominational megachurch.[3] All these groups have at least one commonality: they hope to somehow refresh their Christian walk and renew their witness in the world by revisiting and reclaiming their Christian roots. By reconnecting with the heritage of the ancient church, they are reminded of the "faith once for all delivered to the saints," as well as the particular saints who have lived it out in various forms of

1. See Brian McLaren, *Finding Our Way Again: The Return of the Ancient Practices* (Nashville: Nelson, 2008), and other volumes in that series, which attempts to reclaim and reintroduce the spiritual disciplines to a contemporary audience. The other volumes treat the practices/topics of fasting, pilgrimage, liturgy (of the church year), Sabbath, Eucharist, and prayer.

2. Robert Webber, *Ancient-Future Faith: Rethinking Evangelicalism for a Postmodern World* (Grand Rapids: Baker, 1999), and other volumes in the series. Recent examples of evangelical responses to the New Atheism include Alister McGrath and Joanna McGrath, *The Dawkins Delusion* (Downers Grove, IL: InterVarsity, 2007); John D. Laing, ed., "The New Atheism," *Southwestern Journal of Theology* 54 (Fall 2011); Paul Copan and William Lane Craig, eds., *Contending with Christianity's Critics: Answering New Atheists and Other Objectors* (Nashville: B&H Academic, 2009); William Lane Craig and Chad Meister, eds., *God Is Great, God Is Good* (Downers Grove, IL: IVP Books, 2009); "Evangelical Responses to Neo-Atheist Assaults on God's Goodness and Justice," theme of the Southwest regional meeting of the Evangelical Theological Society, Dallas, Texas, March 1–2, 2013. It should be noted that not many contemporary apologists seem to be delving into the so-called Apologetic Era of the second and third centuries in a sweeping way, but rather they seem to extract smatterings of the apologists' ideas without a broader appropriation of their approach, methodology, and rhetorical strategy. Happily, interest in the ancient church's apologetic tradition is currently rising.

3. See *An Evangelical Manifesto: A Declaration of Evangelical Identity and Public Commitment* (May 7, 2008), http://www.evangelicalmanifesto.com; Guy Davies, "The Great Evangelical Identity Crisis (1980–2010)," *The Gospel Truth Magazine*, November 2010; Jesse Carey, "Perspectives: The Evangelical Identity Crisis," on the Christian Broadcasting Network (May 2008); Lisa Miller, "An Evangelical Identity Crisis," *Newsweek*, November 12, 2006. Albert Mohler has written multiple articles on this issue, including a response to the *Evangelical Manifesto*, which he declines to sign. See, e.g., Mohler, "The Evangelical Identity Crisis: It's Really about Integrity," March 16, 2004, http://www.albertmohler.com/2004/03/16/the-evangelical-identity-crisis-its-really-about-integrity/.

witness down through twenty centuries. Scholars and clerics alike are turning to the fathers for theological as well as homiletic refreshment and renewal. Both Catholics and Protestants have been producing multivolume works—directed at students, pastors, and laypersons—that seek to give access in an accurate English translation to the riches of patristic theology, hermeneutics, and homiletics.[4]

This movement is not limited to clerics and theologians but is also present among the laity. Several personal examples can serve as cases in point. Bonnie, a friend from an evangelical Southern Baptist church, is a mom, director of Awana, and freelance writer for a denominational publication. She became interested in Athanasius, Augustine, and other patristic theologians who set the doctrinal foundations of Christianity. She said that knowing the origins of her faith gave her grounding and confidence in the doctrines that have defined Christians and have endured these twenty centuries. She and about ten others joined me in a discipleship group in which we read and discussed Augustine's *Confessions*. Many of the participants were amazed at the similarities between the philosophical and spiritual issues of the fourth and twenty-first centuries. Another friend, Walker (not his real name), is a dad and works in information technology. He became interested in Athanasius's works. I was stunned (and pleased) when he approached me one day and told me he was reading Athanasius's *On the Incarnation*. When I asked him why, he replied that his interest stemmed from his personal

4. See *Ancient Christian Commentary on Scripture*, ed. Thomas Oden (Downers Grove, IL: InterVarsity, 1998–); *The Church's Bible*, ed. Robert L. Wilken (Grand Rapids: Eerdmans, 2003–); see also the review by R. R. Reno of *The Church's Bible* in *First Things*, April 23, 2009, www.firstthings.com/web-exclusives/2009/04/the-churchs-bible. These projects are ongoing. The effort to provide access to the riches of the patristic corpus in the twentieth century actually began among French scholars like the priest J. P. Migne, who started to produce critical editions of various patristic works (the Patrologia Latina and Patrologia Graeca series between 1844 and 1866). Protestants soon followed, identifying strongly with the church fathers, led by the Tractarians of the Oxford Movement, and later by church historian Philip Schaff, who encouraged Protestants to reclaim the patristic heritage as their own as well, and not simply to abrogate those centuries of (undivided) Christianity to adherents of the "Great Tradition." Between 1886 and 1900, he and other Protestant evangelical scholars aimed to "furnish ministers and intelligent laymen who have no access to the original texts" or are not familiar with Greek and Latin "with a complete apparatus for the study of ancient Christianity" in English (*NPNF*[1] 1:v, preface). Schaff passed away in 1893, before the entire series was completed in 1900. In the twentieth century, Catholic scholars and clergy initiated the (continuing) series of critical editions of the church fathers called Sources chrétiennes beginning in the 1940s. This emphasis on the church fathers was a natural outflow of the ideology of *ressourcement*, which flourished in Catholic theological thought between 1930 and 1960. For a good introduction and overview of the history of patristics as a field of study, see Elizabeth A. Clark, "From Patristics to Early Christian Studies" in *Oxford Handbook of Early Christian Studies*, ed. Susan Ashbrook Harvey and David G. Hunter (Oxford: Oxford University Press, 2008), 7–41.

background. He had suffered from an abusive father and drew comfort from the view of God's fatherhood presented by Athanasius. Yet another friend, Ricky, is a dad and chemical engineer for a pharmaceutical company. He maintains a strong interest in Christianity's doctrinal foundations and is especially intrigued by developments in trinitarian doctrine up to the Council of Nicaea (325) and beyond. By his own account, his interest stems from his evangelistic and apologetic activities. Ricky bears witness to Christ through thoughtful conversations with his work colleagues, and he has become convinced that the nature of truth is under attack in contemporary culture. Through discipleship training classes, he trained others in our church to engage the culture effectively by becoming firmly grounded in Christian doctrine, especially in Christology and the doctrine of the Trinity. In his teaching material on the Trinity, he even developed his own curriculum after conducting some scholarly research, incorporating not only biblical exegesis but also historical study of doctrinal development from the earliest years of the church. Ricky finds value in studying doctrinal and apologetic arguments proffered by earlier Christians because there is no need to reinvent the wheel, so to speak.

An Ancient-Contemporary Example

As Augustine's *Confessions* demonstrate, the psychological and even theological issues of the fourth century offer some unexpected parallels to those of our own era. On many occasions during our discipleship class on Augustine, participants commented, "He could be talking about today!" For example, the tenets of Manichaeanism—a religion in which Augustine was involved for almost a decade—have strong affinities with the New Age teachings of Oprah Winfrey's spiritual guru, Eckhart Tolle. Both deny the reality of personal sin and the necessity for Jesus's atoning, sacrificial death.[5] Both emphasize knowledge, self-realization, and self-actualization.[6] Mani, the founder of Manichae-

5. Cf. Augustine, *Confessions* 4.15, 5.10; and Eckhart Tolle, *A New Earth* (New York: Plume, 2005), 9.

6. These similarities should not surprise us, however, given the Buddhist underpinnings of each system. In *New Earth*, Tolle cites most often the examples of the Buddha and Jesus as ones who lived a fully conscious, awakened, and present life (2, 3, 6, 9, 13, and 14, in the introductory chapter alone). Keith Yandell explains that Mani "claimed a revelation from God and saw himself as a member of a line [of prophets] that included the Buddha, Zoroaster, and Jesus" ("Manichaeanism," in *The Cambridge Dictionary of Philosophy*, ed. Robert Audi [Cambridge: Cambridge University Press, 1995], 460). For Mani, the "object of the practice of religion was to release . . . particles of light . . . and . . . Jesus, Buddha, the Prophets and

anism, also adhered to a dualistic/Gnostic understanding of God and reality. For Mani and his followers, all reality consisted of conflicts between diametrical opposites: light versus darkness, matter versus spirit, body/flesh versus soul, and good versus evil. This dualism pervaded their thought system, extending even to their view of the body (and matter in general) as *hostile* to the soul or mind.[7] For his part, Tolle clearly praises Gnostic thought and its emphasis on "realization and inner transformation."[8] Tolle also posits some degree of dualism in his own spiritual thought, namely, between what he calls the "pain-body" (a somewhat unclear concept) and the consciousness. While the pain-body is associated with darkness and negativity, the consciousness is associated with light and life.[9]

Further, both Tolle and Mani mingled their teachings with Christian concepts. They spoke in biblical terms and infused (if not twisted completely) Jesus's words with their own interpretations, thereby seducing even Christians with their message.[10] Augustine provides an especially illuminating example of the eerie similarity between the tactics of the Manichaeans and Tolle and his contemporary followers:

Mani had been sent to help in this task" (F. L. Cross and E. A. Livingstone, eds., *The Oxford Dictionary of the Christian Church* [Oxford: Oxford University Press, 1997], 1027). Although Cross and Livingstone (ibid.) aver that these particles were "imprisoned in man's brain," they were actually "imprisoned in the fruit" eaten by the Manichaean elect. The release happened through gastronomical processes, as Augustine explains in *Confessions* 3.10 (trans. R. S. Pine-Coffin [London: Penguin, 1961], 67–68); and in *On the Morals of the Manichaeans* 15.36–16.53 (NPNF[1] 4:79–83).

7. Augustine, *Confessions* 4.15, 5.10–11, 7.1–2. Tolle hails Gnosticism as "an intensification of the light of the original teaching" of Christianity, that is, the *true* understanding of Christianity (*New Earth*, 16).

8. Tolle, *New Earth*, 16.

9. The pain-body seems to be "an energy field of pain," that is, a sort of self-existing entity that tries to take over a person, to become that person, and to live through him or her, generating more pain as it feeds off of negative and destructive thinking. He speaks of this pain-body in terms such as "negative," "suffer," "dark shadow" (as opposed to the "light of your consciousness"), "afraid," "negative energy field," and "anti-life" of unconsciousness as opposed to the "life" of consciousness (Tolle, "The Pain Body by Eckhart Tolle," http://www.detoxifynow.com/et_pain_body.html).

10. Tolle writes that "there is only one absolute truth. . . . The Truth is inseparable from who you are. Yes, you *are* the Truth. . . . The very being that you are is Truth. Jesus tried to convey that when he said, 'I am the Truth and the way and the life. . . . Jesus speaks of the innermost I Am, the essence identity of every man and woman, every life-form, in fact." And so Tolle offers the teaching that each person possesses an inner God, a Buddha nature or Atman, "the indwelling God" (*New Earth*, 71, emphasis original). See also James A. Beverley, "Nothing New: Popular spiritual author and Oprah favorite Eckhart Tolle quotes Jesus a lot. Is he a Christian?," *Christianity Today* 52, no. 8 (August 2008): 50. He states that although Tolle "quotes freely from Jesus, Buddha, and others," nonetheless "Jesus is the most quoted teacher in both of Tolle's books."

[The Manichaeans] baited the traps [to reel in converts from Christianity] by confusing the syllables of the names of God the Father, God the Son our Lord Jesus Christ, and God the Holy Ghost, the Paraclete, who comforts us. These names were always on the tips of their tongues, but only as sounds which they mouthed aloud, for in their hearts they had no inkling of the truth. Yet, "Truth and truth alone" was the motto which they repeated to me again and again, although the truth was nowhere to be found in them.[11]

Tolle claims that throughout his life he has been influenced by the Bible, and he purports to impart a true understanding of the Scriptures through his teachings; he believes that currently most biblical teachings are misunderstood by Christians.[12]

The point of this extended comparison is to emphasize the value and even the critical necessity of looking back to the early church's works. As the contemporary church faces current theological and ideological challenges, it is both comforting and instructive to realize that many of these challenges have already been confronted and answered. By rebutting pseudo-Christian ideologies, Augustine and other church fathers helped clarify Christian theology and thus lent definition to Christianity: by combating Manichaeanism, for example, Augustine defined not only what Christians believed, but also what they specifically *did not* and *should not* believe.

Impediments to the Backward Glance

Doctrinal grounding (as in the example above), pastoral needs, evangelism, and apologetic engagement are all good reasons to look back at

11. Augustine, *Confessions* 3.6 (Pine-Coffin, 60). Mani claimed direct revelation from Jesus (among other figures), in addition to styling himself the Paraclete (*Confessions* 5.5).

12. In fact the very title of his book represents a distortion of biblical teaching (Old and New Testaments) regarding the "new heaven" and "new earth." He writes, "We need to understand here that heaven is not a location, but refers to the inner realm of consciousness. This is the esoteric meaning of the word, and this is also its meaning in the teachings of Jesus" (*New Earth*, 23). Having drawn all these comparisons, we must nevertheless acknowledge that an exact one-to-one correspondence between Manichaeanism and Tolle's New Age thinking is lacking. The pantheistic Tolle does not believe in God as an objective entity, let alone a Person, whereas Manichaeans did believe in God, although their understanding was that "God" consisted of two cosmic forces—one good, the other evil—battling one another. Further, the Christologies of these two belief systems are diametrically opposed: the Manichaeans held Jesus to be completely spiritual, without a physical body (that is, they denied the incarnation), a belief known as Docetism; Tolle believes that Jesus was merely human—nothing more than a great, enlightened teacher (like the Buddha), a spiritually awakened man who lived ahead of his time (cf. Augustine, *Confessions* 5.9–10; Tolle, *New Earth*, 6).

the church's history and to mine that history for resources and answers. But some of these reasons are what we might call "cerebral." They contribute to aspects of the life of the mind that are somewhat abstract, and they retrieve information used for theological and/or philosophical engagement or debate. There are also more concrete and practical reasons to look back. Contemporary spirituality, liturgy, and discipleship can all be enriched by turning to past Christians and examining their lives and writings. An interest in these topics might seek to discover how Christians prayed and worshiped, and how they defined and maintained their identity as Christians within their culture.[13]

In addition to these solid but somewhat utilitarian reasons for a backward glance, I also suggest that evangelicals encounter some deeper issues that contribute to historical myopia, as evidenced by many in the Free Church tradition who may reject or be oblivious to the rich and far-reaching historical tradition from which we emerged. Some Reformed-leaning evangelicals are familiar with Reformation ideals and theological commitments, but we must look also to the tradition extending even further back to the patristic and apostolic eras. In my experience, Free Church evangelicals often relinquish the history of the church between the apostles and Luther to so-called Great Tradition churches or mainline liturgical churches, when in fact there is no reason to think that early Christians are not our own forebears as well, and their contributions were clearly acknowledged as foundational by the Reformers themselves.[14] This very phenomenon impelled late nineteenth-century Protestant scholars to produce English translations of the fathers' works in the series *Ante-Nicene Fathers* and *Nicene and Post-Nicene Fathers*.[15]

Although American evangelicals seem to prioritize a sense of community (coffee shops in churches, small-group/cell-group studies, the peppering of the American evangelical landscape with "community" churches), it nonetheless appears that a Christian understanding of "community" in a broader, global, and historical sense is impoverished

13. Robert Wilken, *Remembering the Christian Past* (Grand Rapids: Eerdmans, 1995); Wilken, *The Christians as the Romans Saw Them* (New Haven: Yale University Press, 1984).

14. For example, see Anthony S. Lane, *John Calvin, Student of the Church Fathers* (Grand Rapids: Baker, 1999). Luther's works also demonstrate his conversance with and theological indebtedness to the fathers, as his treatises are liberally peppered with citations from them, and from Augustine above all.

15. *The Ante-Nicene Fathers*, ed. Alexander Roberts and James Donaldson, 10 vols. (1885–87; repr., Peabody, MA: Hendrickson, 1994). A. Cleveland Coxe, in the preface, makes this point, although in doing so Coxe admittedly evinces an anti-Catholic sentiment (*ANF* 1:v). This series was originally edited in Edinburgh from 1866 to 1872. The subsequent, complementary series was edited by the incomparable Swiss-American church historian Philip Schaff (*Nicene and Post-Nicene Fathers*, First Series [1886–89] and Second Series [coedited with Henry Wace [1890–1900]).

by at least three factors: certain denominational/theological commitments, declining biblical literacy in the broader culture as well as within
the church, and an attitude toward history (e.g., the church's memory)
as an impractical and therefore optional discipline.

First, certain denominational convictions sometimes detract from
a full appreciation of the global nature of the body of Christ. One
contributing factor may be the *individualistic* emphasis, which is both
ecclesiologically and soteriologically apparent. On the first count,
many Free Churches are committed to local church autonomy as their
primary ecclesiastical model. A Reformation emphasis on each person's
individual responsibility and accountability to Christ is theologically
and biblically true, but it tends to reinforce a sense of individualism,
where each believer has a primarily vertical spiritual relationship with
Jesus. Just to be clear, I do favor the idea of local church autonomy,
and it does seem that the idea of "local church" is the primary use
of the term "church" in the New Testament. There are good historical reasons for adhering to the idea of local church autonomy, and
an insistence on this ecclesiology guards against any secular or even
denominational group outside the church imposing its will upon a
congregation.

I also hold that every believer's *primary* salvation relationship is with
Jesus and not through any additional mediator (1 Tim. 2:5). Nevertheless, it still seems that this kind of confessional language *inside*
the church, coupled with the American ethos of rugged individualism
that pervades our lives *outside* the church, discourages a broader or
even global sense of community in which the members of the body
are accountable to one another, suffer and rejoice with one another,
and always look to use their gifts for the benefit of the other members.
As a constructive example, the article on the church in the Baptist
Faith and Message 2000 begins with local church autonomy, but then
it moves to the idea of a global and historical church in its final line:
"The New Testament speaks also of the church as the Body of Christ
which includes all of the redeemed of all the ages, believers from every
tribe, and tongue, and people, and nation."[16] This idea of the global
and era-transcending nature of the church seems somewhat secondary,
but it is still affirmed and was historically intended to guard against
the sectarian views of Landmarkism.[17] More positively viewed, the

16. Baptist Faith and Message, Article VI, The Church (June 14, 2000), http://www.sbc.net
/bfm2000/bfm2000.asp.
17. Landmarkism is a belief held by some Baptist groups who believe that "the NT model
for the church is only the local and visible congregation, and that it violates NT principles to
speak of a universal, spiritual church." Mark Noll, "Landmarkism," in *Evangelical Dictionary
of Theology*, ed. Walter A. Elwell (Grand Rapids: Baker, 1984), 619.

statement shows that autonomy with regard to church government and ecumenicity with the faithful of the ages are not mutually exclusive.

I am advocating neither the rejecting of local church autonomy nor the jettisoning of personal and direct accountability before Christ as Lord, grounded as this concept is in the Reformation idea of the priesthood of every believer, and in the Bible itself. However, a more robust focus on the body of Christ as the "redeemed of all the ages" needs to be restored if evangelicals are to have a healthy understanding in both faith and practice of a horizontal (and historical) rather than primarily vertical concept of community. The author of Hebrews used the phrase "so great a cloud of witnesses" (12:1), which included the faithful of many generations going all the way back to the first human family (11:4). The writer believed that reminding the congregation of these powerful stories of faith shaped their perspective; as they experienced hardship themselves, they received encouragement from the faithful witness of their ancestors who proved victorious under adverse circumstances. The testimonies of Christians through the ages can speak powerfully to our own times as well.

A second factor detracting from a historical sense of community involves declining biblical literacy. If we are to believe the alarmist notes sounded throughout evangelicalism for some time now, the decline in biblical literacy in both culture and church bodes disastrously for the life of the church.[18] If biblical literacy is to improve, we must do a better job of teaching biblical terminology and concepts in universities and colleges.

A third factor detracting from a sense of community and historical continuity is the diminishing of the nature and value of history itself. History is perceived as something of a theoretical, impractical discipline, whose relevance is easily outstripped by the concerns of living and working in the world. When Harvard University proposed a curriculum overhaul in 2006, "the question of relevance" came to the fore as educators determined what classes could fulfill program requirements.[19] Students (and some professors) indicated a preference for a curriculum "more connected to life after college," making it possible that some students "could graduate without taking a history course."[20] History, it seems, is optional and not a core requirement, and some students could not articulate the contemporary relevance of ancient history and art history.

18. Stephen Prothero, *Religious Literacy: What Every American Needs to Know—and Doesn't* (San Francisco: HarperSanFrancisco, 2007), 111.

19. Tovia Smith, "Harvard Reconsiders Core-Course Requirements," National Public Radio, December 8, 2006, http://www.npr.org/templates/story/story.php?storyId=6597183.

20. Ibid.

Conventional and popular ideas of history tend to envision formal narratives, characterized by chronology, scientific objectivity, occasional pedantry, a dash of obscurity, and a good dose of deadening dullness. The literature produced between the first and fifth centuries of the church possesses none of these attributes. Even if history is devalued in the culture at large, it should not be so among Christians, who believe and understand the critical importance of a historical grounding for their faith and doctrine, especially as it is manifested in the apostolic preaching and the incarnation, the enfleshed union of God and humanity in time. In fact, the diminution of the value of history contributes directly to the second factor above: a recent (and urgent) emphasis within evangelicalism on restoring biblical literacy is going hand in hand with an emphasis on "metanarrative," that is, the "big picture," the story of God's dealings with his people throughout the Bible.[21] This academic interest has recently given way to denominational interest as well, as exemplified in the current LifeWay-produced Sunday school curriculum, *The Gospel Project*, advertised as a "Christ-centered curriculum that examines the grand narrative of Scripture."[22] The writers emphasize that the Bible is "not a collection of stories," but is "one story, . . . the story of redemption. . . . And it's our story too."[23] Put out by the Southern Baptist Convention, this curriculum is being adopted by other denominations as well, who perceive value in placing the church within the gospel narrative; for example, the Evangelical Free Church in America's Greg Strand connects the value of "the Bible's storyline" with "our identity as Christ's ambassadors."[24] The majority of the story of God's dealings with his people is in the Historical Books of the Old Testament; unfortunately these books seem to be neglected by evangelicals in favor of a focus on end-times prophecy or devotional literature. However, the bedrock of the metanarrative remains the Historical Books (as well as the narrative portions of the Pentateuch), which also provide all the background for the prophetic preaching in the Major and Minor Prophets, and for much of the Wisdom literature (Psalms of David and of the pre- and postexilic

21. See, e.g., Walter Kaiser, *Recovering the Unity of the Bible: One Continuous Story, Plan, and Purpose* (Grand Rapids: Zondervan, 2015); Kaiser, *The Promise-Plan of God: A Biblical Theology of the Old and New Testaments* (Grand Rapids: Zondervan, 2008); Gregory K. Beale, *A New Testament Biblical Theology: The Unfolding of the Old Testament in the New* (Grand Rapids: Baker Academic, 2011); Michael W. Goheen, *A Light to the Nations: The Missional Church and the Biblical Story* (Grand Rapids: Baker Academic, 2011); Christopher J. H. Wright, *The Mission of God: Unlocking the Bible's Grand Narrative* (Downers Grove, IL: IVP Academic, 2006).

22. See www.gospelproject.com.

23. Ibid.

24. See https://www.gospelproject.com/efca.

community, and Proverbs and Song of Songs, which are attributed to Solomon). Without a grasp of the events in the Historical Books of Joshua, Judges, Ruth, 1 and 2 Samuel, 1 and 2 Kings, 1 and 2 Chronicles, Ezra, Nehemiah, and Esther, much of the significance of the Prophets is lost, including prophetic oracles about the Messiah. With respect to the Old Testament, Jesus said that he had come to fulfill the law, not to do away with it, and neither should we ignore the Old Testament since it speaks about him (Luke 24).

Despite these three negative factors, there is a segment of evangelicals who are taking a decided look at the era of the church fathers, and as they do look back to the church of earlier times, certain questions arise: Did the early Christians look back to their own history? For what reasons did they do so? Was their past important to them? Did they seek their place in the grand narrative of God's redemptive plan, both for their own times and for the ages? What was their concept of history, and how did that relate to their understanding of God's historical narrative? The first church historian, Luke, is the traditionally acknowledged author of the Gospel of Luke and the Acts of the Apostles. His historical work, Acts, spans the period from Jesus's earthly departure (ascension) up to Paul's first residence (imprisonment) in Rome. After Luke, the church father chiefly credited with composing the first official history of the church was Eusebius of Caesarea (ca. 263–339). If Luke wrote a history of the church in the first half of the first century, and Eusebius wrote in the early fourth century, the intervening 250 or so years of historiographical silence seem indicative of early Christians' lack of interest in their own history.[25] Can this be true? Did the past hold such little value for them?

Some scholars believe that there indeed was such disinterest. For almost two centuries, beginning in the early nineteenth century, New Testament historical-critical scholars almost completely failed to recognize the church's interest in its own history. The nature of this bias took various forms, including a theological agenda that was virtually divorced from historical contexts. One resultant idea in Christology, for example, was the disparity between the "Jesus of history and the Christ of faith," a phrase coined by Martin Kähler in 1892. This phrase described a bifurcated understanding of Christology in which Jesus the Jew in a historical first-century Semitic context had little or no relationship to the Christ in whom the church confessed its faith.

A closer look at patristic-era documents yields a somewhat more encouraging picture. Although a formal historical treatise on the church's history awaited the hand of Eusebius, historical material

25. R. L. P. Milburn, *Early Christian Interpretations of History* (London: Black, 1954), 25–26.

is not lacking. In fact, it seems that "prior to the fourth century, Christian writers referred to past events, but they did not produce linear, harmonious, pointed historical narrative."[26] What we do find requires different questions. How did early Christians' interest in their own past emerge? What form(s) did it take? Did their recollections stem from particular situations or needs? What events precipitated the written historical forms that have reached us? It is through these historical forms, these documents, that early Christians' lives are allowed to touch ours, essentially allowing the past to reach into the present and affect the church, so that it progresses into the future with a clear identity. Indeed, this goal of identity building is of the essence of "good historical writing," according to Rowan Williams.[27] This kind of writing "constructs that sense of who we are by a real engagement with the strangeness of the past, that establishes my or our identity now with a whole range of things . . . which have to be recognised . . . as both different from us and part of us."[28] While not many of the church fathers were historians per se, a number of them did write a kind of history, depending upon their purposes: apologetic, spiritual and devotional, or doctrinal. What we find, then, are *historical forms* of literature that all demonstrated a particular interest in recording events in the life of the Christian community, and this material was then shaped around a certain rhetorical, ethical, or theological goal.

The concept of collective or corporate memory is helpful as a framework for the discussions undertaken here. To produce a succinct definition of "collective memory" is no easy task, but Elizabeth Castelli's work on this subject is helpful.[29] Collective memory is sometimes called social or corporate memory, and it is actually a fruitful framework for "understanding the work that the past does in the present."[30] Within a community or "collective context," its memory or particular version of the past performs a preserving function, which "emphasizes continuity between the past and the present, establishing an attachment or bond across time."[31] In essence, Castelli writes, "collective memory does the work of 'tradition,' . . . (rendering) past experience meaningful in and

26. Jacob Neusner, "The Birth of History in Christianity and Judaism," in *The Christian and Judaic Invention of History*, ed. Jacob Neusner, AARSR 55 (Atlanta: Scholars Press, 1990), 5.

27. Rowan Williams, *Why Study the Past? The Quest for the Historical Church* (Grand Rapids: Eerdmans, 2005), 23.

28. Ibid., 24.

29. Elizabeth Castelli, "Collective Memory and the Meanings of the Past," in *Martyrdom and Memory: Early Christian Culture Making* (New York: Columbia University Press, 2004), 10–32.

30. Ibid., 9.

31. Ibid., 12.

for present contexts."[32] Collective memory fashions a usable past for later readers, helping them make sense of their present. "Although the relevant modern terms—'collective,' 'social,' 'cultural' memory—are not found in the ancient sources," she continues, "the concern for the preservation of Christian memory is at the heart of early Christian culture."[33] The restoration of collective memory thus poses a positive challenge for Free Church evangelicals, since a retrieval of the past holds powerful promise for bolstering evangelical identity in the present.

The Scope of This Work

Part of the task of this book is to contribute to the establishment and strengthening of a "bond across time." My intent is to focus on historical writing by the Christian community of the first five centuries. In doing so, I delve into early Christian ideas of history and historical writing (historiography), the reasons for undertaking such historical works, and the value of those narratives for the developing Christian communities of the patristic era. By examining four historical forms, I demonstrate that the nature of early Christians' understanding of community was horizontal and corporate in nature, rather than purely vertical and individualistic. Christians' ideas of history and their reasons for recording historical events clearly demonstrate that the early church thought of itself in terms of a corporate memory stretching back to Jesus and the apostles, and including other disciples in the intervening years up to its own time. Their historical accounts also demonstrate how the church viewed itself vis-à-vis its social and religious environs at various stages of its historical and doctrinal development.

I also emphasize that there exists *continuity* between early Christian writers and biblical writers in their understanding of the nature and functions of historical narrative. The Old Testament historians as well as the apostles acknowledged history as the vehicle of God's providential deeds and God's prophetic message; for them, history was a way of understanding God's will and nature. Both groups also held that God was sovereign over history, guiding it in a distinct direction toward a certain goal, or telos, in the future: the eventual establishment of God's eternal kingdom in the world, reflecting the reality of his current reign in heaven. This idea clearly emerges in the Lord's Prayer given to the disciples by Jesus himself ("Your kingdom come, your will be done, on earth as it is in heaven" [Matt. 6:10]), and documents indicate that

32. Ibid.
33. Ibid., 24.

it was a sentiment widely shared by the martyrs of the second- and third-century church, by the fourth-century historian Eusebius as he wrote about the reign of the first Christian emperor, and by the fifth-century Augustine as he penned his massive historical apology, *The City of God*, and longed for God's reign, although not necessarily on earth. History can show how God has worked in past ages and how he still works in the present. God's nature as consistently sovereign ("not at the mercy of historical chance and change"),[34] good, and reliable also emerges. "Thus," continues Williams, "relation to God can be the foundation of a human community unrestricted by time or space, by language or cultural difference."[35]

There is also continuity in historiographical method, in that the church fathers fused the biblical view of history, as reflected in the tradition of the Deuteronomistic Historian and the Chronicler, with the classical methods bequeathed to them by the culture in which they were educated. So in addition to teaching theological truths through narrative, both biblical and patristic historians proffered lessons and models for Christian living. In these ways, historical works make an ongoing and valuable contribution to discipleship. I therefore encourage readers to broaden their understanding of history, memory, and community to include "the redeemed of all the ages,"[36] or as the Apostles' Creed says, "the communion of the saints," thereby recovering a corporate memory to replace the individualistic and almost exclusively vertical understanding of community toward which the Free Church often tends. Corporate memory is valuable precisely because it spells out the uniqueness of Christian salvation. Believers identify not only with Jesus in his relationship to the Father and Holy Spirit—a trinitarian community—but also with other believers across a vast expanse of time and space, all of whom belong to "one network of relations. . . . Historical understanding is not a luxury in such a context."[37]

This volume will first introduce readers to the concept of historical writing in antiquity, its nature and purposes, its importance in the world of the early church, and its contribution to the church's self-understanding (chap. 2). An examination of four related historical forms is then undertaken—roughly in the order in which they arose—followed by individual chapters specifically focused on each form. First examined is *historical apologetic* (chap. 3), which appears early in the book of Acts in the apostolic preaching, as the church found itself unwelcome in Jewish

---

34. Williams, *Why Study the Past?*, 10.

35. Ibid.

36. A phrase from the Baptist Faith and Message (2000), available at http://www.sbc.net /bfm2000/bfm2000.asp.

37. Williams, *Why Study the Past?*, 29.

society and later encountered increased hostility in the broader pagan society as well. Historical apologetic helped Christians to understand themselves as an ancient nation with a unifying faith. This chapter draws chiefly from Christian apologetic material of the second to fifth centuries, and specific authors such as Justin Martyr, Theophilus of Antioch, Tertullian of Carthage, and Augustine of Hippo. As we shall see, apologetic was not limited to the early centuries when Christianity was repressed by violence and punished as a capital crime. Apologetic defense continued to be composed whenever Christians were threatened or accused by outsiders, and it existed even into the later centuries.

Following on the heels of historical apologetic is *heresiology*, which in some way is the other side of the coin, so to speak, and will be subsumed under apologetic. The hostile culture was not the only foe Christian teachers and pastors faced: false doctrine *within* the church had to be combated as well. Although it tended to overlap with other forms, I consider how some of the church fathers (who simultaneously composed apologetic, theological, and antiheretical works) fought to debunk false teachings by using several kinds of historical arguments. Heresiology refers to the process of tracing a heretical notion through its various proponents over time and back to its original source. The historical elements involved here have to do with (on the negative side of things) evaluating the theological and moral integrity of the prime teacher of a heresy (heresiarch) as well as of those who followed him or her, and also deal with (on the positive side) the Christian method of proving the orthodoxy of the church's established teaching via the integrity of teachers in an unbroken line of transmission from its prime teacher, Jesus, through the apostles and the bishops and teachers that followed. This transmission is known as "apostolic succession" and is still followed by those in the Roman Catholic and Eastern Orthodox communions to define correct doctrine over against false doctrine. The most notable example is the pope, who represents the chief teacher in the Roman Catholic Church, purportedly standing faithfully in the doctrinal tradition of Jesus and the apostles, specifically Peter.

To say that heresiology aimed to prove that immoral and misguided teachers bred and transmitted false doctrine, while faithful and virtuous teachers produced correct doctrine, is putting the situation rather nicely. Heresiology was nothing if not strongly polemical, and even orthodox teachers (some of whom we now refer to as saints) could prove virulent protagonists: more often than not, they alleged that the prime teacher of heresiarchs was the devil! Writers adduced in this chapter include Irenaeus of Lyons against the Gnostics, and two other writers who largely followed his methodology and adapted his ideas during the next three centuries: Hippolytus of Rome and Tertullian of Carthage. Heresiology continued to be written into the next several centuries, and many other examples could be offered, such as Theodoret, who also posited a "heretical succession" (from which he distanced himself) parallel to the apostolic succession (with which he associated himself). However, these representative examples suffice to illustrate the method of tracing a heresy's genealogy. Broadly speaking, apologetic engagement with the surrounding culture helped Christians define themselves historically as a noble people of ancient foundations and high ethical commitments leading to proper worship, while a genealogical treatment of heresies within the church helped Christians identify doctrinal boundaries among themselves. That is, the church fathers helped to define the boundaries of orthodoxy by showing its origins to be doctrinally legitimate, while heresies stemmed from illegitimate and false teachers.

After apologetics follow two chapters on the form of *hagiography*, which address issues of discipleship. Here two questions arise: What does a disciple look like in a church under siege (chap. 4)? What does a disciple look like in a church favored by the ruling power in the land (chap. 5)? Under the first scenario (before 312–13), we see martyrs becoming saints, while in the second scenario (after the so-called Peace of the Church), it seems that the saints desired to become martyrs. These chapters draw upon the *acta* (deeds/court proceedings) of the martyrs, as well as devotional or spiritual works (*vitae*, or lives/ biographies) authored by Christians in more peaceful times, which look back to the tumultuous era of the martyrs. The crucible of persecution shaped Christians' consciousness and self-identity, and the formation and consolidation of this identity as primarily *Christian*—above any other loyalty of family, class, ethnicity, or political obligation—proved costly. The value of recording these accounts clearly emerges as later accounts referenced earlier ones, and many accounts of the vicissitudes of persecuted Christians were eventually incorporated into Christian worship as feast days (or anniversaries) of the martyrs, many of whom became inspirational role models for Christian devotional life and practice. While chapter 4 focuses on the martyrs, chapter 5 focuses on three specific lives under peacetime conditions: Antony, whose fourth-century biography was a best seller authored (or redacted) by Athanasius;[38] Macrina, the eldest sister in the illustrious Cappadocian family that included Basil of Caesarea and Gregory of Nyssa; and Melania the Younger, a celebrated fifth-century laywoman who funneled her massive wealth into various ecclesiastical and monastic projects. Each of these accounts demonstrates the desire of Chris-

---

38. Although it is true that Antony was born well before the Constantinian revolution.

tians to practice self-denial in ways that approximated the martyrs' sacrificial discipleship.

The fourth historical form is *ecclesiastical (church) history* (chap. 6). Here Eusebius's *Church History* is especially important, where he recounted the founding and establishment of the church by Jesus and the disciples, then continued the narrative down to his own time. Eusebius's continuators will also receive attention as they carried his historiographical legacy forward. The histories of Socrates Scholasticus, Sozomen, and Theodoret all emphasize the providential guidance of events by the God of history, whose will and rule are inexorable in the face of evil forces. Their works are recognizable as histories that are characteristically Christian in their emphases and interpretation of causes. As we shall see, the bishop-historians (Eusebius and Theodoret) more heavily emphasized the providential intervention of God in human affairs and distinctly appropriated the legacy of the apologetic tradition in attributing negative causation to the devil. The resultant works were simultaneously historical, theological, and apologetic, while the nonclerical historians Socrates Scholasticus and Sozomen kept to the classical models, emphasizing the importance of peace in a unified empire, which denoted a praiseworthy ruler. These historical accounts are critical for preserving Christian memory as the continuing narrative of God's dealings with believers, as well as highlighting the heroic struggles of bishops and teachers, who sought to consolidate and preserve sound doctrine and work for peace within the church.

Let us now travel further back into ancient history, to the era of the Greek wars, when the discipline of historical writing was forged. This foray is necessary to understand classical models and concepts of history with which later Christian writers were familiar, and which they would appropriate and adapt for their own works.

ANCIENT HISTORICAL WRITING AND THE RISE OF HISTORICAL LITERARY FORMS

And with reference to the narrative of events, . . . it rests partly on what I saw myself, partly on what others saw for me, the accuracy of the report being always tried by the most severe and detailed tests possible.
—Thucydides, *Peloponnesian War* 1.22 (ca. 415 BC)

The one function of the historian, then, is to relate things as they happened.
—Lucian of Samosata, *How to Write History* (ca. AD 165)

History writing in ancient Greece was not primarily concerned with relating past events "as they really happened."
—Steven McKenzie, *How to Read the Bible* (2005)

The Nature of Ancient Historical Writing

In our time, history seems to be a fragmented, specialized discipline. It is a subject perceived as dry and dusty and possibly dispensable because it is impractical; in antiquity this was not so. History was considered an artistic literary form akin to poetry. The historian was an artist who crafted his work for the enjoyment and education of the audience and the "enlightenment of posterity."[1] His work was not intended to be purely cold, factual, and analytical. Instead, a historical narrative gave the audience a captivating and instructive story that gripped the hearer's or reader's attention via features like digressions, diversions, and anecdotes, and that also taught the audience lessons in virtue. For the ancients, then, history's "practical use" was character formation; therefore reading and learning history was not optional.

This chapter aims first to set forth the nature of ancient historical writing and to define what it was and was not. It is correct to say that historical works dealt with facts, but they were not just bare-bones time lines, although it is true that chronology served as the *backbone* of history.[2] Two reasons for recording the past will be presented and examined: a *pedagogical* intent to instruct the audience through the narrative by providing examples, and a *providential* purpose, as writers attempted to answer questions about what drives the action in historical events. These twin purposes seem to have been accomplished via four characteristic features: narrative (*narratio* or *historia*), remembrance (*memoria* or *anamnēsis*), imitation (*imitatio* or *mimēsis*), and causation (*aitia*). Second, the question of truth telling in history is a somewhat contentious issue in the field, so this chapter will examine whether ancient historians wrote—or even intended to write—truthfully, whether some standard of truth telling and objectivity in historical reporting existed, or whether the historical ideology of ancient historians was such that their works are by definition unreliable or even misleading. This issue is particularly critical because scholars who want to downplay biblical authority argue that ancient history was more fiction than fact, and then they apply that criterion to the Old Testament Historical Books and New Testament Gospels and Acts. Third, the historical forms that arose or were co-opted by early Christian writers will be presented in more detailed fashion than their introduction in the previous chapter.

Historiographical Features

Detached objectivity was not the *primary* virtue of historical writing (historiography). Like other rhetorical literature, narratives were meant to teach (*docere*), to spur to action (*movere*), and to give plea-

---

1. Quintilian, *Institutio oratoria* 10.1.31 (trans. Winterbottom), in *Ancient Literary Criticism: The Principal Texts in New Translations*, ed. and trans. D. A. Russell and M. Winterbottom (Oxford: Clarendon, 1972), 385.

2. R. L. P. Milburn, *Early Christian Interpretations of History* (London: Black, 1954), 58.

sure (*delectare*).[3] As literary forms go, historical works had two basic parts: a prologue (*prooemium*) and the narrative (*narratio*). Historians strove for some combination of four particular elements. First, they wove together from their sources an absorbing or entertaining *narrative*, as they displayed their storytelling skills for their audience. Second, they aimed for a *remembrance* of epic events of the past that should not be allowed to fall into oblivion. Past events were called to mind through a narrative, which helped the audience to visualize, experience, understand, and learn their own pertinent history as well as the legacy bequeathed to them by past generations. Historians were conscious that they wrote not only for their own generation but also for posterity; indeed, many historians echo this sentiment. The third feature consisted of moral instruction via positive or negative examples fleshed out in the narrative, with an exhortation to *imitate* the noble examples and learn the lesson of the negative examples. Knowing one's own (or even the collective) history both reveals and builds identity; it offers wisdom for the present and future; and it builds character via lessons and observations concerning human nature, motives, and actions. Finally, historians made an attempt to answer questions of *causation* in history. They were concerned with who or what drove the action in either a positive or negative direction; those determinative actions could be ascribed to natural or supernatural forces, or a combination of both.

History's Pedagogical Function

The former three elements (narrative, remembrance, imitation) are interrelated, and taken together they illustrate history's *pedagogical* purpose. The historian selected and crafted his material carefully and appropriately so that moral lessons could be communicated through the *narrative*. In a very illuminating satirical piece titled *How to Write History*, the second-century Greek satirist Lucian of Samosata commented wittily on the nature and features of historical writing.[4] The prologue should identify the subject of the work, stating why it is important and useful and "explaining causes and defining the main heads of events."[5] The narrative should be smooth, even, clear, polished, and logical. The writer must know what to focus upon and

---

3. Basil Studer, "*Eruditio Veterum*," in *History of Theology*, vol. 1, *The Patristic Period*, ed. Angelo Di Berardino and Basil Studer, trans. Matthew J. O'Connell (Collegeville, MN: Liturgical Press, 1997), 290.

4. Lucian, *How to Write History* 6–64 (trans. Russell), in Russell and Winterbottom, *Ancient Literary Criticism*, 537–47.

5. Lucian, *How to Write History* 53 (trans. Russell), in Russell and Winterbottom, *Ancient Literary Criticism*, 545.

what to pass over quickly. Descriptions must be offered in moderation (only what is needed for clarity) and are not intended to give a "tasteless display of virtuosity" while "ignoring history to show off your own talents."[6] As to speeches, which necessarily contain some measure of *inventio*, Lucian advised, "If you have to introduce a character making a speech, let the content of it be first, suitable to the speaker and the situation, secondly (like the rest of the book) as lucid as possible—though you do indeed have license to be rhetorical here and to demonstrate your stylistic ingenuity."[7] Praise and blame should be sparing and rapid—"after all, your characters are not in court." And the historian should not act "as prosecutor rather than historian."[8]

Narratives were frequently—if not exclusively—crafted for the purpose of *remembrance*. Historians wrote to record deeds (and people's lives) that deserved to be praised, commemorated, and emulated, and should not be forgotten. In fact historians usually cited this reason as primary right up front in the introduction (*prooemium*) of their work. For example, the renowned (and somewhat controversial) Greek historian Herodotus began his fifth-century-BC historical work thus:

> Here are presented the results of the enquiry carried out by Herodotus of Halicarnassus. *The purpose is to prevent the traces of human events from being erased by time, and to preserve the fame of the important and remarkable achievements* produced by both Greeks and non-Greeks; among the matters covered is, in particular, the cause of the hostilities between Greeks and non-Greeks.[9]

The church historian Eusebius included similar sentiments in his much more extensive prologue, which laid out the plan for his book, *The History of the Church*:

> If I can *save from oblivion* the successors, not perhaps of all our Saviour's apostles but at least of the most distinguished, in the most famous and still pre-eminent churches, I shall be content.[10]

6. Lucian, *How to Write History* 57 (trans. Russell) in Russell and Winterbottom, *Ancient Literary Criticism*, 546.

7. Lucian, *How to Write History* 58 (trans. Russell) in Russell and Winterbottom, *Ancient Literary Criticism*, 546. See more on invented speeches in the section below.

8. Lucian, *How to Write History* 59 (trans. Russell) in Russell and Winterbottom, *Ancient Literary Criticism*, 546.

9. Herodotus, *Histories* 1, prologue (trans. Robin Waterfield [Oxford: Oxford University Press, 2008]), 3, emphasis added.

10. Eusebius, *Church History* 1.1 (trans. G. A. Williamson, rev. and ed. Andrew Louth [New York: Penguin, 1989]), 2, emphasis added.

The martyrological literature demonstrates this same objective, as seen in the accounts of the passions of Polycarp, Perpetua, Pionius, and the martyrs of Lyons. Sharing "in the remembrance of the saints" brings constantly to mind conspicuous men and women who were champions of the church, indeed, noble athletes of God.[11] Hagiographical literature also aims at remembrance, as for example in the historical biography of Macrina of the great Cappadocian family that included Basil of Caesarea and Gregory of Nyssa. Her younger brother Gregory of Nyssa concluded his prologue with a historical reason for his composition:

> In order, therefore, that *such a life should not be unnoticed in the future* and that the virgin who had raised herself to the highest peak of human virtue through the pursuit of philosophy, *should not remain concealed as a result of our silence*, I thought that it would be good both to obey you and to tell her life-story as shortly as I could and in a simple and unadorned style.[12]

History's paedeutic (educational) function is probably best understood by considering the literary phenomenon of *imitation* (*mimēsis*). In classical Hellenistic education, *mimēsis* meant imitation of any model or representation of something, whether literary or physical. Ideally, one aimed to imitate a good model in order to improve oneself. The process entailed discrimination to determine the model that best achieved both a high caliber of skill and aptitude *and* a high ethical standard. This pedagogical strategy had been widespread in Greco-Roman education (*paideia*) for centuries before Christianity.[13] Its principles were outlined in the teachings of Plato and were more fully expounded for Roman orators by the rhetorician Quintilian.[14] Echoing Plato's discussion of *mimēsis*, Quintilian explained that "every technique in life is founded on our natural desire to do ourselves what we approve in others."[15]

---

11. More details in chap. 4.

12. Gregory of Nyssa, *Life of Macrina* 1, in *Handmaids of the Lord: Holy Women in Late Antiquity and the Early Middle Ages*, ed. and trans. Joan M. Petersen (Kalamazoo, MI: Cistercian, 1996), 52, emphasis added.

13. Several important works on Greco-Roman education include H.-I. Marrou, *L'éducation dans l'antiquité* (Paris: Éditions du Seuil, 1948); Edwin Hatch, *The Influence of Greek Ideas on Christianity* (New York: Harper & Row, 1957). Works that discuss the relationship between Greco-Roman rhetorical education and ancient Christian exegesis are Frances Young, *Biblical Exegesis and the Formation of Christian Culture* (Cambridge: Cambridge University Press, 1997); and Di Berardino and Studer, *Patristic Period*.

14. Quintilian, *Institutio Oratoria* 10.2.1–28 (trans. Winterbottom), in Russell and Winterbottom, *Ancient Literary Criticism*, 400–405; Plato, *Republic* 10, in Russell and Winterbottom, *Ancient Literary Criticism*, 66–74.

15. Quintilian, *Institutio Oratoria* 10.2.2 (trans. Winterbottom), in Russell and Winterbottom, *Ancient Literary Criticism*, 400.

Therefore, persons must have models whose best points they may imitate. Other writers such as Longinus, Tacitus, Plutarch, and Seneca encouraged imitation of ancient writers, echoing Quintilian in their recommendations to imitate examples of both eloquence and virtue.

These ancient authors referred mostly to reading and studying poetry, which was an integral part of classical education, believing that "through the reading, discussion and memorizing of their most famous passages, students were to be led to an esthetic and moral imitation of the most illustrious men of the past."[16] Quintilian considered narrative literature (such as historiography) also a type of poetry. He wrote that history is "very near poetry; in a manner of speaking it *is* a poem written in prose, composed for telling a story, not proving a (legal) case. The whole genre is designed . . . for the enlightenment of posterity and the glory of the writer's genius."[17] Like poetry, the substance of a historical narrative was also pedagogical. Unlike the expectations of modern historical science, classical historical writing entailed weighing moral judgments, so it was characterized by a measure of subjectivity. In his *Rhetoric*, Aristotle had taught that narrative "should be expressive of character" and should evince "moral purpose."[18] Ancient rhetors, therefore, consistently affirmed the usefulness and paedeutic function of history. Down to the patristic era these features of narrative remained themes of historiography and were applied through ethical and spiritual exemplars in historical narratives.

We find that pedagogical purpose with specifically moral overtones is equally present in Old Testament historical material, as in classical and late antique historiography. In the Old Testament narratives, particularly those concerning the period of the conquest of Canaan through that of the Babylonian exile, the standard for assessing the rule of any judge or king was obedience to God manifested by adherence to the torah and the concomitant shunning of Canaanite idols. This assessment rubric is set up in the final chapter of the book of Joshua (Josh. 24)—and even earlier in Moses's farewell speech (Deut. 29–33)—as Moses's successor urged the Israelites, on the basis of God's power and covenant faithfulness demonstrated through a historical review (remembrance), to worship God exclusively and to repudiate any other gods, whether Egyptian or Canaanite. In other words, as the people verged on entering the promised land, as also after its conquest, their leadership urged them to remember the narrative of God's past works

16. Studer, "*Eruditio Veterum*," 300.

17. Quintilian, *Institutio Oratoria* 10.1.31 (trans. Winterbottom), in Russell and Winterbottom, *Ancient Literary Criticism*, 385.

18. Aristotle, *Rhetoric* 1417a (trans. M. E. Hubbard), in Russell and Winterbottom, *Ancient Literary Criticism*, 164.

of faithful deliverance in the exodus and throughout the wilderness wanderings; to heed the lessons of the past with regard to the consequences of idolatry, in the golden calf incident as well as the worship of Baal of Peor (Num. 25:1–9); and to imitate their leaders' faithfulness. Judges 2 further reinforces the standard of evaluation, which will be fleshed out through the book's narratives with examples of political, military, and spiritual successes (like Deborah) and failures (like Samson), each contingent upon covenant obedience or disobedience. The narrative thus teaches later generations (possibly exilic or postexilic) the victorious results of torah observance—especially the injunction at its very head to embrace exclusive monotheism—and equally exemplifies the tragic consequences of flouting covenant obligations. This assessment of the Israelites and their leadership continues throughout the books of Samuel, Kings, and Chronicles. While particularly significant political and military events receive due recognition, the continual refrain of those books pertains more to *spiritual* accomplishments or failures. The spiritual vitality of David, Hezekiah, and Josiah received praise, while the ultimate failures of the idolatrous Jeroboam, Ahab, and Manasseh were denounced.

The classical historical works similarly evince a pedagogical intent, but of course they differ vastly from the primarily religious outlook of the biblical narratives. In the classical works of Greco-Roman antiquity, the rubric of assessment centered on particular vices or virtues. The pedagogical aspect of history was bound up with the ethical understanding of basically four cardinal virtues (justice, temperance, courage, and wisdom) and four vices (distress, inordinate delight, fear, and desire/lust), although they were more correctly termed "passions" in Hellenistic antiquity. This set of virtues and passions derived from a combination of Platonic, Aristotelian, and Stoic philosophy. Every citizen was expected to cultivate virtues and root out vices, while rulers were held to a more rigorous standard, being expected to exhibit the cardinal virtues to a heightened degree. As to the substance of these classical works, historians like Herodotus, Thucydides, Tacitus, and Ammianus Marcellinus focused on the grand narrative of war and statecraft, constantly weighing the motives, diplomatic skills, and military might of the players involved. Their vivid descriptions and colorful sketches placed the audience in the drama itself and offered both enjoyment and instruction, for the moral aspect of the episodes was never far from the author's mind. Indeed, they adhered to the insistence of classical *paideia* that the very purpose of history is to teach lessons from the past that can be applied to help a person better navigate the exigencies of the present and future. The Greek Thucydides, for example, stated as much in his own prologue to the *History of the Peloponnesian War*.

He wrote that if his account "be judged useful by those inquirers who desire an exact knowledge of the past as an aid to the interpretation of the future, which in the course of human things must resemble if it does not reflect it, I shall be content."[19] The philosopher Aristotle stated much the same in his work on rhetoric, which includes narrative material: "In political oratory, . . . if there is narration, it should tell what has happened, so that people can deliberate better about the future for being reminded of the past."[20] Narrative material should also "be expressive of character, and will be so if we know what produces this effect. One thing is what reveals moral purpose."[21] The first-century historian Tacitus constantly made ethical judgments through his historical writing; while he treated the expected conventional themes of a history, describing the Roman Empire's domestic politics, economics, and foreign affairs under the Julio-Claudian dynasty, he also consistently drew out moral teachings. His character portraits of the Caesars (esp. the "morose," "cryptic," and degenerate Tiberius) are stark, unforgettable, and ethically loaded.[22] While the fourth-century soldier-historian Marcellinus painted a vivid picture of the military campaigns in which he served, he also did not neglect to offer a glowing portrait of his commander, the self-proclaimed philosopher-monarch Julian (the Apostate), whose character and virtues—in Marcellinus's opinion—rivaled those of Socrates and Alexander the Great.[23] The moral impetus was even stronger in biographical works, such as those by Plutarch and Suetonius. They offered basic personal information about each subject, but all the stories lent themselves to shedding light upon some aspect of the person's character—virtuous or otherwise—for the moral improvement of the reader.[24]

    In the historical works of the early church, the rubric was much the same. The martyr narratives commended virtues like fortitude and monotheistic faith, while the chief vice was capitulation to the sacrifice (i.e.,

19. Thucydides, *History of the Peloponnesian War* 1.22 (trans. Richard Crawley, ed. W. Robert Connor [London: Everyman, 1993], 11).

20. Aristotle, *Rhetoric* 1417b (trans. Hubbard), in Russell and Winterbottom, *Ancient Literary Criticism*, 165.

21. Aristotle, *Rhetoric* 1417a (trans. Hubbard), in Russell and Winterbottom, *Ancient Literary Criticism*, 164.

22. Tacitus, *Annals of Imperial Rome*, rev. ed., trans. Michael Grant (Harmondsworth, UK: Penguin, 1971), 39.

23. Ammianus Marcellinus, *The Later Roman Empire* 16.5 (trans. Walter Hamilton [New York: Penguin, 1986], 91–94).

24. Suetonius, *Lives of the Twelve Caesars*, trans. Robert Graves and Michael Grant (London: Penguin, 1979); Plutarch, *Makers of Rome*, trans. Ian Scott-Kilvert (London: Penguin, 1965); Plutarch, *The Rise and Fall of Athens*, trans. Ian Scott-Kilvert (London: Penguin, 1960); Plutarch, *Fall of the Roman Republic*, trans. Rex Warner (London: Penguin, 1972).

idolatry) demanded by the state. In Christian biographies of subsequent centuries, writers combined the Hellenistic rubric of classic virtues and vices with Jesus's kingdom ethic as set out in the Gospels. These late antique Christians strove to emulate the martyrs' ideal of discipleship through self-denial (via ascetic discipline) and love of neighbor. In the church histories produced by Eusebius and his continuators, the writers assessed various secular leaders according to their friendliness or hostility toward Christianity, and later according to their orthodoxy in light of continuing doctrinal developments, synodal creeds, and conciliar decrees. These assessments sound strikingly like the biblical historical material in Kings and Chronicles. Christian writers, therefore, took into account the historiographical principles of the biblical materials as well as the moral framework of Greco-Roman society and fused these together to produce a distinctively Christian historical work.

Causation or History's Providential Aspect

Another purpose for historiography involves explanations of how and why events happen, that is, *causation*. History is not only pedagogical but also *providential*. Historians sought to explain to their audience the causes of events, whether noble or tragic, and the working out of a greater purpose in them. Sometimes they tried to identify historical patterns such as cycles that played out and then came around again in another era. While some pagan historiography tended to explain causation in cyclic or fortuitous terms (e.g., hints in Tacitus), Jewish-Christian historical thinking was linear, with a clear goal, or telos, toward which history was progressing. Although a classical historian like Herodotus included "the gods" in his historical vocabulary when composing *The Histories* about the Greco-Persian wars, he was nonetheless ambivalent about their intervention. He apparently did not attribute serious historical causation to the gods, but rather to human personalities and their ambitions. His emphasis on the cunning and ambitious Themistocles on the Greek side, or the grasping and overconfident tyrant Xerxes on the Persian side, rendered a consideration of "the gods" as a cause merely conventional. Classical Greek and Roman historians tended to explain causation in terms of Fate (*Moira/Fatum*) or Fortune (*Tychē/Fortuna*), the latter concept increasingly personified as a goddess: this is evident in the *Histories* of Polybius (second century BC), in the two works of Sallust (first century BC), and in Cassius Dio (second and third centuries AD), who actually considered himself her devotee.[25]

25. Glenn F. Chesnut, *The First Christian Histories: Eusebius, Socrates, Sozomen, Theodoret, and Evagrius*, 2nd ed. (Macon, GA: Mercer University Press, 1986), 8–9.

Later the medievals personified *Fortuna* as a fickle female spinning a wheel, symbolizing that both good and bad events came and went, cyclically and unpredictably, in the lives of individuals and nations.

Although we might think ourselves at a vast cultural, religious, and scientific remove from these historians, we may still express ourselves in terms of "Mother Nature" in the face of a natural disaster, even if we do not actually believe in the existence of a deity named "Mother Nature." Similarly, secularists may refer to "acts of God" even if in actual fact they are agnostics. These two phrases function for us much as the references to *Fortuna* and *Tychē* functioned for most Greco-Romans. Such terms, along with other derivatives, formed a part of their vocabulary for the uncertainty in human life.[26] They seemed to be a conventional but necessary admission that human knowledge about the future is limited, that we do not always fully understand natural phenomena, and that inscrutable factors are often at work in human and superhuman decision making at critical historical junctures.

Apart from the identification of *Tychē* as a goddess, other concepts of Fortune existed—for example, as just a generic historical concept to explain causation. However, by the third century AD, her cult statues and altars flourished throughout the ancient Near East, so usage of the term *tychē* by Christian historians carried idolatrous baggage. The need to explain causation still remained in Christian historiography, though. For pagans, Fortune as a more general historical concept expressed the unknown, unplanned, paradoxical, unexpected, uncontrollable, and unpredictable elements in the chain or web of human events. Christian historians, for their part, consciously avoided terms for Fortune and appealed instead to the biblical God and the concept of Providence (*pronoia*). This concept involved an overarching plan of God for the ages, a plan that began at the dawn of creation, or even earlier, as we can gauge from the Pauline and Petrine perspectives.[27] In other words, Christians espoused a linear metanarrative that spanned both the Old and New Testaments, further extending to their own time and beyond. The concept of Providence included ideas of cosmological organization and purpose, so the workings of the universe could be in some measure predictable, fathomable, purposeful, and above all, beneficial to human life (rather than hostile or random). Christian historians also made use of a related concept, the "*kairos* moment," often invoked by secular historians as well. This moment refers to a critical point in a chain of events where one person's resolute decision turns the course of events. This idea seemed to give real historical importance

---

26. Ibid., 10–14.

27. Ephesians 1:4 and 1 Pet. 1:20 both use the phrase "before the foundation of the world."

to human decision making (rather than attributing turns of events to supernatural or impersonal influences), but Glenn Chesnut calls it "simply another face of Fortune."[28] As an example, the conversion of Constantine would constitute such a *kairos* moment for the late Roman Empire.

Along with a beneficent providential agent, historians also understood that there could be opposing (but unequal) agents. As one aspect of the pagan understanding of Fate, writers identified a retributive (revenging, punishing) element. Sometimes historians referred to the "jealousy of the gods" or to the envy of a particular god or goddess as a cause of trouble. Discord (*Eris*) or Envy (*Phthonos*) could also manifest as a personified force in the universe, who cannot tolerate prosperity and peace among mortals. For various reasons there seemed to be a need to throw human events into upheaval and chaos. Christian historiography incorporated this concept, using the biblical figure of the devil (together with his demons), who fits perfectly the role of the malignant power in the universe, the enemy of God and of God's people, the church. Christians understood that this agent (although subordinate) had some measure of freedom to oppose God's work through the church by various means: sometimes through persecution, other times through heresy. For example, the author of the account of events in Lyons in AD 177 attributed the outbreak of persecution against the Christians to Satan, variously called the "enemy," "demon," "evil one," and "the wild Beast."[29] In another example, the bishop Theodoret of Cyrus, who composed a history of the church between 448 and 450, attributed the outbreak of the Arian heresy to the "all evil [*pamponēros*] and envious demon [*baskanos daimon*]," who could not bear to see the church enjoying its newfound peace under Constantine.[30]

It becomes clear, therefore, that the most important features of history involved narration, remembrance, instruction in morality, and causal explanations. These aims remain consistent from the historians of antiquity, through to the church historians of the fourth century, and beyond. After this survey of the literary characteristics of historical writing, we turn to an issue that is at the heart of the importance of history, expressed in the question, Is it true?

28. Chesnut, *First Christian Histories*, 16. Ephesians 1 refers to the "fullness of time" in v. 10, using the term *kairos* (*plērōmatos tōn kairōn*).

29. *Martyrs of Lyons* 1.5, 1.6, 1.23, 1.57, 2.6, in *The Acts of the Christian Martyrs*, vol. 2, ed. and trans. Herbert Musurillo (Oxford: Clarendon, 1972), 63, 67, 69, 71, 81, 85.

30. Theodoret, *Church History* 1.2.5, in *Théodoret de Cyr: Histoire ecclésiastique, Livres I–II*, trans. L. Parmentier and G. C. Hansen, SC 501 (Paris: Cerf, 2006), 146–47, with my English translation.

Truth Telling in History: Standards of Truth in Ancient Historical Writing

While history as a literary form was somewhat closer to an art than a science in antiquity, nonetheless sufficient evidence remains to confirm that there did exist a standard of veracity in gathering and recording data and in critical assessment of the sources of data. History was not a bare chronicle—"bald narrative," in R. L. P. Milburn's words—but neither was it a fantastic mythical epic.[31] The author was concerned for accuracy but also desired to relate his story attractively, especially in an oral culture where literary works were most often publicly presented or performed. From its inception in the fifth century BC, Greek history reflected a narrative genre distinct from myth. Herodotus of Halicarnassus is commonly hailed as the "father of history" (though some may call him the "father of lies"), so scholars may feel justified in assessing the nature of ancient historical writing through the prism of his *Histories*. Herodotus (in)famously wove local myths and legends—essentially numerous "travelers' tales"—into the tapestry of his narrative, despite doubting the truthful provenance of many of the stories.[32] Still, he claimed to record the stories as he had received them, seemingly unconcerned as to their accuracy, allowing his readers to weigh that likelihood themselves after having enjoyed a good story.[33] Rather than being seen as the first to offer a work of true history (despite the shortcomings of his era), perhaps Herodotus ought better to be considered as a critical *link* between mythological stories and ethnographic legends on the one hand, and a more rigorously critical work of history such as Thucydides produced on the other hand. It seems that the witness of later writers, although unsparing in their admiration for Herodotus's skill as a raconteur, prefers the more severe work of Thucydides as a trustworthy historical work that defines the genre and can be commended as a model for future historians.

Steven McKenzie's *How to Read the Bible* amply illustrates the disparaging view of truth telling in ancient historiography.[34] In McKenzie's view (following John Van Seters), accuracy and truth telling were low priorities in ancient historiography. It is worth examining

---

31. Milburn, *Early Christian Interpretations of History*, 5.

32. Michael Grant, *Readings in the Classical Historians* (New York: Scribners, Macmillan, 1992), 23.

33. Herodotus, *Histories* 2.123, 7.152 (Waterfield, 144, 457).

34. Steven L. McKenzie, *How to Read the Bible: History, Prophecy, Literature—Why Modern Readers Need to Know the Difference and What It Means for Faith Today* (Oxford: Oxford University Press, 2005).

McKenzie's argumentation and examples because, as one reads his interpretation of ancient historiography, his cherry-picking of ancient sources becomes patently obvious, along with his theological agenda. Citing Richard Nelson to help him define ancient historiography, McKenzie writes, "Consequently, history is not the same thing as objective, detached reporting. It is a type of literature, and as such, it has a literary intent. The writer of history seeks to make the past alive for the reader by telling a story."[35] As it stands, this definition is not in dispute, but McKenzie follows up with several more assertions that lead his reader to despair of finding truthful historical accounts in antiquity.

> History writing in ancient Greece was not primarily concerned with relating past events "as they really happened." This is surprising to modern readers because it is how we now tend to define history. But telling exactly what happened in the past was "neither an important consideration nor a claim one could substantiate."[36]

He also declares,

> The ancient readers understood this. . . . Ancient historians may have occasionally invented stories and other materials for inclusion in their histories. Inevitably, their sources were incomplete and left gaps in the coverage of history. . . . [He cites Finley once more:] "But ancient writers, like historians ever since, could not tolerate a void, and they filled it in one way or another, ultimately by *pure invention*."[37]

McKenzie lays out his rationale for the conclusions he will draw by citing Herodotus and Thucydides as examples of ancient historians. He proceeds to latch on to historical speeches, stating that they were usually invented (a mostly true claim). He offers examples from Herodotus and then turns to Thucydides's *Peloponnesian War* 1.22, omitting several sentences in which Thucydides gives the rather exacting criteria by which he determined what to write in a speech and how to give a narrative account of events. Citing Nelson again, McKenzie writes, "We have no good reason for taking the speeches to be *anything but inventions* by the historians, not only in their precise *wording* but also in their *substance*."[38] This assessment is a far cry from the intentions

35. Ibid., 27, citing Richard Nelson, *The Historical Books* (Nashville: Abingdon, 1998), 25.
36. McKenzie, *How to Read the Bible*, 28, citing Moses Finley, *The Use and Abuse of History* (New York: Viking, 1975), 29.
37. McKenzie, *How to Read the Bible*, 27–28, emphasis added, citing Moses Finley, *Ancient History: Evidence and Models* (New York: Viking, 1986), 9.
38. McKenzie, *How to Read the Bible*, 27, emphasis added.

and scrupulously careful historical methodology of Thucydides, as we shall see below. McKenzie continues,

> The point is that Herodotus and other ancient Greek historians exercised *considerable freedom* in their literary *creations*, especially in the arrangement of materials, but also sometimes in the basic *content*. . . . Again, the ancient historian's primary concern was *not* with detailing exactly what happened in the past. Rather it was with interpreting the meaning of the past for the present, with showing how the "causes" of the past brought about the "effects" of the present.[39]

This series of quotes follows a discussion on ancient historiography, whose conclusions he then applies to Old Testament historical material, even though the legitimacy of drawing these kinds of parallels between ancient Greek historiography and the Old Testament is in no way self-evident. As he consistently emphasizes his point, he prepares the reader to accept his thesis as he applies it to Old Testament historiography, by which he strips particular passages of historical viability and relegates them to the status of "etiologies."[40] Although there are some similarities between the two (like the rubric of vice and virtue), we shall see that Greek methodological ideas concerning historiography will not allow McKenzie's points to stand firmly.

One would have to be foolhardy indeed to attempt to prove McKenzie and his sources wrong on *every* point, or to portray the ancients as unbiased, objective observers who accumulated evidence and deployed resources with the skill and technological advantages offered by modern journalism. But neither should the ancients be broadly portrayed as purveyors of pure invention, dressing up events at the expense of truth. Historical bias and journalistic limitations will always exist, but this is no reason to portray the ancient historians as if they had no standards of objective truth whatsoever and did not aspire to any, or that ancient historical narratives only cloaked themselves in the respectable garb of fact while underhandedly advancing their own agenda, playing fast and loose with information, and even willfully misinforming the audience.

In fact, there is evidence from antiquity for a standard or ideal historical product, and this standard included truthfulness, a clear distinction from other literary genres, selectivity of evidence, and a critical assessment of various accounts. The classical historians expressed a concern for truth telling in historiography and deprecated an exaggerated or patently untrue product. Thucydides's magnum opus clearly fits these truth-seeking parameters, and later writers recognized his achievement.

39. Ibid., 28–29, emphasis added.
40. Ibid., 29–46.

He opens his work with a few programmatic comments on the nature of history, how it has been done in the past, and how he proposes to go about his task: "The way that most men deal with traditions, even traditions of their own country, is to receive them all alike as they are delivered, without applying any critical test whatever."[41]

Thucydides mentions several examples in both ancient history as well as contemporary history, then continues: "So little pains do the vulgar take in the investigation of *truth*, accepting readily the first story that comes to hand," making oblique reference to (the unnamed) Herodotus, his older contemporary.[42] He explains further that, "on the whole," his own conclusions may "safely be relied upon." Thucydides intends to avoid "the lays of a poet displaying the exaggeration of his craft," as well as "the compositions of the chroniclers that are attractive at *truth's* expense."[43] Many of these prior accounts treat events that occurred so long ago that they basically possess legendary or mythical status. "Turning from these, we can rest satisfied with having proceeded upon the clearest data, and having arrived at conclusions as exact as can be expected in matters of such antiquity."[44] Early on, Thucydides acknowledges the limitations of his evidence, but also clearly states his intention to present a truthful account.

It is worth citing in full the portion of Thucydides's prologue concerning invented speeches used selectively by McKenzie to make his own point. Rather than proving McKenzie's argument about speeches being "pure invention" and historians exercising "considerable freedom" in both form and content, Thucydides seems to say something quite different.

> *With reference to the speeches in this history*, some were delivered before the war began, others while it was going on; *some I heard myself, others I got from various quarters; it was in all cases difficult to carry them word for word in one's memory, so my habit has been to make the speakers say what was in my opinion demanded of them by the various occasions, of course adhering as closely as possible to the general sense of what they really said.* And with reference to the narrative of events, far from permitting myself to derive it from the first source that came to hand, I did not even trust my own impressions, but it rests partly on what I saw myself, partly on what others saw for me, the accuracy of the report being always tried by the most severe and detailed tests possible.[45]

41. Thucydides, *Peloponnesian War* 1.20 (Crawley, 10).
42. Thucydides, *Peloponnesian War* 1.20 (Crawley, 10, emphasis added).
43. Thucydides, *Peloponnesian War* 1.21 (Crawley, 10, emphasis added).
44. Thucydides, *Peloponnesian War* 1.21 (Crawley, 10).
45. Thucydides, *Peloponnesian War* 1.22 (Crawley, 11, emphasis reflects McKenzie's selection from Thucydides).

In order to be exacting in getting to the truth of a matter, Thucydides states that he had to expend some effort to weigh the likelihood of the veracity of one or another account if eyewitness reports of the same event did not match. He also intended his history to be sober writing rather than merely entertaining: "The absence of romance in my history will, I fear, detract somewhat from its interest; but if it be judged useful by those inquirers who desire an exact knowledge of the past as an aid to the interpretation of the future, which in the course of human things must resemble [the past] if it does not reflect it, I shall be content."[46]

Long after his time, Thucydides's influence was felt and his work admired as a benchmark for future historical works. Later rhetoricians recognized both him and Herodotus as leaders in the field of historiography, but Thucydides appeared to take the palm for truthfulness, while Herodotus received accolades for his evocative narrative and dramatic skills. The great rhetor Quintilian wrote, "Many have written history with distinction, but no one doubts that two are far ahead of the rest. . . . Thucydides is close-knit, concise, always pressing on. Herodotus is charming, clear, discursive."[47] Additionally, Quintilian affirms that history as a genre clearly differs from the rhetoric of the courts in both its form (narration, not argument) and purpose (to aim for posterity and the future, not to argue a case in the present). It is true, Quintilian writes, that orators could benefit from some aspects of the discipline of history, but legal oratory and history were clearly different genres and were not to be inappropriately mixed (although history could provide precedents of which it would behoove a lawyer to apprise himself, and indeed a number of Christian apologists certainly used historical data to make their cases).[48] Another writer, Longinus, also commended Thucydides as one of the best historians of the past whose works endure and who is worthy of imitation.[49]

Thucydides's most fervent fan was the mid-second-century satirist, Lucian of Samosata, who reiterated half of a millennium later the same emphases on historians' rigorous and dogged pursuit of truth, above all in historical narrative. While Lucian's piece *How to Write History* is largely satirical and maintains a light tone, it nonetheless makes the serious point that, by and large, many contemporary historians wrote with a self-serving eye to the present and were egregiously biased and

---

46. Thucydides, *Peloponnesian War* 1.22 (Crawley, 11).

47. Quintilian, *Institutio Oratoria* 10.1.73–75 (trans. Winterbottom), in Russell and Winterbottom, *Ancient Literary Criticism*, 391.

48. Quintilian, *Institutio Oratoria* 10.1.73 (trans. Winterbottom), in Russell and Winterbottom, *Ancient Literary Criticism*, 385. More on the usable past in chapter 3.

49. Longinus, *On Sublimity* 14.1 (trans. D. A. Russell), in Russell and Winterbottom, *Ancient Literary Criticism*, 476.

sometimes downright deceptive. Some will no doubt object that this is satire and should not be taken seriously; I reply that Lucian's satire is driven by a need for critique but also self-preservation. His humorous critique demonstrates that ancient writers understood what the genre of history entailed and recognized that accuracy should be a central feature. It seems that his satire was driven by the existence of so-called histories whose flattering and self-serving motives were unmistakably transparent. Also, his satire is more than an offhanded critique; it is extensive and pointed. Thucydides had made similar comments in his preface to the *Peloponnesian War*, and it seems that Lucian is indebted to him, or engaging in a bit of historical retrieval himself, borrowing from Thucydides's high standard to critique the historians of his own day.

In his *How to Write History*, Lucian makes several strong points regarding the characteristics of good historiography. First, history is not panegyric—that is, an extensive work of praise and occasional flattery. Second, history is not poetry. Third, historical writing is oriented toward the future. Fourth, history must be truthful if it is to be useful. It does not necessarily have to be adorned and pleasing to the reader. It should not be so "dressed up" in fable, fiction, and encomia that it no longer resembles *history*. Next, Lucian describes the ideal historian as one who has political understanding and good literary technique, not an "armchair" historian. He is independent minded and fearless, disinterested and with no stake in either side of a story. He must tell things as they happened, not catering to the reputations of one or another figure, since if he does so he will necessarily have to lie. "History, on the other hand, cannot tolerate the least fragment of untruth."[50] His example of this unbiased and evenhanded reporting is Thucydides.[51]

Further, he believed that "the one function of the historian, then, is to relate things as they happened." Referring again to Thucydides, he writes the following regarding the historian:

> Even if he dislikes people for private reasons, he will put the public interest far higher, and think truth more important than his personal feud. . . . This, as I said, is the one special feature of history. *Truth* is the only goddess to whom the potential historian has to sacrifice; he need not trouble with anything else. His single criterion, his one exact standard, is to bear in mind not his present hearers, but his future readers.[52]

50. Lucian, *How to Write History* 7, in Russell and Winterbottom, *Ancient Literary Criticism*, 537.
51. Lucian, *How to Write History* 38, in Russell and Winterbottom, *Ancient Literary Criticism*, 541.
52. Lucian, *How to Write History* 39, in Russell and Winterbottom, *Ancient Literary Criticism*, 542, emphasis added.

"This, then," Lucian continues, "is the historian I want—fearless, incorruptible, free, the friend of truth, and plain speaking. Let him . . . call a fig a fig, a tub a tub."[53] Thucydides's work endures as a hard-hitting piece of critical historical writing, while Herodotus's endures because it is an enjoyable read, "an exhibition-piece for the moment."[54]

> [Thucydides] laid down these rules [of balanced and independent-minded historical reporting] definitively, distinguishing the good from the bad in history with great wisdom. . . . He does not welcome fable, but bequeaths to posterity a *true account* of events. He introduces also an argument from utility, and defines the purpose of history in a very sensible way: "If the same sort of thing happens again," he says, "people will be able to handle their problems better by referring to the record of the past."[55]

After treating the historian's style, which should be clear and plain, and understandable to "the masses," he turns his attention to data collection.[56] "A historian must not be careless about the collection of facts. He must investigate the same matters over and over again, with pain and effort. If he can, he should go to the site, and see with his own eyes. If this is impossible, he must pay attention to the most impartial informants, those whom he thinks least likely to add to or subtract from the facts out of favor or prejudice."[57] Lucian's next section rebuts McKenzie's emphasis on ancient historians blurring the boundary between factual history and rhetorical narrative, commenting, "Historians are not like orators. What they have to say exists . . . because it really happened."[58] Historians are like "artists" whose materials were provided, and "their art consisted in managing the material for the purposes required. Well that is also the historian's position. He has to organize his facts skillfully, and express them as vividly as he can."[59] The historian does not make up the facts; he fashions his history out of information about real events that he gathers, organizes, and assesses critically.

53. Lucian, *How to Write History* 41, in Russell and Winterbottom, *Ancient Literary Criticism*, 542.
54. Lucian, *How to Write History* 42, citing Thucydides, *Peloponnesian War* 1.22, in Russell and Winterbottom, *Ancient Literary Criticism*, 542.
55. Lucian, *How to Write History* 42, in Russell and Winterbottom, *Ancient Literary Criticism*, 542–43, emphasis added.
56. Lucian, *How to Write History* 44, in Russell and Winterbottom, *Ancient Literary Criticism*, 543.
57. Lucian, *How to Write History* 47, in Russell and Winterbottom, *Ancient Literary Criticism*, 544.
58. Lucian, *How to Write History* 51, in Russell and Winterbottom, *Ancient Literary Criticism*, 544.
59. Lucian, *How to Write History* 51, in Russell and Winterbottom, *Ancient Literary Criticism*, 544–45.

After a section on features of a proper history (several of which are mentioned in the first portion of this chapter), Lucian concludes,

> Remember, in general, my refrain: don't write with your eyes only on the present, for your contemporaries to praise and honour you; make all eternity your goal, write for posterity, ask the future to reward your writing, so that it can be said of you, . . . "He was always for the *truth*." . . . And so must history also be written—with honesty and hope for the future, not with flattery to gratify present recipients of praise. Here is your standard and rule for a proper history.[60]

Rise of Historical Forms

The historical forms that arose in the first few centuries of the church seemed to be oriented toward questions and issues pertinent to each century; although they were certainly written for posterity, they were not unrelated to previous centuries. In fact, arguments, questions, and topics frequently built upon those in previous writers. Clearly, most writers knew they followed in a tradition. As the gospel spread throughout the gentile world, elements of *historical apologetic* can be found in the preaching of the New Testament church. The Old Testament was critically important in Peter's, Stephen's, and Paul's explanations of the relationship between torah/law and promise/grace, as they tried to communicate the significance of Jesus's saving life and atoning work for both Jews and gentiles.[61] Also significant was Peter's Pentecost sermon (Acts 2:14–36, 38–39), which demonstrates the idea of the God of history as foremost in the apostles' minds for explaining their experiences with Jesus as well as the events of the day of Pentecost witnessed by the audience in Jerusalem. The God who spoke his promises through the prophets David and Joel fulfilled his plan of redemption in the apostles' day through the life, death, and resurrection of Jesus, David's descendant, and through the descent of the Holy Spirit by whom the prophets had spoken (Acts 4:25). In addition, Peter's address on Solomon's porch (Acts 3:12–26) affirms the axiom that "the God of our fathers" is the sovereign God who fulfilled his eternal plan through the suffering and resurrection of Jesus (Acts 3:13–15, 18). Further, God's plan of redemption remains to be fully consummated in the future, at "the time for restoring all the

---

60. Lucian, *How to Write History* 61, in Russell and Winterbottom, *Ancient Literary Criticism*, 547, emphasis added.

61. This line of argument appears especially strong in the Epistles to the Romans and Galatians in the figure of Abraham.

things about which God spoke by the mouth of his holy prophets long ago" (Acts 3:21). This genre continued to develop as the second- and third-century church defended itself and its teachings against various theological, civil, and philosophical opponents. The church's intense apologetic efforts extended even into the fifth century, as exemplified by Augustine's masterpiece, *The City of God.*

In its continuing growth and expansion, the church also encountered doctrinal challenges (heresies) as it sought to develop its theological principles, especially regarding the doctrines of creation, Christ, and the Trinity. Standing in the firm tradition of the apostles, the church vehemently opposed heretical ideas and practices, and the bishops especially served in this capacity, in an effort both to instruct the flock and to protect it from false doctrine. Some of these bishops undertook to write a kind of *doctrinal* history of the particular heresy they were fighting; their treatises produced a historical form known as *heresiology*, a history of heresy.

As early opposition to Christianity intensified and the church suffered intermittent persecution during the first three centuries, Christians recorded accounts of the martyrs' ordeals as they attempted to walk faithfully in discipleship after their Master, who had exhorted them to take up their cross and follow him. This historical form is known as *hagiography*, the biographies of holy men and women (from *hagios*, meaning "holy"). This form did not cease with the conclusion of persecution in the fourth century as the church was legalized under Emperor Constantine via the Edict of Milan in AD 313. Rather, the lives of martyred men and women served as heroic narratives, and examples of holy living and sacrificial discipleship for Christians of later generations to remember and imitate. Further, new biographies emerged, portraying holy men and women whose lives were extraordinary in their realization of the ascetic ideal of self-denial and control of the passions. These Christians served as role models of sacrificial discipleship in a context of peace, political favor, and prosperity for the church: to use a contemporary term, they were the "Radical" Christians of antiquity.

As Christianity experienced the boon of freedom in 312 after a terrifying decade of persecution (most intensely prosecuted in the eastern portion of the Roman Empire—Palestine and Egypt until 324), we find that *chronological narrative* in the Christian tradition made its debut. This genre (which came to be called *ecclesiastical history*) fused the biblical understanding of history as reflected in the traditions of the Deuteronomistic Historian and the Chronicler, with the classical form of history as it was taught in classical *paideia*. The result was a work focused on God's providential acts in history to bring about the triumph of the church. Its ideological principles were derived from the Old Testament while its format was familiar to a classical audience. Another facet of chronological narrative is the *Chronicles* produced by several writers such as Eusebius, Jerome, and others. These were not written in the classical style of a history, but rather attempted to put all of world history into a universal chronicle and to show where Christianity fit into the historical world scheme. Often there was an apologetic point so that these works defy easy classification as history or apologetic. These works will be briefly addressed in chapter 6.

Moving through these forms in order from historical apologetic to chronological narrative, it will be helpful to provide some examples of each before delving into them separately over the following chapters.

Apologetic: The Story of an Argument

The church's apologetic tradition began at its inception, on the day of Pentecost. The apostolic preaching contained the gospel *in nuce*, and apologetic often served as its vehicle. The preaching of Peter and Paul consistently conveyed the same facts of Jesus's prophesied life, death, and resurrection, but this kerygma was pitched differently according to context or need. For example, in his Pentecost sermon (Acts 2, see above), Peter defended the events of the day in terms of prophetic fulfillment, as an outworking of the prophecy of Joel 2. In a later chapter, Stephen defended himself with an *apologia* based on the form of "historical retrospect—a form well established in the Jewish tradition."[62] He countered the allegations of his accusers by rehearsing Old Testament history with respect to the two accusations against him: deprecating the temple's importance and speaking against the torah. As he reviewed the place of the tabernacle—the temple's precursor—and then the temple in the religious life of Israel, he built an argument that the age of temple worship had passed with the coming of Jesus, whose focus was on the "temple of his body" (John 2:21), one "not made with hands" (Mark 14:58). He also indicted his accusers based on their very respect for the law and the giver of that law, Moses: although they upheld the law's importance as being divinely derived and venerated Moses the mediator, they did not keep that law, and they rejected God's latest prophetic spokesperson (Christ), just as their fathers rejected Moses (even in his own lifetime) as well as every other prophet who spoke from God (Acts 7:35, 39, 51–53).

62. F. F. Bruce, *The Book of the Acts*, NICNT (Grand Rapids: Eerdmans, 1988), 133.

The second and third centuries have been broadly known in church history as the "Age of the Apologists," although current scholarship indicates that this is an increasingly problematic phrase and concept. In the early centuries, when Christianity was still a minority religion in the Roman Empire, the church felt compelled to defend itself against various accusations by both pagan and Jewish challengers. Apologists such as Justin and Tertullian defended their monotheistic faith against accusations of atheism; they defended their refusal to participate in civic ceremonies that required idolatrous sacrifices (either to a god or to the emperor); they defended themselves against accusations of antisocial tendencies, lack of patriotism, and an unthinking faith; and they defended their sacred communal rites and fellowship meal against allegations of incest and cannibalism. Among other rhetorical strategies, many apologists included historical arguments, such as demonstrating the reasonableness of their faith and practice by appealing to how Christian doctrine and ethics were similar to classic philosophical ideas and ideals, like those in the life of the venerable and ancient Socrates. Another historical argument involved tracing a time line from Moses forward in an attempt to demonstrate the antiquity of Christianity and to show how it superseded the antiquity of pagan religion, proving that it was not a recently invented religion.

Apologies, or works of a clearly apologetic nature, did not cease with the toleration of Christianity resulting in the end of persecution. In the early fourth century, just after the church's legalization, the rhetorician Lactantius wrote a historical and somewhat apologetic work, *On the Deaths of the Persecutors*, arguing that persecuting emperors were severely punished by God through foreign captivity, usurpation, or debilitating disease, while those friendly to the growing church were rewarded by God with a lengthy life and reign (a theme that also appears in Lactantius's contemporary Eusebius and those historians who continued his legacy). Although the work is mainly rhetorical, it may serve as something of a triumphalistic counterpart to the accounts of the martyrs, as a vindication of their innocence and proof of "God's intervention in human history," borne out by the historical record.[63] More directly apologetic in nature is Eusebius's massive two-part opus *Demonstration of the Gospel* (composed after 313), which includes the treatise *Preparation for the Gospel*. Against some of the blistering criticisms of the pagan philosopher Porphyry, Eusebius compares Greek literature to the Bible and finds Christian teachings superior to pagan philosophy. He also demonstrates how the historical life of Jesus

---

63. Timothy Barnes, *Early Christian Hagiography and Roman History* (Tübingen: Mohr Siebeck, 2010), 115.

fulfilled the Old Testament prophecies, thereby making Christians the true heirs of Old Testament promises.[64] In another example of later historical apologetic, the great North African bishop Augustine also engaged in historical apologetic in order to defend the church against charges of inviting barbarian invasions of the Roman Empire due to its abandonment of the traditional veneration of Roman gods. In *The City of God*, Augustine composed his arguments on the basis of respected pagan Roman historians like Sallust and Cicero, countering the church's accusers by using the facts of their own national histories against them.

Heresiology: The Story of Heresy/Doctrine

This historical and literary form is one that current evangelicals subsume under apologetics. In addition to engaging the broader culture outside the church with arguments defending against various accusations or caricatures, many apologists challenged false doctrines within the church. The bishop Irenaeus—followed by Tertullian, Hippolytus, and others whose publishing ministries combated heretical doctrines— wrote a kind of history of heresies; hence these writers are also known as *heresiologists*. They will be examined more closely, but they were not alone in composing focused works against heretics. Theologians and bishops like Athanasius and Augustine composed heresiological treatises that may be classified as doctrinal polemic. The difference between heresiology and doctrinal polemic tended to be that the former model (like Irenaeus's) was more like a genealogy of multiple heresies (sometimes called "filiation"), resembling a family tree of heretical ideas and groups; while the latter model targeted one group (or founder) at a time, like Mani, Arius, Pelagius, Marcion, or Praxeas (possibly a symbolic name). A work of heresiology usually involved tracing the historical lineage of heretical teachers, aiming to show a morally or doctrinally corrupt originator. Thus Irenaeus traced the heresy of Gnosticism back to Simon Magus, whose story is found in Acts 8. Athanasius made it almost his life's work to combat Arianism, a Christological heresy teaching that Christ was an exalted creature rather than equal to (coessential with) God the Father. Athanasius traced Arianism back to Satan himself![65] These fathers wrote to show

---

64. Rebecca Lyman, "Eusebius of Caesarea (ca. 260–ca. 339)," in *Encyclopedia of Early Christianity*, ed. Everett Ferguson, 2nd ed. (New York: Garland, 1998), 399–402.

65. Athanasius, *Four Discourses against the Arians* 1.1.1 (NPNF² 4:306). For Irenaeus's tracing of Gnosticism back to Simon the Magician, see Irenaeus, *Against the Heresies*, 1.22.2–1.23.5, in *St. Irenaeus of Lyons: Against the Heresies*, trans. Dominic J. Unger, ACW 55 (New York: Paulist Press, 1992), 81–84.

that Gnosticism and Arianism, respectively, did not constitute true (orthodox) Christianity. And while correct doctrine on the issues of creation and Christology was critically important, pastoral concerns equally motivated these authors. For example, some members of Irenaeus's church were led astray and abused by Gnostic charlatans.[66] A number of women (including a deacon's wife) were seduced and "defiled in mind and body" by Marcus, a Gnostic teacher.[67] Some of these women, Irenaeus writes, returned to the church, but "gradually withdrew themselves in silence and despaired of the life of God; some of them apostasized completely."[68]

Interestingly, these authors' criticisms have a charge in common with Augustine's observations against the Manichaeans and evangelicals' criticism of Tolle: heretical teachers were misleading Christians by cloaking their messages in biblical language.[69] Augustine complained that the Manichaeans "baited the traps [to reel in converts from Christianity] by confusing the syllables of the names of God the Father, God the Son our Lord Jesus Christ, and God the Holy Ghost, the Paraclete, who comforts us. These names were always on the tips of their tongues, but only as sounds which they mouthed aloud, for in their hearts they had no inkling of the truth."[70] Irenaeus wrote that the Gnostics "select passages from the Scriptures in order to prove that Our Lord announced another Father beside the Creator of the universe, who, as we have already mentioned, was the product of Degeneracy."[71] What he means is that Gnostics taught that there was one god of the Old Testament, who was wicked, ignorant, and wrathful; and another God of the New Testament, the loving Father revealed by Jesus Christ. As examples, he gave the misinterpretation by Marcus and his followers of passages such as Isaiah 1:3; Hosea 4:1; Romans 3:11–12; and Exodus 33:20, which they twisted to show a distinction between the good God, also called Father or Profundity, and the evil god, the creator of matter.[72] Ultimately this dualistic view of God also posited a radical disparity between the Old and New Testaments. Similarly to Irenaeus, Athanasius wrote that the Arian heresy, "which has now risen as harbinger of Antichrist . . . in her craft and cunning, affects to array herself in Scripture language, like her father the devil, and is forcing her way back into the church's paradise,—that with the pretence of

---

66. Irenaeus, *Against Heresies* 1.13 (ACW 55:55–59).
67. Irenaeus, *Against Heresies* 1.13.5 (ACW 55:57–58).
68. Irenaeus, *Against Heresies* 1.13.7 (ACW 55:58–59).
69. See chap. 1.
70. Augustine, *Confessions* 3.6 (trans. R. S. Pine-Coffin [London: Penguin, 1961], 60).
71. Irenaeus, *Against Heresies* 1.19.1 (ACW 55:75).
72. Irenaeus, *Against Heresies* 1.19.1 (ACW 55:75).

Christianity, her smooth sophistry . . . may deceive men into wrong thoughts of Christ."[73] It was imperative, therefore, that those skilled in teaching doctrine could argue persuasively against erroneous teachings and discredit them by revealing their origins. The accusation that heretics deceptively twisted Scripture was also a theme in the work of Tertullian, who insisted that heretics thus had no right to Scripture since they were mangling its meaning. In opposing heresy, apologists defined the boundaries of orthodoxy, and in doing so they defined themselves as authoritative interpreters and constructors of Christian doctrine. Their doctrinal origins are apostolic, and their authoritative text, the Bible, is their privilege alone to interpret, since they alone have the interpretive key, the incarnate and resurrected redeemer Jesus Christ, truly God and truly human. Affirming the historicity of the incarnation was critical for the gospel, since many heterodox groups opposed either the human or divine nature of Christ. Further, affirming Christ's fulfillment of Old Testament prophecies ensured the integrity and unity of the scriptural canon.

Hagiography/Sacred Biography: The Story of a Witness

This type of history may also be termed "devotional history" and will be accorded two chapters in this volume. The documents here consist mostly of martyrdom accounts (known as *acta*) and the spiritual lives (*vitae*) of Christians, whether they were "professional" Christians—clergy or monastics—or lay Christians. Hagiography encompasses the dramatic stories of men and women, youth and elders, citizens of the empire from all walks of life and diverse vocations, who bore witness to Jesus—not Caesar—as their Lord. In fact, the word "martyr" (*martys* in Greek) means "a witness" or "one who gives testimony." The witness these people gave cost them their very lives.

Such stories deliver a powerful impact because of the natural drama of the weaker individual up against a powerful and hostile state, where the stakes are enormously high. Ancient techniques of historical narrative also highlight dramatic elements of the story, which carry the audience along. Devotional history is intended to connect with its reader, and it picks up on two important features of history's pedagogical function: (1) the intent to instruct through object lessons (morals) drawn from historical events, and (2) the intent to edify and exhort through personal examples. The intention of history was to teach through events and to motivate the reader to imitate noble models provided by the author;

73. Athanasius, *Four Discourses against the Arians* 1.1.1 (NPNF[2] 4:306).

this also is overwhelmingly the case in the stories of martyrs and saints. The concept of *imitatio*, which undergirds much ancient historical writing, appropriated biblical examples as models for Christian living (and dying). Eventually historical Christian figures who lived after the apostles would be looked to as models in a similar way.[74] The reasons for recording and retelling these accounts included commemoration of a life given in service to Christ, exhortation to faithfulness in Christian living in the face of the government's hostility, and a demonstration of true discipleship.

A good example of all three of these aims may be found in the ordeal of the famous second-century martyr Polycarp of Smyrna.[75] His story is retold in the style of the Gospel narrative of Jesus's passion. The narrative clearly shows that, as Polycarp modeled his life and death on that of Jesus, so Polycarp's followers modeled their own lives upon his: "Just as the Lord did, he [Polycarp] too waited that he might be delivered up, that we might become his imitators [*mimētai*]."[76] Polycarp's followers sought to "come into the kingdom of Jesus Christ following his [Polycarp's] footsteps."[77] In the account of Polycarp's martyrdom, we find a tradition of discipleship. Polycarp looked to Jesus as his model, while Polycarp's followers in Smyrna looked to their pastor as their model. It is clear that Jesus is always the "king and master," while the martyrs who are commemorated (whether Polycarp, as here, or any other martyr) are "imitators of the Lord" and our "fellow disciples."[78] They were not to be worshiped; that privilege was reserved for Christ alone. They should be remembered, however, and their lives of discipleship—in both living and dying according to the example of their (and our) master, Jesus—should be imitated. Their remains were often treated with great respect, commensurate with their lives of holiness and with the greatness of their sacrifice, not unlike the treatment of the remains of John the Baptist (Mark 6:29) and Stephen the deacon (Acts 8:2). In addition to Polycarp, we will become acquainted with many other men and women from the second to the fourth centuries who testified by their deaths that Christ is Lord, not Caesar.

What effect did these accounts have on later Christians? Persecution rapidly clarifies priorities and confronts a person with a choice between ultimate allegiance to God or to the current world order (i.e., Caesar); between a desire for heavenly, eternal realities or for earthly,

---

74. See Robert L. Wilken, *Remembering the Christian Past* (Grand Rapids: Eerdmans, 1995), 121–33.

75. For an account of his death, see Musurillo, *Acts of the Christian Martyrs*, 1–21.

76. *Martyrdom of Polycarp* 1.2 (Musurillo, 2).

77. *Martyrdom of Polycarp* 22.1 (Musurillo, 19).

78. *Martyrdom of Polycarp* 17.2–3 (Musurillo, 17).

temporal realities. Under the threat of death, will a believer demonstrate steadfastness in suffering discipleship or prefer the expediency of compromise? By hearing or reading the accounts we possess, martyrs received strength and endurance to face death, and later Christians were inspired to die daily to self. In a different way each experienced the privilege of sharing in the sufferings of Christ. The phenomenon is akin to the effects for the church in the book of Hebrews: much of the letter/sermon—especially chapter 11, the so-called hall of faith—lends itself to clarifying the Christian's identity as a cosufferer with Christ, but equally as a citizen with him in a heavenly rather than an earthly city. Additionally, the surviving accounts give a sense that God accords the martyrs glimpses of the eschatological reality toward which God providentially moves history. Part of this reality involves the ultimate conquest of evil forces (specifically, the devil himself), a conquest in which both martyrs and any true disciple are privileged to participate.[79]

After the era of martyrs had passed, men and women still sought to be radical followers of Jesus. In a number of ways, the biographies of the late third century and onward reflect themes similar to those of the martyr stories. Three stories selected for discussion in this volume are the *Life of Antony*, *Life of Macrina*, and the *Life of Melania the Younger*. All three reflect the authors' desire to memorialize their subject, their pedagogical intention to instruct readers in holy living by providing examples of holiness and self-denial from their subjects' lives, and their focus on their subjects' frequent victories over the devil. The story of Macrina evidences a special emphasis on sanctity, the life of Melania focuses heavily on asceticism, and Antony of Egypt's biography concentrates on his violent conflicts with demons.

Ecclesiastical History: The Story of the Church

Chronological narrative often involved some sort of apologetic motivation, so that chronicle and apologetic often appeared together in Christian historiography.[80] This seems to be the case, for example, in the preaching of the New Testament church, where the pairing of narrative history and apologetic appears in the sermons of Peter (Acts 2:14–40), Stephen (Acts 7:2–53), and Paul (Acts 13:16–41). The historiographical

79. For example, Tertullian wrote to a group of imprisoned martyrs, "The prison, indeed, is the devil's house as well, wherein he keeps his family. But you have come within its walls for the very purpose of trampling the wicked one under foot in his chosen abode" (*Ad Martyras* 1 [*ANF* 3:693]).

80. The same was often the case in classical and Jewish historiography as well.

themes of causation and providential fulfillment loomed large in narrative. By the time Eusebius put pen to paper to write his *Church History*, these themes were well established and developed in Christian apologetic, and even based on older patterns and historical paradigms evident in the Historical Books of the Old Testament, especially Judges, Samuel, Kings, and Chronicles. These themes, as well as the chronological framework of the *Church History*, were sometimes expressed through straight narrative and sometimes through a proliferation of documents about particular events, while at other times they undergirded apologetic arguments. For example, Eusebius's account chronicling the beginnings of the church from the apostles to his own time under the emperor Constantine was recorded for multiple purposes: praising the emperor, with whom he had developed a special friendship; venerating those he considered heroes of the faith (esp. the martyrs); highlighting and promoting the bishops of the church as the legitimate and doctrinally sound successors of the apostles of Jesus, proving the antiquity and hence the validity and authenticity of Christianity as a logical continuation and fulfillment of Judaism; and attempting to explain how the incredible situation of the church's newly favored status had been brought about by God.[81] In contrast to classical historical works, which consisted chiefly of heroic speeches, epic battles, and a focus on principal political figures, the new genre of church history offered copious documentation (rarely invented speeches), warfare waged against demonically instigated heresies and persecutions, and a focus on virtuous and orthodox ecclesiastical leaders (bishops and teachers) and eventually Christian rulers.

After this overview of the nature of historiography and its features, as well as an introduction to four historical forms in the early church's literature, the chapters that follow will examine each historical form in more detail, seeking to answer two questions: First, what is the historical dimension of each form presented? That is, which of the historiographical features does each contain, and how do they operate in that type of literature? Second, how does each form contribute to the formation of Christian identity?

---

81. Most of these reasons can be found in Eusebius's preface to the *History*. For the genesis and rationale of church history as a genre, see Jacob Neusner, "The Birth of History in Christianity and Judaism," in *The Christian and Judaic Invention of History*, ed. Jacob Neusner, AARSR 55 (Atlanta: Scholars Press, 1990), 3–4. See also Glenn Chesnut, *First Christian Histories*, chaps. 3–6; Arnaldo Momigliano, *The Classical Foundations of Modern Historiography* (Berkeley: University of California Press, 1990), 132–52; Arnaldo Momigliano, *Essays in Ancient and Modern Historiography* (Middletown, CT: Wesleyan University Press, 1982), 107–26; Gregory E. Sterling, *Historiography and Self-Definition: Josephos, Luke-Acts and Apologetic Historiography*, NovTSup 64 (Leiden: Brill, 1992; repr., Atlanta: SBL, 2005).

HISTORY AS APOLOGETIC

Harnessing a Usable Past

The prefect turned to Justin: "If you are scourged and beheaded, do you believe that you will ascend to heaven?" . . . Justin said: "We are confident that if we suffer the penalty we shall be saved." The prefect Rusticus passed judgement: "Those who have refused to sacrifice to the gods are to be scourged and executed in accordance with the laws." Then the holy martyrs went out to the customary spot, glorifying God, and fulfilled their testimony by their act of faith in our Saviour.

—*Acts of the Christian Martyrs* (trans. Musurillo), 47

PERSECUTION OF CHRISTIANS across the Roman Empire was not virulent at all times in all places; nonetheless it was a real threat in both East and West at various times. In his *Church History*, Eusebius identifies as imperial persecutors first Nero (64) and then Domitian (ca. 93–96), who followed his predecessor's bad example.[1] In the mid-third century, Eusebius cites the emperor Decius's brief persecution (249–51), which resulted in lapses of faith among some Christians and produced the Novatian schism in the West. Decius's policies demanded religious conformity and empire-wide sacrifice in a bid to return homage to the traditional gods of Rome, hoping for

1. Eusebius, *Church History* 3.17 (trans. G. A. Williamson, rev. and ed. Andrew Louth [New York: Penguin, 1989], 80–82).

their protection and assistance in Rome's military conflicts with the Goths along the Danube. Relative peace obtained under Gallienus, who declared toleration for Christianity in 260. During the Great Persecution, which began in 303, Diocletian and his imperial partner Galerius (esp. the latter) oppressed the Christians, causing horrific scenes that Eusebius narrates from his own memories as an eyewitness and from documents of the period. The accession of Constantine, who dispatched the imperial persecutor Maximinus Daia, ended the Great Persecution around 312, and peace reigned in the church, allowing a recovery. In 324 a final onslaught came against the church from Licinius, Constantine's co-ruler, and concluded with Licinius's death in 325. In between these date markers, there were sporadic regional outbreaks of hostility, much of it seemingly mob violence rather than instigated by the state.

Recent research in late antique literary culture, anthropology, and archaeology has rendered our picture of the church's history in the second to fifth centuries somewhat less certain than Eusebius's narrative would indicate. Narratives constructed by Christian historians like Eusebius and his continuators are seen as triumphalistic, not doing justice to the actual situation that obtained in Christian relations with Jews, pagans, and heterodox Christian groups. Christian self-definition vis-à-vis these other groups required them to draw stark and certain boundaries, which in reality were certainly more nuanced and complex. Therefore the scholarly approach to these rhetorical pieces of apologetic must be cautious, balanced, historically responsible, and aware that their construal of reality cannot always be taken at face value, especially in light of Christians' destruction of many adversarial pagan writings. These cautionary measures help us insofar as we do not seek simply to retrieve a mere ideology from the texts (although that does help us understand Christian perceptions), but we are also interested in recovering *truth*. This latter aim may be somewhat elusive; however, as exampled in the epigraph to this chapter, Christian confession entailed suffering and death often enough that there is an uncomfortably substantial body of extant apologetic and martyrological literature. That is a sobering and stark reality that confronts any attempt to retrieve the truth of past events from ancient literature. Rhetorical or not, Christians were open to prosecution and execution for a common core of accusations identified by apologists in both East and West.

In this chapter we will concern ourselves with Christian apologetic in a rather narrow sense. With this genre, it is easy to answer some questions about Christians' interest in their own past and what events precipitated that interest. Apologetic historical narratives arise when a group (usually ethnic) feels itself to be a disempowered (or persecuted) minority under the rule of a dominant power. By delineating the group's history, the apologist or historian makes claims about the antiquity of the group's past, the superiority of the group's achievements, its contributions to the dominant culture, and often the indebtedness of the dominant power to the minority group. This was the case in the ethnic history of the Babylonians composed by Berossus early in the third century BC, the history of the Egyptians attributed to the priest Manetho from the early third century BC, and the history of the Jews by Josephus in the first century AD.[2] Apologetic historiography (distinct from historical apologetic) was sometimes directed at the dominant power and other times at its own ethnic or religious group.[3] Often it was directed to both. In any case, these types of works by Christian apologists helped Christians know their place and assert their rights with respect to the Roman Empire and its politics.[4]

While the authors of historical apologetic are not historians composing narratives but rather orators arguing a particular case, their writing illustrates some advice regarding history given by Quintilian to orators. Quintilian believed that "history too can nourish the orator, with a rich and pleasant juice."[5] Of course he knew it was inappropriate to tell stories or to entertain in court while defending a client, but he writes, "History has a further use . . . in its supply of knowledge of events and precedents: in these an orator must be well versed."[6] Importantly, Quintilian taught that drawing examples from the past as evidence guards against bias that would be present with current examples.[7] The apologists put this advice into practice as they harnessed a usable past (events, trends, biographical information) in order to make their cases against their accusers' allegations.

The field of late antique apologetics is vast, so our focus will rest not on apologetic in general but on apologetic arguments that used history in some way to defend Christian beliefs and practices. This treatment is in no way exhaustive yet provides examples of historical arguments in defense of Christianity from representative apologists in both the Greek and Latin traditions. The literature on apologetics,

---

2. Gregory E. Sterling, *Historiography and Self-Definition: Josephus, Luke-Acts, and Apologetic Historiography*, NovTSup 64 (Atlanta: SBL, 1992), 136, 163, 175–78, 225, 392–93.

3. The distinction between the two phrases is subtle but significant. Apologetic historiographies were full-scale narrative works written from an ethnic minority standpoint. Historical apologetic (the device covered in this chapter) consists of rhetorical works of defense (apologies) written from the standpoint of the persecuted. The genres overlap to some degree when Christian apologists use the histories or parts thereof to make their case.

4. Sterling, *Historiography and Self-Definition*, 385–86.

5. Quintilian, *Institutio Oratoria* 10.1.31 (Winterbottom, 385).

6. Quintilian, *Institutio Oratoria* 10.1.34 (Winterbottom, 385).

7. Quintilian, *Institutio Oratoria* 10.1.34 (Winterbottom, 385).

ancient and modern, is currently burgeoning, and in view of monographs and articles now appearing on apologetic topics (esp. regarding the second century), interested evangelicals are afforded the opportunity for a healthy dialogue with the ancients on methods and approaches to defending our common faith.[8]

This chapter is laid out in three parts: after (1) an introduction to the apologists' historical context and biblical models, we next turn to what we shall call (2) *apologia* proper, concluding with (3) the form of heresiology. The section on *apologia* proper will identify historical arguments or themes apologists used to defend against pagan accusations of atheism, novelty, intellectual deficiency/credulity, and worship of a human being (who was, moreover, a criminal); the next part will treat heresiology, a polemical tracing of the history of false doctrines and their proponents. With regard to the former, representative second- and third-century selections from Justin Martyr's and Tertullian's *Apologies* will be adduced, as well as contributions from Theophilus of Antioch's *To Autolycus*. In the third century, opposition grew more shrill, and Christian apologists responded with greater sophistication, though still building on the foundation of earlier arguments, repeating them and incorporating them into their own projects. Pagan detractors such as the intellectual Celsus and the philosopher Porphyry drew rejoinders from the great Alexandrian theologian Origen (to Celsus), as well as Eusebius, Jerome, Apollinarius, and Augustine (to Porphyry, even long after his death).[9] Toward the end of the third century and into the early fourth, apologetic lagged somewhat, especially after the Constantinian achievement of imperial toleration for the church. Nonetheless, along with Christianity, paganism was still tolerated and did not disappear; Christian apologies could still be written in the style of the early apologists and with similar themes, but with the friendlier tone of a victor rather than of a persecuted and endangered minority sect.

From about the middle of the fourth century, Christian defensiveness steadily intensified because of the pagan reaction to Christian rule.

---

8. Examples of recent apologetics publications include Sara Parvis and Paul Foster, eds., *Justin Martyr and His Worlds* (Minneapolis: Fortress, 2007); William Edgar and K. Scott Oliphint, eds., *Apologetics Past and Present: A Primary Source Reader*, vol. 1, *To 1500* (Wheaton: Crossway, 2009); Jörg Ulrich, Anders-Christian Jacobsen, and Maijastina Kahlos, eds., *Continuity and Discontinuity in Early Christian Apologetics*, Early Christianity in the Context of Antiquity 5 (Frankfurt: Peter Lang, 2009); Mark J. Edwards, Martin Goodman, Simon Price, and Chris Rowland, eds., *Apologetics in the Roman Empire: Pagans, Jews, and Christians* (Oxford: Oxford University Press, 2009); Denis Minns and Paul Parvis, eds., *Justin, Philosopher and Martyr: Apologies*, Oxford Early Christian Texts (Oxford: Oxford University Press, 2009). Much more literature exists for popular audiences.

9. See Robert Wilken, *The Christians as the Romans Saw Them* (New Haven: Yale University Press, 1984), 126–63.

One powerful pagan opponent was the emperor Julian, the so-called
Apostate (r. 360–63). He sought to return the empire to its worship of
traditional deities, with himself as pontifex maximus (chief priest);
and he restored to the Senate House the Altar of Victory, which had
been installed by Augustus but removed by Constantius, Constantine's son. After Julian's demise, the empire was restored to Christian
rulers, like Gratian, who again removed the altar. Pagan aristocrats,
politicians, and intellectuals objected to its removal, and men like the
senator Symmachus petitioned the young Western emperor Valentinian
for the altar's restoration. His request (as well as subsequent requests)
was repeatedly denied, and Emperor Theodosius I (r. 379–95) actually
declared Christianity to be the official religion of the empire, taking
measures to legally suppress paganism. Pagan hostility was mount-
ing and culminated in the 390s. Accusations were leveled against the
church—namely, that desertion of the traditional gods had deprived
Rome of its protectors and had allowed Rome to fall prey to barbarian
devastations. When Rome was invaded and pillaged by the Visigoths
under their leader Alaric in 410, the Christians were once again on the
defensive, and men like Augustine and the Spanish priest Orosius set
about planning a response. Augustine's response was by far the most
complex, captivating, and enduring. Building upon prior theological
and apologetic historical understanding, Augustine set out a philosophy
of history as a process with a definite goal (telos), completely rejecting the influence of Fate or the possibility of cyclic history, and also
rejecting an imperial theology—a theology that had been clinched with
Eusebius's vision of history, which Orosius had accepted.

The third part of the chapter will concern itself with a different but
related kind of historical literature, heresiology, which flowed naturally
out of apologetic as the other side of the coin.[10] While heresiology
frequently blurred the line between polemic and apologetic, heresiology and apology are closely enough related to be treated together:
in fact some apologists wrote separate treatises of both kinds (like
Tertullian), while others evince elements of heresiology within their
apologies (like Justin). These writers are mainly doctrinal apologists, or
perhaps *polemicists* might be a more apt descriptor, since this kind of
argumentation does not remain defensive but rather attacks false ideas
and exposes them as such. As the apologists who defended Christianity
sought to define themselves over against Jews and pagans, heresiologists represent a further, narrowed self-definition as properly orthodox

---

10. Frederick Norris includes "histories of heresies" in his category of historiography ("Historiography," *EEC*, 532–35). See also Jeremy Schott, "Heresiology as World History in Epiphanius's *Panarion*," *Zeitschrift für Antikes Christentum* 10 (2007): 546–63.

(correctly thinking or worshiping) Christians, whose theological benchmark was basically the Rule of Faith (*regula fidei*), or Rule of Truth, and the apostolic tradition in the pre-Nicene centuries, and in subsequent centuries the Nicene Creed and orthodox creeds determined by later conciliar decisions and decrees.

Definition and Elements of an *Apologia*

An apology is usually defined as a "reasoned defense of belief or behavior," and the forensic *apologia* was a "speech offered by the accused in a judicial proceeding."[11] There was no set form for the apologies generally, but only for these forensic apologies, which were, strictly speaking, a legal defense systematically rebutting charges. For example, a famous *apologia* by Plato was Socrates's defense of his own controversial philosophical beliefs, teachings, and lifestyle. Interestingly, Socrates is an oft-referenced figure from antiquity that Christian apologists like Justin and Tertullian used in their own defense against charges of atheism in the empire.

Apologetic evinces both positive and negative aspects. The positive side has to do with defending Christianity by laying out its beliefs in a way that shows its reasonableness and logic, and even its consistency with and similarity to what pagans would acknowledge as true, noble, and virtuous. For example, Justin wrote that Christianity is a philosophy, believers worship the same Logos who inspired Socrates with true ideas, and that Christians are not atheists but monotheists like the philosophers. Justin's defense was logical and persuasive, addressing the emperor and his sons as fellow pursuers of the philosophical ideals of reason, truth, and wisdom.

Negative aspects of apologetics usually involved delving into polemic, moving from the defensive to the offensive, attack mode, and laying out and systematically refuting the opponent's errors of belief and practice. This style mainly appears in heresiology, but apologies whose titles contain the term "Against" (*Adversus*) indicate their controversial intent. Several apologists composed works against the Jews (*Adversus Judaeos*), modeled upon Josephus's work *Against Apion*, in which he defended Judaism as venerable and ancient. The Christians, of course, defended Christianity and its ties to Judaism in the face of Jewish counterassertions that Christians do not keep the Sabbath, practice circumcision, keep the feast days, and (in general) practice torah. From the very beginning and over subsequent

11. Harry Gamble, "Apologetics," *EEC*, 81.

centuries, Christians continued to see "themselves and Judaism as successive moments in the same story."[12] These particular treatises, then, revealed Christians' dual and somewhat uneasy relationship to Judaism: they believed that the church was the new Israel, "the Israel of God" (Gal. 6:16), which had superseded the old, disobedient Israel; yet the church's history was the Old Testament narrative, and Christians refused to discard their Jewish heritage. In fact, when Marcion of Sinope in Pontus (modern Turkey) came on the scene in the mid-second century AD, teaching a discontinuity with Judaism, his ideas were sharply and vehemently rejected by multiple apologists as heretical and dangerous, cutting off the church from its historical roots, as well as impugning the Old Testament revelation of God. Tertullian branded him "the Wolf of Pontus" (and a slew of other derogatory titles) and accused him of using "the knife, not the pen, since he made such an excision of the Scriptures as suited his own subject-matter."[13] Marcion, in other words, was prepared to discard the Jewish heritage entirely.

Other adversarial works were written against pagans, who most of the time were referred to as Greeks or Hellenists. This negative apologetic extended into heresiology, and some apologists, like Tertullian and Theodoret, wrote both kinds of works. The relationship between defensive and offensive apologetics is evident even in the current study of apologetics among evangelicals, where one finds both positive engagement with the culture, defending and explaining Christian belief and practice, as well as negative attacks on those who profess false doctrine, such as Jehovah's Witnesses and Mormon groups. For both ancient and current apologists, it is important to counter false teaching because it could confuse new believers as well as unbelievers. For ancient Christians, moreover, the stakes were even higher: false teaching could misrepresent Christianity to the civil authorities, resulting in persecution and death, especially in light of accusations of disrespect for (not sacrificing to) the emperor, disrespectful attitudes toward the state, or competing political loyalties or secret meetings, which could be construed as obstinacy, antisocial tendencies, or sedition.[14]

12. Frederick Norris, "Articulating Identity," in *The Cambridge History of Early Christian Literature*, ed. Frances Young, Lewis Ayres, and Andrew Louth (Cambridge: Cambridge University Press, 2004), 78.

13. Tertullian, *Prescription against Heretics* 38 (ANF 3:262).

14. The accusation of antisocial tendencies had been around since the first century, recorded in the second by Tacitus (*Annals of Imperial Rome* 15.41); their punishments under Nero for novelty, their "new and mischievous religious belief," is recorded in Suetonius (*Lives of the Twelve Caesars* 6.16, "Nero," translated by Robert Graves [London: Penguin, 1979], 221).

Biblical Models: Self-Definition against Judaism

In the time of the New Testament church, the major charges against
Christians included proclaiming Jesus as Messiah, worshiping him,
and proclaiming the gospel to the gentiles in order to share with them
the heritage of God's people. These beliefs and actions drew accusations of disrespect, blasphemy, and the defilement of Jewish law and
traditions of the fathers. As the (probable) writer of Acts, Luke makes
the case through the apologetic speeches/sermons of Peter (3:11–26),
Stephen (7:2–53), and Paul (22:1–21; 26:1–23; 28:17–28) that there is
continuity between the old covenant and the new covenant; and that
the Spirit-given prophecies proclaimed by Israel's prophets throughout
the nation's history are fulfilled by Jesus in his suffering, death, and
resurrection. These preachers reminded their accusers that Christians
did not reject the fathers or Moses or the prophets; rather, the Jews
had historically rejected God's messengers and dealt faithlessly with
them, even though they were confirmed through signs and wonders as
bearers of God's message and agents of his deliverance (Moses was a
prime example). Israel's historic patterns of faithlessness, rejection,
persecution, and even murder had recently recurred in bringing about
the death of Jesus, and also recurred in the rejection, persecution,
and murder of his followers (like Stephen). The historical argument
is brought polemically into the present as accusations are leveled at
those who considered themselves keepers of the law and teachers of
the people. These accusers bear an unattractive family resemblance to
other members of their "family," their forefathers: Stephen referred
to them as "stiff-necked people with uncircumcised hearts and ears"
and "betrayers and murderers" of the "Righteous One" (Acts 7:51–52
HCSB); Paul used Isaiah's words to describe them as spiritually "cal-
lous," "hard of hearing," and blind (28:25–27 HCSB); Peter called them
murderers of Jesus (5:29–30).

While defining their Christian identity over against and in relation to
the Jews, that is, in terms of both continuity in heritage yet discontinuity in their understandings of prophetic fulfillment, encounters such as
Paul's in Athens in Acts 17 invited Greek pagan philosophers to hear
the gospel as well. Paul did not shy away from discussing controversial
Christian ideas like the resurrection, but neither did he intentionally
offend his hearers, instead dialoging with them in terms of their own
interests. While Stephen and Peter appealed to fulfilled Old Testament
prophecies for their apologetic (as did Paul when he preached in the
synagogues), Paul also appealed to philosophy and the Greek interest
in religion and the gods. The New Testament Christians, then, saw
themselves as the new Israel and looked to the Old Testament as their

own ancient story.[15] The historical work of God in sending the Messiah as promised by the prophets was Christians' proof of the gospel's truth and the validity of their belief and practice. In looking back to the Old Testament for their history, Christians saw themselves as a distinct movement in world history, as the gospel was driven forth by the empowering of the Holy Spirit.[16] They also presented to the ancient world a totalizing definition of history as salvation history, with its understanding of God's redemptive plan and divine will as encompassing all nations, not just the Jews.[17] Luke's historical narrative helped "Christians understand their place in the Roman Empire."[18] Since Christianity distinguished itself from Judaism, it became vulnerable to persecution as a novel sect; therefore the church argued for continuity with Judaism and its antiquity, thereby gaining social and political standing in the Roman Empire.[19] Luke also defines for the church the apostolic tradition, so important for the church's self-understanding. Gregory Sterling explains, "Identity as a Christian meant maintaining a continuity with the tradition of the past, specifically the tradition of the apostles."[20] Significantly, of course, this aspect eventually became enshrined in the final lines of the Nicene-Constantinopolitan Creed (381).

History as Apologetic: Self-Definition against Pagan Culture

Justin, First Apology (ca. 150–60)

Just as Paul in Athens looked around at all the city's idols and was perturbed, so the early apologists and martyrs saw idolatrous statues that they associated with demons. The philosopher Justin's *First Apology* included both positive and negative apologetic, but the treatise is mostly conciliatory. Justin answers the common pagan accusation ridiculing the novelty of Christianity by claiming that the ancient Old Testament prophecies are fulfilled in Christ and the church. He begins his *First Apology* by addressing himself—a philosopher—to the philosopher-king Antoninus Pius and his two adopted sons and co-Caesars, Marcus Aurelius (Verissimus the philosopher) and Lucius Verus (Lucius the

---

15. Norris, "Historiography," 532.
16. Sterling, *Historiography and Self-Definition*, 360–63, 378–79.
17. Ibid., 363.
18. Ibid., 385.
19. Ibid., 385–86.
20. Ibid., 380–81.

philosopher).[21] Justin repeatedly emphasizes truth and justice, not as a disinterested party, but as one for whom the upholding of truth and justice is a matter of life and death. He presents Christian beliefs as "reasonable" and "true," two virtues that every philosopher strives for in gaining knowledge. Justin also appeals to kings as lovers of learning and dispensers of justice.[22]

As he appeals to imperial philosophical commitments, Justin brings up a crucial figure of the past. First, Justin equates Christians with philosophers and explains that their beliefs, worship, and way of life are rational. Next, he compares Jesus to the ancient and venerable Socrates, one whom pagan intellectuals might consider the ultimate philosopher, thus elevating Christianity to a high level of philosophical respectability. Justin also highlights the tragic story of Socrates's fate, similar to Christians' own deaths. Although universally respected and honored, Socrates had died as a martyr of sorts, having fallen victim to the unreasoning passions of Athens' ruling authorities. Since Rome's ruling authorities style themselves as enlightened philosophers, Justin seems to urge them not to repeat a historical tragedy by killing Christians.

In the course of defending Christians from charges of atheism, immorality, rebelliousness, and irrationality, Justin also defends them from the charge of practicing magic (which was illegal) by pointing out that Christians consider (and had considered for decades) one like Simon the Magician (Magus) to be an apostate and heretic. This Simon (Acts 8), from Samaria, Justin's own hometown, practiced magical arts, claimed to be a god, and allowed himself to receive worship, even receiving a statue in Rome. Simon and another compatriot, Menander, both carried on these deceptive and demonic activities.[23] The question naturally turned to Jesus and his miracles. Was Jesus a magician or truly the Son of God? Was he a crucified criminal worshiped by Christians? Justin turned to truthful prophecies and their fulfillment by Jesus through his life and death. These prophecies had been written down and "carefully preserved" by historical persons who wrote books under the reigns of historical kings, like Ptolemy Philadelphus, who included the Septuagint in his library.[24] Christ's incarnation was predicted as long ago as the time of Moses, and other prophets also predicted specifics of Christ's life, such as his virgin birth at Bethlehem and his crucifixion

---

21. Justin, *1 Apology* 1 (*ANF* 1:163). For a more detailed explanation of the imperial and familial relationships among the three addressees, see Denis Minns and Paul Parvis, eds. and translators, *Justin: Philosopher and Martyr* (Oxford: Oxford University Press, 2009), 34–41.

22. Justin, *1 Apology* 1.1–2 (*ANF* 1:163).

23. Justin, *1 Apology* 26 (*ANF* 1:171). This information is further confirmed (or repeated) by Irenaeus in *Against Heresies* 1.23.1–5 (ACW 55:81–84).

24. Justin, *1 Apology* 31 (*ANF* 1:173).

under Pontius Pilate.[25] Justin argues that, although the evidence of
Christ's virgin birth, suffering, and death is contained in these Jewish
documents (the Old Testament), the Jews do not understand them and
count Christians as apostates and blasphemers, persecuting them and
cursing them even recently during the Bar Kokhba rebellion (132–36).
Justin locates Christ's identity within Roman history and states that
this Christ is also God the Word (Logos)/Son, who became incarnate
as a human being.[26] The prophecies show Christ's divine origin, while
the genealogies demonstrate his humanity. In this discussion, Justin is
careful to distinguish these historical facts from the mythical fables of
the Greeks and Romans.

As Justin defends the church against charges of atheism and lack of
reverence for the gods, he lays out an explanation repeated subsequently
in the apologetic tradition. The stories of the gods are deceptions by
wicked demons, he insists.[27] These demons both lead people into heresy
(via agents like the unscrupulous Simon, Menander, and Marcion) and
cause persecution against Christians, perpetrated by people blinded to
true doctrine. Clearly, as a causal factor, demonic activity is front and
center in his *First Apology*, through deceivers, imitators, and counter-
feiters of true religion via pagan myths; demons also are persecutors
and disturbers of the church's peace.[28]

Justin turns to a more positive approach as he lays out Christian
doctrine and practice, showing its antiquity as well as its rationality
and compatibility with Plato. Demonstrating the church's antiquity
was critical to his defense, since Romans made a distinction between
the recent (*nova*) and the ancient (*vetera*), favoring the latter. What was
new and recent, the Romans considered faddish and perhaps ephem-
eral, neither reliable nor respectable, and a bit suspect. The old ways of
thinking and worshiping were tried and true, venerable and respectable.
Therefore the charge of "novelty" was serious, and Justin would not
be the last to counter it.

In Justin's view, the similarity of ideas between Plato and the church
regarding the Godhead and the concept of the Logos is due to Plato's
indebtedness to Moses, indicating the antiquity of Christian doctrine
and its priority over the respectable philosophical ideas of Platonism.
"It is not, then," Justin writes, "that we hold the same opinions as
others, but that all speak in imitation of ours."[29] Justin's appeal to the
indebtedness of Greek philosophy and ethics to one of Christianity's

25. Justin, *1 Apology* 33–35 (*ANF* 1:174).
26. Justin, *1 Apology* 32 (*ANF* 1:173).
27. Justin, *1 Apology* 54 (*ANF* 1:181).
28. Justin, *1 Apology* 57 (*ANF* 1:182).
29. Justin, *1 Apology* 60 (*ANF* 1:183).

forefathers is an example of his use of apologetic historiographical tradition, where the dominant group is indebted in an important way to the weaker group. By using this motif, Justin emphasizes Christianity's antiquity and moral and philosophical superiority vis-à-vis the Romans. In fact, Clement of Alexandria, born around the time of Justin's death, makes an expansive argument along the same lines in one of his own works, the *Stromata* (*Miscellanies*). He claims that even the philosopher (and mathematician) Pythagoras had acknowledged the indebtedness of Plato to Moses, asking, "For what is Plato, but Moses speaking in Attic Greek?"[30] Justin concludes his *apologia* by appealing once again to the emperors' justice and fairness in considering Christian teachings that are "reasonable and true," asking that the sovereigns abide by the ruling of Hadrian to refrain from hunting down Christians, and giving them a fair hearing if put on trial for lawbreaking.[31] Justin's arguments regarding Christianity's antiquity, priority, and superiority to pagan religions, and the intellectual and ethical merits of its doctrines, would bear fruit in the later apologetic tradition as apologists continued to draw upon historical material to extend these arguments.[32]

Theophilus, To Autolycus (ca. 180)

In an effort to defend Scripture against pagan error, many early apologists argued that Scripture predates the best of pagan history and literature, and therefore its doctrine is the original and most reliable religion. Theophilus, bishop of Antioch, made this twofold argument in his treatise *To Autolycus*, composed around 180, probably addressed to a friend whom he was trying to persuade to embrace Christianity. The progress of his argument, mirroring other apologetic arguments, reinforces an important point in contextualizing historical apologetic: the historical angle is brought into the apology as part of a broader theological polemic against the vanity of pagan idolatry.

In book 1, Theophilus begins by arguing that demons deceive people into worshiping false gods, and by book 2 he appeals to the antiquity

---

30. Clement of Alexandria, *Miscellanies* 1.22, in *ANF* 2:334–35. For Clement's more complete treatment, see *ANF* 2:324–29, and *Miscellanies* 2.1–5 (*ANF* 2:347–53). In the above-cited section of book 1, Clement cites several of the Jewish apologetic historiographers treated in Sterling's monograph, *Historiography and Self-Definition*: Eupolemus, Artapanus, and Josephus. Clement also cites several other ethnic and religious historians and chronographers such as Euphorus, Demetrius, Apion, and Apollodorus.

31. Justin, *1 Apology* 68 (*ANF* 1:186).

32. In a later section of *Miscellanies*, Clement also brings out the distinction between the new and the old, arguing that it is actually the Greeks who occupy themselves with ideas that are "things of yesterday and of recent date," while Christian Scripture belongs to "remote antiquity" (*Miscellanies* 1.29, in *ANF* 2:341).

of Christianity to demonstrate its chronological priority over other ancient cultures, and the superiority and truth of Christian Scripture and worship (therefore, pagan worship is false). Starting with a genealogy of Adam and Eve, Theophilus claims Cain as the founder of a city, in contradiction to Homer, who had said that there were no cities before the flood. He concludes that the Bible is "more ancient, yes, and . . . more truthful than all writers and poets," an obvious reference to the pagan canon of literary classics.[33] Christian civilization even preceded the flood, after which the rest of the great civilizations sprang forth as descendants from Noah's line: Babylon, Assyria, Canaan, and Egypt. According to Theophilus, all the records of these great civilizations are "recent" in "comparison with our books."[34] This appeal to the antiquity of the Judeo-Christian writings emphasizes their superiority since they are foundational to human civilization.

Autolycus is unconvinced by Theophilus's reasoning thus far, although he still seems open to listening.[35] In book 3, Theophilus moves to argue for the antiquity of Moses. Perhaps too trusting, Theophilus draws on earlier ethnic histories, like the work of the Babylonian priest and astronomer Berossus, and the Egyptian priest Manetho, whose histories containing dynastic pharaoh lists had been previously used by Jewish apologists like Josephus to prove Jewish antiquity.[36] Theophilus writes that the Hebrews built cities for the pharaoh; therefore, "the Hebrews, who also are our ancestors and from whom we have those sacred books which are older than all authors, . . . are proved to be more ancient than the cities which were at that time renowned among the Egyptians."[37] He claims that Moses is also older than the ancient Greek settlement of Argos, founded by its first king Inachus after the flood, and that Moses also predates the Trojan War (of Homeric fame) by at least nine hundred or one thousand years. To further drive home his point about the antiquity and priority of Judaism (and therefore Christianity) with respect to Greek culture, Theophilus delineates a universal chronology from Adam to Marcus Aurelius—an ambitious undertaking indeed![38] In

33. Theophilus of Antioch, *To Autolycus* 2.30 (*ANF* 2:106).

34. Theophilus of Antioch, *To Autolycus* 2.31 (*ANF* 2:107).

35. Theophilus of Antioch, *To Autolycus* 3.1 (*ANF* 2:111).

36. Avery Dulles explains that Christian apologists sometimes appropriated too naively the arguments they found in various sources and greatly exaggerated the antiquity of Moses and the priority of Christianity's intellectual and religious heritage to suit their argument (*A History of Apologetics* [Eugene, OR: Wipf & Stock, 1999], 28, 30).

37. Theophilus of Antioch, *To Autolycus* 3.20 (*ANF* 2:117).

38. This portion of the apology is perhaps a précis of a lost work by Autolycus, *The History*, which was a chronography.

the course of the genealogy, he integrates Jewish history with that of the Romans. "Hence," he boasts, "one can see how our sacred writings are shown to be more ancient and true than those of the Greeks, Egyptians or any other historians. For Herodotus and Thucydides, as also Xenophon, and most other historians began their relations from about the reign of Cyrus and Darius, . . . not being able to speak with accuracy about prior and ancient times."[39] For Theophilus, it was no great thing if the classical historians wrote the history of their own times: they were at a disadvantage when it came to writing with certainty about antiquity, and they were therefore forced to relegate that period and even the primordial times of universal origins—shrouded as they were in myth and speculation—to poets like Homer and Hesiod, and to philosophers like Plato and Thales. Christianity, by contrast, is not a religion of uncertainties, conjectures, fables, and myths. Rather, because of carefully kept records in the Sacred Scriptures, and recorded events that are corroborated by external documents, Christians can speak factually and with confidence about events from the foundation of the world and even from Adam, the first human being![40] Further, not only can Christians speak about the past because of the priority of their heritage, but they can also speak with authority about theological truth because the content of those most ancient records is God's revelation to his chosen people. He is the creator, the Jews are his people, and the church is the fulfillment of his cosmic plan for history.[41] Thus Theophilus brings the discussion back around to his primary interest, that of persuading his friend to accept the truths of this noble and ancient religion. A biblical tour through Christianity's past has served Theophilus well, helping his friend "to see the antiquity of the prophetical writings and the divinity of our doctrine, and that the doctrine is not recent, nor our tenets mythical and false, as some think, but very ancient and true."[42] Most pagans (Greeks), Theophilus laments, are ignorant of these historical truths because they live in idolatrous sin; blinded to the truth, they continue to persecute as they "put to death" and "subject . . . to savage tortures" those who worship the true God.[43]

39. Theophilus, *To Autolycus* 3.26 (*ANF* 2:119).
40. Theophilus, *To Autolycus* 3.26 (*ANF* 2:119).
41. Theophilus, *To Autolycus* 3.29 (*ANF* 2:120). Theophilus even accuses pagan writers (Plato and Apollonius) of getting dates wrong by up to fifty years. He suggests that they dishonestly reported earlier dates in an effort to make Greek culture appear more ancient than it actually was.
42. Theophilus, *To Autolycus* 3.29 (*ANF* 2:120).
43. Theophilus, *To Autolycus* 3.30 (*ANF* 2:121).

Tertullian, Apology (ca. 193–211)

After Justin and Theophilus made historical arguments for the antiquity of Christianity along biblical, philosophical, and theological lines, Tertullian built on their foundations in his own *Apologia*, delivering a decisive historical blow to the Romans' self-understanding as ancient and virtuous. In a powerful historical and rhetorical tour de force that Mark Burrows labels "forensic retorsion," Tertullian turns the Romans' accusations of novelty, atheism, and lawlessness back around to condemn the Romans themselves.[44] As previously with Justin, "apologetics could not afford to avoid the question of history," so Tertullian employs Quintilian's advice to the rhetor to be well apprised of historical *exempla* that may be put to good use in a legal argument.[45] Tertullian offers a "forensic defense of the legitimacy of Christianity" in the Roman Empire, but he also pushes back offensively with "a treatise on origins," both of the Romans and of the Christians (by way of the Jewish Scriptures).[46] The final result shows that in persecuting Christians, Romans are on the wrong side of history.

Although Tertullian addressed his *Apology* to the "rulers of the Roman Empire," there is no evidence that those rulers ever actually read it.[47] However, it is clear that many other Christians—and possibly pagan intellectuals—did read it. For example, Eusebius quotes several portions of it in his *Church History* to show that only bad emperors had persecuted the church, while other emperors like Tiberius or Marcus Aurelius admitted the truth of Christianity and sought to accord it a place in Roman society.[48] Tertullian, then, appeals to the rulers' sense of justice (as Justin had done), urges the Romans to "consult your histories," by which he means the works of Tacitus, and offers historical examples of Roman rulers who did and did not issue persecutory legislation: Tiberius was friendly; Marcus Aurelius, Trajan, Hadrian, Pius, and Verus (all philosopher-kings / enlightened monarchs) were protectors; while Nero and Domitian, universally reviled monarchs, were singled out as persecutors.[49] The argument goes that if the well-respected emperors had regarded Christians well, they ought still to be well regarded and well treated. If the Romans uphold laws inimical

---

44. Mark S. Burrows, "Christianity in the Roman Forum: Tertullian and the Apologetic Use of History," in *The Christian and Judaic Invention of History*, ed. Jacob Neusner, AARSR 55 (Atlanta: Scholars Press, 1990), 53.

45. Ibid., 52.

46. Ibid.

47. Tertullian, *Apology* 1 (*ANF* 3:17).

48. Eusebius, *Church History* 2.2 (Williamson, 38–39).

49. Tertullian, *Apology* 5 (*ANF* 3:22); Eusebius, *Church History* 2.25 (Williamson, 62).

to Christians, they are not in line with the "good" emperors but rather with the vile ones, who are "unjust, impious, base, of whom even you yourselves have no good to say."[50]

After impugning the Romans' sense of justice, Tertullian turns to the concept of antiquity and challenges Romans to be consistent with their supposed veneration of the past. With respect to the accusation that Christians dishonor the ancients and therefore also the traditional gods, Tertullian shows that Roman society only claims to honor the ancients and their virtuous ways. He asks, "What has come to your religion—of the veneration due by you to your ancestors? In your dress, in your food, in your style of life, in your opinions . . . you have renounced your progenitors. You are always praising antiquity, and yet every day you have novelties in your way of living."[51] Roman consuls, even before Christ, honored virtuous gods and expelled immoral deities, specifically Bacchus and Egyptian deities. These deities have since been restored, proving that the ancient ways of virtuous religion—even if it did entail idolatry, which is wrong—are cast aside and trampled by Romans, just as they accuse Christians of doing.[52] In fact, Romans are guilty of a steady moral and religious decline since the time of their forefathers. This historical argument is drawn from the tradition of the ancients, which was vitally important to the Romans.

In view of the importance attached to antiquity and tradition, Tertullian affirms the church's continuity with Judaism and offers examples of the Christians' antiquity, beginning with the history of their Scriptures. Scripture's "high antiquity . . . claims authority for these writings," so that the apologist is on common ideological ground with his audience; arguing for Scripture's authority is unnecessary, since the audience already accepts that authority on the basis of Scripture's antiquity. Furthermore, the long history of the Jews is historically witnessed by the ethnic apologetic historians we have seen previously, listed by Tertullian in a long catalog.[53] Tertullian relates the story of the production of the Septuagint at the request of Ptolemy Philadelphus in the mid-third century BC. The Hebrew Scriptures are much older than that, though, since the books of the Law were originally given to Moses, another ancient and venerable figure, older than Inachus, king of Argos (as in Theophilus), earlier than the destruction of Troy by about 1,000 years, and 1,500 years

50. Tertullian, *Apology* 5 (*ANF* 3:22).
51. Tertullian, *Apology* 6 (*ANF* 3:23).
52. Tertullian, *Apology* 6 (*ANF* 3:23).
53. In *Apology* 19 (*ANF* 3:33), Tertullian lists Manetho, Berossus, Hiram the king of Tyre (Hieromus), Ptolemy of Mendes, Demetrius of Phalerum, Apion, and Josephus.

older than Homer.[54] Tertullian admits that Christians have only existed since the reign of Tiberius, but through their Jewish heritage, the Scriptures and the prophets, they are much older.[55] Therefore, ironically, it is rather the Romans who are novel and the Christians who are ancient.[56]

After affirming Christians' continuity with Judaism, however, Tertullian also must explain their discontinuity since the Jews rejected the Messiah whom God had sent to them. Christ was intended as the savior of the human race, but the Jews misunderstood this revelation and crucified him instead (another historical event Tertullian can point out to the readers). Therefore the church has become the true heir of God's fulfilled Old Testament promises, and its ancient Scriptures have become the "treasure-source" from which "all later wisdom has been taken," effectively putting the Romans in the Christians' debt for any philosophical wisdom or religious truth they possess.[57]

Another path that Tertullian pursues into antiquity goes to the very heart of Roman religion and its gods. Tertullian examines classical sources for the gods' origins and finds that based on the writings of Greek and Latin "theologians" (or rather, mythographers), there is a consensus that the earliest gods had been humans.[58] Figures like Saturn, Hercules, and Jupiter had once been humans who were later declared gods and worshiped. These human-made gods who depended upon humans for their deity are laughable to Tertullian. In sacred mythology, the gods are prone to very human foibles and passions, unworthy in both word and deed to receive worship, and they also appear vulnerable to harm from humans. In fact, Tertullian unveils quite an extensive tradition of poetic, dramatic, and philosophical disdain of the gods in Greco-Roman sources and sometimes outright vilification of them.[59] Tertullian bluntly wraps up his theological argument: Christians do not venerate the Roman religion because those gods do not exist; therefore

54. These dates are Tertullian's calculations based on either apologetic tradition or his reading of the ethnic histories. They are quite out of line with current dating schemes for the life of Moses. See note 36 above for a cautionary note from Avery Dulles regarding Christian apologists.

55. Tertullian, *Apology* 21 (*ANF* 3:34).

56. Burrows, "Christianity in the Roman Forum," 68–71.

57. Tertullian, *Apology* 21, 47 (*ANF* 3:33–36, 51).

58. This concept is known as Euhemerism, named after the fourth-century BC Greek mythographer Euhemerus, largely considered an atheist in his own day. Euhemerus had written that the gods had once existed as humans, after whose deaths people exaggerated accounts of their lives and exploits, and developed myths over time. Other Christian apologists mention this concept as well in their polemics against idolatry.

59. Tertullian, *Apology* 13–15 (*ANF* 3:29–30). Chapters 14 (*ANF* 3:29–30) and 46 (*ANF* 3:50–51) mention the trial and death of Socrates for his supposed atheism.

there is actually no Roman religion to speak of, leaving Christians innocent of the charge of atheism.[60]

As he draws his *Apology* to a close, he anticipates the historical apology of Augustine, still almost two hundred years into the future. In a famous passage, Tertullian complains that Christians are perceived as the cause of all ills that befall the empire and therefore expected to pay with their lives when disaster strikes: "They think the Christians the cause of every public disaster. . . . If the Tiber rises as high as the city walls, if the Nile does not send its waters up over the fields, if the heavens give no rain, if there is an earthquake, if there is famine or pestilence, straightaway the cry is, 'Away with the Christians to the lion!' . . . Pray tell me, how many calamities befell the world and particular cities before Tiberius reigned—before the coming, that is, of Christ?"[61] There follows a long historical catalog of natural disasters and barbarian invasions, and the human death toll in various Roman military defeats. This evidence is the culmination of Tertullian's method of historical retorsion. "The truth is," Tertullian argues, "the human race has always deserved ill at God's hand" because it chose to worship idols, not God, and later rejected Christ.[62] He points accusingly at pagan society: "You, therefore, are the sources of trouble in human affairs; on you lies the blame of public adversities," since pagans ignore the one true god and worship idols.[63] The injustice done to both God and his people will be rectified in a last historical phase: the final judgment. In the consummation of time, it will be the Romans rather than the Christians who will be summoned before a tribunal, and in that court, idolaters will be condemned while Christians will be "acquitted by the Highest."[64] In the end, through the weapon of historical evidence, Tertullian shows his pagan persecutors to be on the wrong side of history in multiple ways: legally, ethically, theologically (religiously), and eschatologically, although they do not yet perceive this final aspect.

Augustine, The City of God (ca. 413–26)

Augustine's massive apology, *The City of God*, defended Christians against accusations of being the cause of military defeats that led to the sack of Rome in 410. These accusations apparently built upon already extant animosities due to the refusal by Christian emperors to restore the Altar of Victory with its attendant rituals to the Sen-

60. Tertullian, *Apology* 24 (*ANF* 3:38).
61. Tertullian, *Apology* 40 (*ANF* 3:47).
62. Tertullian, *Apology* 40 (*ANF* 3:48).
63. Tertullian, *Apology* 41 (*ANF* 3:48).
64. Tertullian, *Apology* 48–50 (*ANF* 3:53–55).

ate House, as well as to restore public subsidies to support the vestal virgins and their religious rituals, or *cultus*. Additionally, pagans felt increasingly repressed by the government, especially under the rule of the enthusiastically Christian emperor Theodosius I. To help him with his intended project, Augustine had asked a young Spanish priest, Paulus Orosius, to gather for him examples of disasters that had befallen the Roman Empire before the advent of Christ. Orosius far exceeded that assignment with his work titled *Seven Books of Histories against the Pagans*. However, Augustine disagreed with Orosius's interpretation of events and the too-close connection that Orosius had drawn (in line with Eusebius's imperial theology) between the church and empire. According to Augustine, the idea that the destinies of the church and the kingdom were intertwined was false and could no longer stand: they were two completely different entities ("cities") with divergent ends.

As Augustine begins his own apologetic, he uses the Old Testament, going back in primeval history to the first family, and he traces the "history" of Rome, a manifestation of the Earthly City established and ruled by humans. He begins with the very first city, established by none other than Cain, a citizen of the Earthly City, who desired to have primacy and out of envy slew his brother Abel, a sojourner and citizen of the Heavenly City. The narrative progresses from Cain and Abel to Romulus and Remus, showing that the Earthly City was founded upon violence, bloodshed, and murder and continued to be reestablished by new rulers upon the same principles. As Augustine proceeds, he integrates the history of the Hebrews with that of other great civilizations like Assyria, Greece, and Rome (Orosius had also included Carthage), raising Jewish (and therefore Christian) history to the level of great ancient world empires.

Understanding his audience perfectly, Augustine knew his culture's deep veneration of past empires and their glory, and how they are admired and considered in some sense paradigmatic. Augustine therefore dismantled the Romans' rosy view of their past not only by appealing to the Bible but also by drawing from the Romans' own sources. After the city established by Cain, Augustine moves next to Nimrod's Babylon, considered a mighty ancient empire that prefigures Rome, which Augustine brands a second Babylon. Babylon's name, he explains, means "confusion," and so its greatness is belied by its origin in pride and haughtiness, and in treachery and rebellion against God.[65] Using the words of Rome's own historians, like Sallust, and philosophers like Cicero, Augustine asserts that Rome never had morality as the basis for its greatness, even during what Sallust called

---

65. Augustine, *City of God* 16.4 (trans. Henry Bettenson [London: Penguin, 1972], 656–57).

its finest days.[66] Even after the Romans expelled their kings (who had oppressed them), fear and tyranny ruled between the Roman social classes; and after the Second Punic War (which ended with the defeat of Carthage in 201 BC), moral vices increased and worsened, until Rome reached "the depth of depravity."[67] Additionally, he concludes from Cicero's definition of a "republic" that there never had been a true republic, for this ideal required justice in the ruling of the people. In fact, there is not even a "people" without a "'consent to the law' which makes a mob into a people, and it is the 'weal of the people' that is said to make a commonwealth."[68] Rome also thought it had the approval and patronage of the gods, but Augustine argues that their worship is actually another kind of injustice—idolatry—in which the gracious and true and just Ruler of humanity is deprived of the worship he deserves, a worship instead offered to demons.[69] Contrasting Rome's self-imagined greatness, then, with a true republic even by the standards of the ancients, Augustine shows that Rome—as the epitome of the Earthly City—never achieved the greatness of its best intentions. He asserts that the City of God, "that commonwealth whose founder and ruler is Christ," is the only city where justice can truly exist on all levels.[70]

Moving forward in his apologetic, Augustine goes backward into history. He reminds his pagan readers, who are of an inferior earthly city and enemies of the City of God, that in the recent sack of Rome by Alaric, both pagans and Christians fled for sanctuary to Christian churches and were spared. This proves that *God* is their benefactor, not the gods of Rome. In fact, before rites for the gods were established under King Numa (the successor of Romulus), he had already reigned for forty-three peaceful years. Yet between his reign (ca. 715–673 BC) and the Augustan settlement (27 BC), when all the while the Romans venerated their gods, the temple of Janus closed its doors—indicating peacetime—only once. Additionally, Rome had experienced "famine, disease, war, spoliation, captivity, massacre and the like" for centuries before the advent of Christ, so if Christians are to blame for the recent sack of Rome, who bears the blame for previous disasters if not the supposed protector gods of the city?[71]

Augustine's interest in classical (secular) history extends only so far as he needed it for his apologetic concerns: he was no historian but

---

66. Augustine, *City of God* 2.18 (Bettenson, 68–69).
67. Augustine, *City of God* 2.18 (Bettenson, 69).
68. Augustine, *City of God* 19.21 (Bettenson, 883).
69. Augustine, *City of God* 19.21–22 (Bettenson, 883–84).
70. Augustine, *City of God* 2.21 (Bettenson, 75).
71. Augustine, *City of God* 3.1, 3.9 (Bettenson, 89, 96–97).

primarily a theologian.[72] He largely relied on traditional apologetic arguments as foundational (as we have seen from Tertullian above), but from the beginning of the fifth century, his view of history and his vision of the future were transformed, so that he rejected the conclusions of his predecessors with respect to the historical significance they assigned to the Roman Empire in the grand scheme of the history of the ages.[73] Eusebius and Orosius had used a seven-age theory (based on the six days of the creation, plus a final Sabbath) in which, with the advent of Christ, world history entered the final age of blessedness (Sabbath) and historical consummation, and the Roman Empire was a part of that betterment as an agent of progress, helping spread the gospel of the kingdom of God. The Christian rhetorician Lactantius had also adopted this historical-progress scheme, intimating that the current age was the best and highest, the consummation of the ages. After previously adopting similar schemes himself earlier in his career (before about 400), Augustine, watching the empire crumble around him, discards this pattern in favor of a three-part scheme of ages: the age before the law, the age under the law, and the age under grace, inaugurated by the incarnation.[74] As for the age of blessedness to come, Augustine remained "steadfastly agnostic about the time of the world's end," refusing to speculate or to indulge in scriptural calculations to predict the parousia, final conflagration, transformation of the earth, and establishment of God's eternal kingdom.[75] In the current age, he believed, there are no guarantees of a complete end to persecution. As long as the church is in the world and its members comingled with citizens of the Earthly City, we can neither know the future nor expect progress, moral improvement, continued peace, and united rule under a wise and godly sovereign. We must continue to journey as pilgrims toward the City of God and expect perfect bliss only there.

Heresiology: History as Doctrinal Succession

The apologetic tradition concerned itself with defining the Christian movement as distinct from paganism and Judaism; heresiologists further

72. See R. A. Markus, "History," in *Augustine through the Ages: An Encyclopedia*, ed. Allan D. Fitzgerald (Grand Rapids: Eerdmans, 1999), 432–33.

73. Ibid., 433.

74. Ibid. Augustine also previously favored a traditional Roman theme of the six stages of human life (infancy, childhood, youth, young adulthood, mature adulthood, and old age) followed by a final golden age of worldwide peace (Brian E. Daley, *The Hope of the Early Church: A Handbook of Patristic Eschatology* [1991; repr., Peabody, MA: Hendrickson, 2003], 133).

75. Daley, *Hope of the Early Church*, 134.

defined Christian doctrine as orthodox, as distinct from heterodox or aberrant doctrine. Irenaeus, Tertullian, Hippolytus, and other heresiologists made it their aim to uphold ecclesiastical and doctrinal purity, many of them finding themselves at the intersection of orthodoxy (as theologians) and orthopraxy (as bishops). One way was to show continuity by demonstrating an unbroken chain of a succession of teachers, as Eusebius would do later in his *Church History*.

The Literary Form of Heresiology

Many heresiologists proceeded on the model of Irenaeus, seeking to show the doctrinal lineage of an ideology like Gnosticism and to trace it to its originator, known as a heresiarch or arch-heretic. The origin of a heresiarch was identified by tracing a succession of teachers. Just as sound doctrine was traced back to the apostles, so also heresy was traced back to heretics and persons of low character. Probably following Justin, Irenaeus's "candidate for that role" was Simon the magician from Samaria, who had accepted Christianity but sought to use it for personal profit by offering the disciples money for the power to work miracles like they were performing (Acts 8).[76] Simon gained a following in Rome, and according to Justin, he styled himself a god and received worship. His low character suggests a similar status for the beliefs he spawned as well as later movements born from them. John Henderson states that once the "genealogy of heresy" was "established, later heresiologists found it both effective and economical to attack later heresies by linking them with already refuted and discredited earlier ones."[77] Looking at the spectrum of histories of heresy, this picture is borne out from the earlier to the later materials.

Many examples of heresiology exist, but time and space constraints prohibit proper treatment of even well-known examples. Epiphanius's (bishop of Salamis) *Panarion* (*Medicine Chest*) is an exposé of multiple heresies, using the metaphor of the medicine box in the sense of a stash of poisons rather than medicine for healing. It is quite extensive, confirming its author's well-deserved reputation as a heresy hunter. A number of works were undertaken against heresies in general, such as the ones that follow, and several writers pressed on to compose much more substantial and detailed works against specific heresies—for example, Tertullian's massive project *Against Marcion*, Athanasius's *History of the Arians*, and Augus-

---

76. Antti Marjanen, "Gnosticism," in *The Oxford Handbook of Early Christian Studies*, ed. Susan Ashbrook Harvey and David Hunter (Oxford: Oxford University Press, 2008), 204.

77. Cited in ibid., 205.

tine's anti-Manichaean works. In all of these treatises, to a greater or lesser degree, an examination of a doctrine is undertaken, and its illegitimacy is determined partly by its lack of conformity to Scripture and church tradition as embodied in the Rule of Faith, and partly by tracing its origins to its prime teacher and ultimately to the devil. Here we examine representative works by Irenaeus of Lyons, Tertullian of Carthage, and Hippolytus of Rome.

Irenaeus, Against Heresies (ca. 180s)

Irenaeus is probably the first of the church fathers to compose a detailed, sustained heresiology against Gnosticism in its many divisions and groups.[78] In book 1 of his five-book work *On the Exposition and Overthrow of the Knowledge Falsely So-Called* (also called *Against Heresies*), Irenaeus sets out an exposé of various Gnostic groups and their beliefs and mythologies. This first book fits most properly the form of a heresiology as Irenaeus scrutinizes the Gnostic doctrines he has encountered, while subsequent books in the treatise take a more positive and constructive approach (after demolishing the heretical arguments, of course) to formulating theological concepts, especially concerning the doctrine of Scripture, the doctrines of creation and redemption, and principles for correct biblical hermeneutics. Exposing aberrant beliefs brought their most secret ideas reserved only for the privileged—the so-called secret gnosis—out into the open, and Irenaeus presents their esoteric teachings as ridiculous, scandalous, and fractured. He shows that they are fragmented and contradictory, based on an amalgamation of myths and philosophical ideas, and most importantly, not at all in line with the apostolic teaching and the Rule of Truth, which encapsulated the church's basic doctrine at the time.[79] He states clearly about the Valentinian system, "Such is their system which neither the prophets preached, nor the Lord taught, nor the apostles handed down."[80] This group and the groups they spawn intentionally pervert and misuse Scripture to suit their fantastic

78. Some scholars would use the term "Gnosticisms," indicating that Gnosticism was not a monolithic and uniform theological system, but that there existed variety within what is loosely called Gnosticism.

79. For a fuller explanation of the interplay between the Rule of Truth and the Scriptures in the patristic period as well as its ramifications for evangelicals, see D. H. Williams's volume in the Evangelical *Ressourcement* series, *Evangelicals and Tradition: The Formative Influence of the Early Church* (Grand Rapids: Baker Academic, 2005), as well as the companion volume, D. H. Williams, *Tradition, Scripture, and Interpretation: A Sourcebook of the Ancient Church* (Grand Rapids: Baker Academic, 2006).

80. Irenaeus, *Against Heresies* 1.8.1, in *St. Irenaeus of Lyons: Against the Heresies*, trans. Dominic J. Unger, ACW 55 (New York: Paulist Press, 1992), 41.

myths.[81] In section 10, Irenaeus lays out the Rule of Truth, juxtaposing it with the Valentinian system, whose doctrines he calls "unstable,"[82] and condemns them again for straying from apostolic teachings.[83]

Irenaeus's basic strategy was to identify Simon the arch-heretic and demonstrate a "clearly observable genealogy of heretical movements" traceable to other groups and ending with the Valentinians active in his own area.[84] By labeling all the diverse groups as Gnostics and showing their lack of social and theological cohesiveness, Irenaeus intended to show that the Gnostics had a common origin, a common name, and "formed a chain of heretical succession" apart from orthodoxy.[85] Simon was succeeded by Menander, and they both inspired Saturninus and Basilides. Cerdo "also got his start from the disciples of Simon," and he in turn was succeeded by Marcion.[86] These spawned the Encratites, who then drew Tatian away from the good teacher he had in Justin Martyr.[87] Then, from other Gnostics that had sprung up "out of the ground like mushrooms," the "wild beast with many heads" was produced, a reference to the "Valentinian school."[88] He shows that Marcus the magician, "the forerunner of the Antichrist," derives from the Valentinians.[89] The genealogical approach is clearly acknowledged in his conclusion to book 1: "By such mothers and fathers and ancestors it was necessary to expose clearly the followers of Valentinus."[90] Although he expressed some vitriol toward Marcus, this was largely because this man had caused theological and moral problems locally in Irenaeus's parish. It is a mark of Irenaeus's pastoral greatness and a wonderful lesson to all theologians who expose heresies that this bishop was nonetheless so concerned about these misguided souls, who are prodded by satanic illusions, that he hoped some could "be saved," that "others will no longer be misled by their . . . persuasion," and that "some will have pity on them."[91] In his conclusion to book 3, Irenaeus also states that the church must pray for these heretics and love them "more expediently than they . . . love themselves."[92] Even though it is

81. Irenaeus, *Against Heresies* 1.8.1 (ACW 55:41). See also Irenaeus, *Against Heresies* 1.9.4 (ACW 55:47).

82. Irenaeus, *Against Heresies* 1.11.1 (ACW 55:51).

83. Irenaeus, *Against Heresies* 1.22.1–2 (ACW 55:80–81).

84. Marjanen, "Gnosticism," 205.

85. Ibid.

86. Irenaeus, *Against Heresies* 1.27.1–2 (ACW 55:91).

87. Irenaeus, *Against Heresies* 1.28.1 (ACW 55:93).

88. Irenaeus, *Against Heresies* 1.30.15 (ACW 55:102).

89. Irenaeus, *Against Heresies* 1.13.1 (ACW 55:55).

90. Irenaeus, *Against Heresies* 1.31.3 (ACW 55:103).

91. Irenaeus, *Against Heresies* 1.31.3 (ACW 55:103).

92. Irenaeus, *Against Heresies* 3.25.7 (ACW 55:143).

a tough love, to expose their errors and humiliate them, its end is to save them for the truth of the gospel, and therefore Irenaeus says he and the church should continue to "try, with all our strength and without weariness, to offer our hand to them."[93] In the meantime, these kinds of "splits and tensions" helped the church to "clarify its own identity as a communal body of interpretation and ecclesial practice," united in its understanding and practice of the Scriptures, determining what constituted orthodoxy based on the Rule of Faith and what deviated from it.[94]

Tertullian, Prescription against Heretics *(ca. 200)*

Like Irenaeus, Tertullian held high the Rule of Faith as a baseline for interpreting the Scriptures. In this brief work, possibly an introduction to further antiheretical pieces, Tertullian assigns the causes of heresy to the inordinate curiosity and speculation about divine matters inspired by philosophy. He also identifies a progenitor of all heresy: rather than Simon Magus, as Irenaeus and others contend, Tertullian goes further back to the devil, who is still trying to rival God by destroying the church through internal conflict.[95] Tertullian singles out, for example, the demonically inspired Gnostic doctrine of a second God who rivals the wrathful and corrupt Old Testament God, as the Gnostics believed. The devil has deluded the Valentinian heretics into thinking that they have exclusive insight into the nature of God as dual, when no other group had posited a second God.

Recognizing that Jesus and the apostles had foretold the rise of heresies in the church,[96] Tertullian states that heresies test a person's faith;[97] he lists a number of heresies and heretical groups and teachers of his own day, historically locating the source of many of those heresies in pagan philosophy. For example, the Gnostic teachings of Valentinus stem from Platonism, while Marcion's ideas stem from Stoicism.[98] Tertullian locates other non-Christian ideas regarding the body, the nature and origin of God, the problem of evil, and so on in the teachings of other various philosophers (Epicurus, Zeno, Heraclitus).[99]

---

93. Irenaeus, *Against Heresies* 3.25.7 (ACW 55:143), cited in Robert M. Grant, *Irenaeus of Lyons*, Early Church Fathers (London: Routledge, 1997), 143.

94. John Behr, *Irenaeus of Lyons: Identifying Christianity* (Oxford: Oxford University Press, 2015), 9.

95. Tertullian, *Prescription against Heretics* 34 (ANF 3:259).

96. Tertullian, *Prescription against Heretics* 1–2 (ANF 3:243–44).

97. Tertullian, *Prescription against Heretics* 5 (ANF 3:245).

98. Tertullian, *Prescription against Heretics* 7 (ANF 3:246).

99. Tertullian, *Prescription against Heretics* 7 (ANF 3:246).

Above all, he castigates Aristotle, whose dialectics provided a methodology for arguing over the intricacies of these questions and persuading people of their validity—in essence, deceiving people and spreading heresies.[100] This catalog of philosophers draws from Tertullian the famous exclamation, "What indeed has Athens to do with Jerusalem? What concord is there between the Academy and the Church? What between heretics and Christians? . . . Away with all attempts to produce a mottled Christianity of Stoic, Platonic and dialectic composition!"[101] This exclamation follows Tertullian's description of Paul's visit to Athens, where Paul had become convinced through his conversations with philosophers that they teach "human wisdom which pretends to know the truth whilst it only corrupts it and is itself divided into its own manifold heresies."[102] Tertullian also blames "restless curiosity," which seeks to go beyond the Rule of Faith, a trespass which oversteps the standard for Christian self-definition.[103]

The "prescription" part of his work has to do with a legal feature of Roman law. Tertullian makes an argument involving apostolic succession and the Rule of Faith. Arguing over Scripture using *only* Scripture is useless with heretics because they misuse and misinterpret it.[104] They are in essence trespassers on Christian property. Tertullian therefore argues that heretics have no right to Scripture, which they distort and abuse because they disbelieve the Rule of Faith. He knows this charge to be true because after heretics have been taught the Rule, their inordinate curiosity continues to inquire after points of doctrine, for which the Rule should suffice.

He argues further that genuine Christian doctrine issues only from apostolic successors. Tertullian insists on the necessary continuity of sound doctrine from Christ to the apostles, a teaching that they passed on to the churches they established. Therefore, only if teachers can trace their doctrine back to an apostolic origin is that teaching genuine. Sound teaching is to be accepted upon authority (by faith in its origin as authentic), not by philosophical argumentation and Scripture twisting. "Indeed, it is on this account only that they will be able to deem themselves apostolic, as being the offspring of apostolic churches. Every sort of thing must necessarily revert to its original for classification."[105] That is, ideas must be traced back to a valid origin in order to be classified as orthodox or heterodox. While the apostolic churches have been

100. Tertullian, *Prescription against Heretics* 7 (*ANF* 3:246).
101. Tertullian, *Prescription against Heretics* 7 (*ANF* 3:246).
102. Tertullian, *Prescription against Heretics* 7 (*ANF* 3:246).
103. Tertullian, *Prescription against Heretics* 13–14 (*ANF* 3:249–50).
104. Tertullian, *Prescription against Heretics* 15, 17, 19, 37, 44 (*ANF* 3:250–52, 261, 264).
105. Tertullian, *Prescription against Heretics* 20 (*ANF* 3:252).

founded upon the teachings, suffering, and martyrdom of the apostles, the heretics' sects by contrast are associated with plagiarism, idolatry, and the devil, who is the author of both heresy and idolatry.[106]

Tertullian proceeds with a double-pronged strategy. First, he asserts that the heretics cannot trace their teachings to the apostles and were not contemporary with them to receive apostolic approval. He challenges them to "produce the original records of their churches," proving their legitimacy by bishops' rolls "running down in due succession from the beginning" and showing that their originator was apostolic or apostolically ordained.[107] Second, the apostles did not approve but instead condemned heretical ideas that already existed in their time. For example, going back into the apostolic history of the New Testament, Tertullian shows that the apostles "both exposed and denounced" various heresies: denials of the resurrection (1 Cor. 15), characteristic of Marcion, Apelles, and Valentinus; prohibition against marriage (1 Tim. 4), taught by Marcion and Apelles; a preoccupation with endless genealogies (1 Tim. 1), an obsession of Valentinus and the Gnostics; deification of the elements (Gal. 4:9), characteristic of Hermogenes; Docetism (1 John 4:3), as taught by Marcion and other Gnostics; and the worship of angels (Col. 2:18), as required by Simon Magus, who was condemned directly by the apostle Peter for his sorcery (Acts 8:20–23).[108] Thus Tertullian finds a historical argument from apostolic succession (or lack of it among the heretics) to argue against the counterfeit doctrines of the various heterodox groups of his day.

Hippolytus, Refutation of All Heresies *(ca. 222–35)*

Of Hippolytus the person (170–236), not much information is available. He wrote in Greek, was said to be a disciple of Irenaeus (whose theology he reflects), and seems to have the stern tone of Tertullian, his older contemporary. He was known as a rival bishop of a morally rigorist group at Rome who was eventually (likely) reconciled to the church. Hippolytus was also an older contemporary of Origen, who as a young man was impressed by his preaching. He ended his life in exile, sentenced to work in the mines (gold, silver, or lead) on the island of Sardinia.

In *Refutation of All Heresies*, a work originally in ten books (now lacking books 2 and 3), Hippolytus shows familiarity with the arguments of Irenaeus and possibly Clement of Alexandria. In the style of

---

106. Tertullian, *Prescription against Heretics* 21–40 (*ANF* 3:252–62).
107. Tertullian, *Prescription against Heretics* 32 (*ANF* 3:258).
108. Tertullian, *Prescription against Heretics* 33 (*ANF* 3:258–59).

Irenaeus, he sets out an ordered catalog of the heretical doctrines of his time. Although some Greek apologists accord much credit to philosophy (but not mythology) as compatible with Christian ideas about virtue and the divine, Hippolytus takes a somewhat dimmer view, perhaps thinking that too much is conceded to pagans in trying to create a bridge to Greco-Roman culture. Instead, he traces heresies and heretical teachers to various philosophical schools (like the Pythagoreans and Platonists), and he accuses heretics such as Simon Magus, Marcion, and others of plagiarizing philosophers like Aristotle and Empedocles and trying to pass them off as divinely revealed doctrines.[109]

Hippolytus's plan to expose the heresiarchs as plagiarists of the philosophers effectively makes these teachers the equals of atheists in both word and lifestyle. These teachers' ideas are not from the Bible but are derived from philosophers, astrologers, and other charlatans or speculators, so that no one who follows them should be deceived into thinking that they are "preserving the succession of any saint." Hippolytus lays out this thesis in the prologue (*prooemium*) of book 1.[110] He criticizes the teachings of Simon, Valentinus, and Marcus (a disciple of Valentinus), doctrines known to Hippolytus through Irenaeus.[111] Basilides plagiarizes the ideas of Aristotle, and Marcion plagiarizes from Empedocles.

His final chapter (book 10) constitutes a wrap-up of the entire work, and "as a sort of finishing stroke," Hippolytus concludes by summarizing the heresies and heresiarchs he has covered, as well as the philosophies he has discussed.[112] He also gives a brief exposé of the true doctrine, "simple and unadorned," proving that it derives neither from Greek philosophy nor from the mythologies and strange teachings of any other nation (e.g., Egyptians, Babylonians, Chaldeans, etc.).[113] In a move similar to the apologists of his time, Hippolytus makes a point of demonstrating the antiquity of the true Christian teaching, showing that it predates the philosophers. Previously Hippolytus had written a chronography, but in this present work he only briefly runs down the generations in Genesis from the righteous Abraham to Kohath, the son of Levi, and to the migration of this faithful family to Canaan; then he traces the generations backward from Abraham to Noah, intending to demonstrate "clearly . . . the existence of a nation of worshippers of the true God, more ancient than all the Chaldeans, Egyptians, and Greeks," who would logically be more recent than the true believers (i.e.,

109. Hippolytus, *Refutation of All Heresies* 9.26 (ANF 5:138).
110. Hippolytus, *Refutation of All Heresies*, prologue (ANF 5:10).
111. Hippolytus, *Refutation of All Heresies* 6.37 (ANF 5:93), 6.50 (ANF 5:99).
112. Hippolytus, *Refutation of All Heresies* 10.1 (ANF 5:140).
113. Hippolytus, *Refutation of All Heresies* 10.1 (ANF 5:140).

the Christians).[114] He shows in this way "the antiquity of the people of God" in an argument we have seen to be rather common by this point.[115] Since the true worshipers, the "friends of God," practice a faith that predates the wisdom of any other group, those groups as well as the heretics are exhorted to learn true doctrine from the Christians.[116] Since Hippolytus had concerned himself with Christian heretical groups (like the Gnostics) as well as philosophical schools who misconceived the nature of God and the true nature of creation and fell into idolatry, he lays out simply and directly a doctrine of theology proper and of creation, including the place of evil in the created order. Hippolytus asserts that everything God created is good and glorious, not evil, and that evil is nonexistent in the original creation, stemming instead from humans' misuse of free will. He affirms that human beings were created with worth, dignity, and freedom. To confirm the goodness of the creation, God the Logos entered into creation through the incarnation, to redeem and regenerate humanity, lifting it up and sanctifying believers to the highest level of godliness.

Historiographical Features in Christian Apologies

The historiographical features delineated in the foregoing chapters are present to varying degrees in apologetic. They are a bit trickier to identify because *narrative* histories (or parts thereof) of nations or even personal testimonies of conversion are embedded within a different literary form and are only adduced when convenient to the argument. Sometimes they may not appear as a historical argument but rather as a biblical argument, moving through prophetic proofs of the Old Testament and culminating in the historical life, death, and resurrection of Christ in the New Testament. Common arguments include appealing to the antiquity of Moses as an ancient leader and lawgiver of a nation; examining biblical genealogies to date the religious histories of civilizations, thereby demonstrating the Abrahamic-Israelite nation's priority to events of other kingdoms; and examining the successions of kingdoms themselves, usually to prove which kingdoms were indebted to Judaism—and ultimately to Christianity. Finally, there are narratives of historical tragedies that befell the Roman Empire before the church's establishment, *exempla* after the advice of Quintilian, adduced to exonerate the church of blame for more recent invasions of

---

114. Hippolytus, *Refutation of All Heresies* 10.26–27 (ANF 5:149).
115. Hippolytus, *Refutation of All Heresies* 10.26 (ANF 5:149).
116. Hippolytus, *Refutation of All Heresies* 10.27 (ANF 5:150).

the empire. If there is a sense that *remembrance* is valued, it is found in the ideas of *vetera et nova* (ancient and new), that whatever is ancient and venerable is good and desirable. The Romans also venerated the past, its victories and accomplishments, its virtues and greatness, but they remembered that past in accordance with the identity they chose for themselves as just, enlightened, religious, and traditional. When this supposed historical reputation was being used to accuse Christians, Tertullian, Augustine, and others reexamined the Romans' own history books and, event by event, dismantled the idyllic and noble picture Romans had built of their past (helped in this endeavor no doubt by poets and satirists). There is some overlap between narrative and *mimēsis*, as exemplars of different kinds are brought up from antiquity. Men and women from Greek and Roman history (like Socrates and the peaceful King Numa) are highlighted as examples of so-called atheism, self-sacrifice, martyrdom, enlightened rulership, and personal virtue. Elements of *causation* also emerge, though they are muted. Causative forces include both evil influences like deceitful demons, and equally free human decisions to pursue virtuous or heretical courses of action. Some apologists make direct statements about causation that show up in properly historical works, such as defense of the idea of providential oversight of history (the divine plan) and rejection of Fate and Fortune as central forces operating in history and driving it forward to a telos. For example, Tertullian writes of the eschatological judgment tribunal and the fact that at the time of God's choosing, God will bring an end to time—and as sovereign judge, God will render judgment on the nations, with the world as his courtroom. This emphasis on God's sovereignty as causative, and on God as ruler above Caesar and all nations, is evident in the later works of Lactantius (e.g., *Divine Institutes*), Eusebius, and Theodoret.

Self-Definition through Apologetics

Through their rhetorical efforts, the apologists, heresiologists, lawyers, theologians, philosophers, and bishops fought for the truth of Christian doctrine. Through their testimonies and arguments, they helped to establish several key points of Christians' identity, so important to consolidate the faith of many who felt victimized, marginalized, and disempowered in the Roman Empire. The apologists helped Christians see their own religious, social, and political legitimacy within the empire, as Christians made up just one religious group among many others. They were law-abiding folks and maintained a high ethical standard. Although they may appear to be in violation of the Roman laws and customs obligating veneration of the gods, the apologists felt that a fair and impartial hearing—not condemnation on the basis of "the Name" (a phrase frequently used in the apologetic literature for Christians) alone—would exonerate them. If the Romans were true to their own professed religious values and enlightened ideals of toleration and justice, they would embrace Christianity.

By their use of various historical strategies, the early apologists encouraged Christians to see themselves as ancient rather than recent and to recognize the practice of their faith as actually constituting the original and true religion intended for all nations. The church itself was a distinct *ethnos*, a people with a noble calling to bear witness to the God of the nations. In their relationship to Judaism and to philosophy, Christians were characterized by both continuity and discontinuity. The antiquity of their "race" and their faith relied on Judaism, yet the Jews had rejected God's Messiah, thereby disqualifying themselves from their inheritance. The church, then, is the heir of God's Old Testament promises of blessing and eternal salvation. With respect to philosophy, Christianity may bear some similarities to ideological trends and spiritual wisdom from Greco-Roman culture, but Christianity has temporal priority, and pagan philosophy is inferior. Although the Greeks drew inspiration and truth from the Judaic religious and ethical heritage, they nonetheless misunderstood the nature of God and fell into the error of idolatry. Some apologists strike discordant notes of discontinuity with philosophy, not only because they saw it as pagan and idolatrous but also because elements of the philosophical heritage have been twisted by humans under demonic influence and have misled the faithful and fractured the church. It was possible, then, for philosophy to be a bridge or a bane.

The ancient apologists should be viewed with a critical eye for their time-bound approaches, so we must appropriate their ideas responsibly. Yet we should also regard them with a heart of gratitude for standing up as advocates on behalf of the church to engage, challenge, and invite the wider culture to take a closer look at Christian life, convictions, and doctrine. The apologetic task, undertaken in uncertain times, was a way of discipleship for these believers. When later apologists wrote, they did so by taking the mantle of previous writers upon themselves, quite aware of their participation in a Christian tradition.

MARTYROLOGY

Remembering the Martyrs' Noble Example

It is our battle to be summoned to your tribunals that there, under fear
of execution, we may battle for the truth. But the day is won when the
object of the struggle is gained, . . . the glory of pleasing God and the
spoil of life eternal. . . . Therefore we conquer in dying.

—Tertullian, *Apology* 50 (ANF 3:54)

What Is Hagiography?

Hagiography (from Gk. *hagios* + *graphō*) is an umbrella term referring
to any narrative of a holy person's life that strives to inculcate lessons of
Christian orthodoxy, piety, and virtuous character, generally providing
examples of discipleship for a Christian audience. Some contest the
idea that hagiography is "real" or factual history, and argue that the
genre is most useful for providing contextual clues about the social,
religious, or historical situation behind the text. In other words, the
text is not to be looked at for itself, but to be looked *through* and hence
in some way to be disregarded.[1] However, other scholars reply that

---

1. See Candida R. Moss, *Ancient Christian Martyrdom: Diverse Practices, Theologies, and
Traditions* (New Haven: Yale University Press, 2012), 1–22.

hagiography does constitute "history" in certain ways[2] and can be critically investigated through solid historical research methods that can confirm some long-held ideas, challenge or overturn others, and even lead to some new and important conclusions, as in the excellent study by Timothy D. Barnes.[3] Hagiographical literature includes the struggles of the martyrs as they faced death, as well as the struggles of later Christian men and women as they faced sinful, fleshly temptations. This chapter will concern itself with the former (the *acta* of the martyrs), and the next chapter will deal with the latter (the *vitae* of later Christians).

The term "martyr" (from Gk. *martys*) refers to a witness who bears testimony (Gk. *martyria*) to facts about which one is so convinced that death is preferable to denying those facts. The martyrs are those who testified to the truth of Christ's sovereign lordship in their own lives as well as over the entire world. Another sense in which the idea of witness functions is as a memorial. The Old Testament records many instances of memorial objects that bear witness to pacts, covenants, promises, or particular events in Israel's history. For example, a pile of twelve stones memorialized Israel's crossing the Jordan into Canaan (Josh. 4:4–7), functioning as a reminder and a prompt for conversations with future generations about the holy and omnipotent God who had redeemed his people from Egypt and fulfilled his promises completely. Joshua admonished the people, "In the future, when your children ask you, 'What do these stones mean to you?' you should tell them, 'The waters of the Jordan were cut off in front of the ark of the LORD's covenant. When it crossed the Jordan, the Jordan's waters were cut off.' Therefore these stones will always be a memorial for the Israelites" (4:6–7 HCSB).

Memorials both remind and inspire. As stones and altars and Scriptures reminded Israel of its past with the Lord, the early Christians looked to graves (in the catacombs and elsewhere) where they gathered to remember the martyrs' combat on the anniversary of their deaths. Later the commemorative shrines built over the sites of martyrs' burials would be called *martyria*, as the church built on the site of Calvary was known as the *Martyrium* by pilgrims to the Holy Land in subsequent centuries.[4] In her travel diary the pilgrim nun Egeria explains that the church is "called the *Martyrium* because it is on Golgotha, behind the

---

2. For such a counterargument, see Eric Brook, "Hagiography, Modern Historiography, and Historical Representation," *Fides et Historia* 42, no. 2 (2010): 1–26.

3. Barnes, *Early Christian Hagiography and Roman History* (Tübingen: Mohr Siebeck, 2010).

4. This information is found in the travel journal of Egeria as well as in the catechetical sermons of Cyril of Jerusalem. See George E. Gingras, ed. and trans., *Egeria: Diary of a Pilgrimage*, ACW 38 (New York: Newman, 1970).

Cross, where the Lord suffered His Passion, and is therefore a shrine of martyrdom."[5] In addition to graves and other memorials, Christians produced commemorative narratives that preserved a written witness to prior events. From our sources, it is plain that remembering, although highly valued in itself, was not an act performed purely for ceremonial reasons. It was intended rather as training for spiritual combat, to inspire courage in future spiritual athletes who might face martyrdom. The literature of the first three centuries AD especially evinces the understanding that public confession of Christ proves costly, so the disciple requires both training in doctrine and stalwart witness in word and deed. Even in the following centuries when Christians no longer stared in the face a government-mandated death, they still retained the same understanding of the entire world as an arena of combat and dire contest between two competing agendas, two competing loyalties, with the Christian at the nexus of that clash.

Biblical Models

The periods of intense persecution in the second to fourth centuries produced a literature among Christians that focused very decidedly on discipleship. Whatever else might attract readers to martyrdom accounts, the twin themes of sacrificial discipleship—self-denial and a willingness to carry one's cross—emerge prominently. Jesus had warned his followers that they would experience suffering via rejection and even loss of life (John 15:20–21). Both the New Testament and the martyrological literature portray the cross-bearing life as a contest (Gk. *agōn*) or a competition in which believers are athletes. As a Pauline example, 2 Timothy 2:5 (HCSB) reads, "If anyone competes like an athlete [*athlē*] . . . [he must] compete [*athlēsē*] according to the rules." In the same letter to Timothy, Paul urges the young pastor to "share in suffering [*synkakopathēson*] as a good soldier [*stratiōtēs*] of Christ Jesus" (2:3 [HCSB], a metaphor that continues in 2:4). Similarly, early Christian writers also used military imagery to depict the Christian life as a fight, indeed, an all-out war against the church's perennial enemy, the devil. As Christians read the Gospel narratives of Christ's passion, they formed a powerful and intimate identification as disciples with the master (*kyrios*) who was ill-treated (or hated, Gk. *miseō*) (John 15:18–19) and persecuted (Gk. *diōkō*) (15:20), and the shepherd who was beaten (Gk. *patassō*) (Matt. 26:31). They expressed passionate love and a deep and personal attachment to Christ as Savior and Lord

5. Egeria, *Diary of a Pilgrimage* 30 (ACW 38:103).

in the terms used by Paul in Philippians 3:10–11 (HCSB), desiring to "know [Christ]," especially the "fellowship of His sufferings, being conformed to His death" so that they might attain to the "resurrection from among the dead." Their attachment to and identification with Christ took literary form as features of Christ's passion narrative appeared in martyrdom accounts. These include (but are not limited to) an arrest, an interrogation or trial before Rome's representative, giving a defense in terms of another kingdom and a competing spiritual reality (John 18:36), the presence of "the Jews" who incited the crowd to call for punishment (or simply the involvement of the crowd) (John 19:15), language of self-sacrifice or self-offering, and prayer(s) of relinquishment, yielding one's spirit to the Father, and requesting forgiveness for malefactors. An interesting difference is that whereas Jesus did not say much in his own defense, knowing that his death was prophesied and eternally redemptive for the world (John 12:27–33), the *acta* contain both brief and lengthy accounts of Christians defending themselves.[6] In the martyrologies, sometimes this polemical apologetic takes place over a few days and consists of several addresses, as in the cases of Apollonius and Pionius.

One early figure who gave a lengthy defense (*apologia*) immediately before his death was Stephen the deacon, commonly called the "protomartyr" (Acts 6:8–8:2). Saul (Paul) had heard Stephen's speech (disapprovingly, we assume) and confessed later that, "when the blood of Stephen your witness [*martyros*] was being shed, I myself was standing by and approving and watching over the garments of those who killed him" (Acts 22:20). That event powerfully affected Paul: the guilt he felt at his involvement and agreement with Stephen's executioners became part of his testimony to prove that he was a changed man. The biblical details of Stephen's passion also appear in some measure as a pattern for later martyrdom accounts. Featured details include the martyr's face glowing "like the face of an angel" (Acts 6:15); his character as powerful, gracious, Spirit filled, and able to work wonders (6:5, 8, 10); his receiving visions of Christ and heaven (7:55–56); his death preceded by a sermon or *apologia* of some sort (7:2–53); and prayer(s) of relinquishment, as the martyr ends his life while praying to Christ (7:59–60). Stephen himself followed Christ's example of relinquishing his spirit to Jesus (as he had done to the Father) and also forgiving his persecutors.

6. But see Robin Darling Young's view that the martyrs did indeed perceive their deaths to be redemptive in some respects for the Christian community (*In Procession before the World: Martyrdom as Public Liturgy*, The Père Marquette Lecture in Theology [Milwaukee: Marquette University Press, 2001], 9–10, 12).

In addition to the exhortations Paul gave to his disciples—especially his protégés, Timothy and Titus—regarding willingness to compete in the contest and "fight [agōnizou] the good fight [agōna] of the faith" (1 Tim. 6:12), he also encouraged them to accept suffering and persecution if they came. Paul did not shrink from persecution, but he did make efforts toward self-preservation in order to continue the proclamation and propagation of the gospel (e.g., Acts 9:23–25; 2 Cor. 11:32–33). To this end, Paul also defended himself on numerous occasions, most notably before Felix and Agrippa (Acts 24:10–21; 26:2–29), or when he was persecuted for the gospel he preached about Jesus as the Messiah, the resurrection, the "judgment to come" (Acts 24:25 HCSB), and the gentile mission. His military and athletic metaphors became popular themes in the martyrologies and were especially appropriate since the deaths of Christians came to be staged in amphitheaters and arenas where sporting events and gladiatorial combats took place as spectacles to please the crowds. His efforts at self-defense and challenging his persecutors or escaping their clutches and further abuse became a policy of sorts among Christians, especially bishops, who could continue their pastoral and episcopal work from temporary obscurity during a wave of persecution and ostensibly could better serve their communities alive than dead.

What Do Our Historical Sources Look Like?

The so-called Acts of the Martyrs (acta martyrum) contain accounts that are more or less based on eyewitness testimony or have been orally transmitted, recorded, and preserved for the benefit of the Christian community. These accounts derive from all parts of the Roman Empire of the first three centuries AD, while Christianity was illegal and subject to occasional, regional, or empire-wide persecution. The stories contain the exploits of famous martyrs like Polycarp of Smyrna, the bishop and disciple of John; Justin Martyr, the famous Roman Christian philosopher and apologist; the martyrs of Lyons and Vienne, including the illustrious and venerable Blandina; the North African bishop Cyprian, an important contributor to the doctrine of the church (ecclesiology); and Perpetua and Felicitas, the two brave young North African women who faced the beasts in an arena, as part of a birthday celebration for the emperor's son.

The accounts also include the heroic feats of lesser known (to us) martyrs, such as Attalus of Pergamum and Sanctus of Vienne (a deacon in that city), both of whom suffered along with Blandina in Gaul; Pionius, a presbyter from Smyrna; Bishop Carpus, his deacon Papylus (or

Pamphilus), and a noblewoman from their congregation, Agathonike, all from Pergamum; the Spanish bishop Fructuosus and his two deacons; Julius the Veteran, a soldier who had served in the empire's legions for twenty-seven years and seven deployments, and was eventually martyred in Durostorum on the border of modern-day Romania and Bulgaria; the Greek (Thessalonian) girls Agape, Chione, and Irene, and several others with them, who were martyred upon refusing to hand over precious copies of the Scriptures and other Christian materials under Maximian's persecution; and finally the dignified and beloved Egyptian bishop Phileas of Thmuis, who commanded such respect that he was begged even by the prefect interrogating him to reconsider his decision not to sacrifice—Phileas, however, did not veer from his course.

Before launching into historical aspects of the *acta*, a word about criteria for inclusion or exclusion of particular sources is in order. Many more martyrological accounts exist than those presented in this book, and many more martyrs are commemorated in Christian tradition than those for whom narratives have survived. The sources that follow (and those cited above) are deemed generally reliable, with a broad scholarly consensus for their historical authenticity. The texts used here derive mostly from the collection made by Herbert Musurillo.[7] Where he indicates uncertainty or implausibility regarding the events described, I have used those narratives cautiously or not at all. Nonetheless, even dubious accounts (e.g., the martyrdoms of Conon, Marian and James, and Montanus and Lucius) were produced by particular communities in an attempt to achieve the same kind of effect achieved by the authentic accounts. Furthermore, it is possible that there had existed a true story, unwritten or no longer extant, that provided the basic elements of an elaborate account like the *Martyrdom of Montanus and Lucius*. Nonetheless, we ought to be mindful of what Elizabeth Castelli terms "the malleability . . . of the commemorative traditions" associated with particular saints, such as Thecla the "protomartyr" whom she references.[8] Thecla was a "martyr" whose story, reputation, and veneration were widespread throughout the Mediterranean.[9] Unfortunately, the historical narrative of her life is ambiguous and is classified among the apocryphal literature

---

7. Herbert Musurillo, ed. and trans., *The Acts of the Christian Martyrs*, vol. 2 (Oxford: Clarendon, 1972).

8. Elizabeth Castelli, *Martyrdom and Memory: Early Christian Culture Making* (New York: Columbia University Press, 2004), 8.

9. Her story is related in the apocryphal work *The Acts of Paul and Thecla*. For further study of her veneration and the popularity of her *cultus* among women pledged to lifelong virginity or chastity, see the excellent work by Stephen J. Davis, *The Cult of Saint Thecla: A Tradition of Women's Piety in Late Antiquity* (Oxford: Oxford University Press, 2001).

related to the New Testament.[10] It appears even from the apocryphal account that she did not, in fact, die a martyr's death, and therefore (in my opinion) she is not to be classified with martyrs such as Polycarp, Pionius, Blandina, Perpetua, and others of whose deaths we are quite certain, given the personal or eyewitness accounts that have survived.

Historiographical Features of the *Acta*

The historiographical features discussed in chapter 2 will be considered here in terms of their incorporation into the *acta*. These features include narrative, remembrance, imitation, and causation.

Narrative

With few variations, virtually all the sources recount the story of the martyr's arrest, trial, witness, and death. Sometimes the narrative account emerges from a *trial or court document*. An editor may provide a brief historical introduction and narrative framework, then usually an account of the interrogation follows. Sometimes the interrogation contains dramatic verbal exchanges and interactions with the judge (e.g., the sermon/apology of Pionius).[11] At other times victims (e.g., Phileas) serenely and calmly confess their faith and accept or even urge on their fate.[12] Some martyrdom accounts have been transmitted in an extended *epistolary format*—a long letter that reads like a short story.[13] In these accounts, the editor elucidates moral and spiritual lessons for the audience through the polished narrative, a process well in keeping with classic educational methods of the time. One document stands out as technically fitting neither of these formats: the *Passion of Perpetua and Felicitas* does contain some introductory and concluding editorial material, but the intervening content derives substantially from the first-person narrative account in Perpetua's own prison diary.

The intent of the narrator or editor (and later, the preacher) was often to draw listeners into the story, according them something of a

---

10. See also *New Testament Apocrypha*, vol. 2, *Writings Related to the Apostles*, ed. Wilhelm Schneemelcher, English trans. ed. Robert McL. Wilson (Philadelphia: Westminster, 1964), esp. 322–64.

11. Out of a total of 23 sections, Pionius speaks at length in sections 4–6 and 12–14. He also speaks when being interrogated by the proconsul or others who are witnesses to the proceedings in sections 3, 7–10, and 15–20 (*Martyrdom of Pionius the Presbyter and His Companions* [Musurillo, 136–67]).

12. See *Acts of Phileas* (Musurillo, 341, 349).

13. E.g., *Martyrs of Lyons and Vienne*; *Martyrdom of Polycarp*; *Martyrdom of Marian and James*; and *Martyrdom of Montanus and Lucius*.

front-row seat. This effect was accomplished by a "collapsing of time" within the text.[14] Elizabeth Castelli sees in the martyr narratives

> a desire to situate contemporary readers/hearers in continuous relation to events in the distant and more recent past in which divine activity has touched human existence directly. The writer promises that the text will create an intimacy between those who suffered, those who were direct witnesses to that suffering, and those who hear or read about it all later. The writing is about bringing the reader into the event, and situating that event within a continuous historical passage.[15]

This strategy enabled the listeners to participate in or experience the action in some way, even as they stood removed from the events by decades or even centuries. Descriptions of sights, smells, sounds, and touch are all used masterfully to engineer this effect for later listeners. So in the account of Polycarp's martyrdom, the narrator describes the manhandling of this elderly saint, citing a small detail: as Polycarp was threatened and removed from the carriage that had transported him to the amphitheater, the guards "took him down so hastily that he scraped his shin."[16] When he entered the amphitheater, the mob unleashed "such an uproar that no one could be heard."[17] When Polycarp was finally sentenced to execution by burning, the narrator describes the mob's actions to gather wood and brush "from workshops and baths" as happening "with great speed, more quickly than it takes to tell the story," re-creating an ominous and frenetic atmosphere of unruliness and savage intent.[18] As the pyre was lit and the flames billowed in a vault around Polycarp, those present described "a delightful fragrance, as though it were smoking incense . . . or perfume."[19] Depictions of the crowd are especially vivid in the story of Perpetua and Felicitas, as the people exhibit a spectrum of emotions and reactions: sometimes showing sympathy toward the martyrs and horror at their plight, other times showing rage, satisfaction, or cruel jubilation at the bloody spectacle of martyrs mauled by beasts, a grisly voyeurism in desiring the gory sight of their bodies laid out in public view.[20]

A further advantage for later readers of martyrdom accounts is the vantage point of the omniscient narrator. The reader or hearer expe-

14. Daniel Boyarin, *Dying for God: Martyrdom and the Making of Christianity and Judaism* (Stanford, CA: Stanford University Press, 1999), 111.

15. Castelli, *Visions and Voyeurism* (Berkeley, CA: Center for Hermeneutical Studies, 1995), 9.

16. *Martyrdom of Polycarp* 8 (Musurillo, 9).

17. *Martyrdom of Polycarp* 9 (Musurillo, 9).

18. *Martyrdom of Polycarp* 13 (Musurillo, 13).

19. *Martyrdom of Polycarp* 15 (Musurillo, 15).

20. *Passion of Perpetua and Felicitas* 18, 19, 21 (Musurillo, 127–31).

riences the public drama of the crowd's reactions and is also privy to
the story behind the scenes, the private drama occasioned by congre-
gational and family members. Often these stood by to minister and to
witness, but the accounts are clear that at other times they proved to
be a liability, as in the story of Perpetua. While some family members,
like her brother and mother, were apparently believers and offered support for her, especially concerning the welfare of her infant, Perpetua's
father behaved otherwise.[21] Perpetua describes her father as one who
clearly loved and valued his daughter highly and thus felt deep grief and
anxiety for his daughter's plight. He visited her in prison, attempting to
dissuade her from her faith choice, and came to her before and during
her trial. He was "worn with grief" and kissed her hands, "throwing
himself down" in front of her. The account continues as her turn to
be interrogated comes: "My father appeared with my [infant] son,
dragged me from the step, and said: 'Perform the sacrifice—have pity
on your baby!'" He himself suffered a rain of blows with a rod from
Hilarianus, the interrogating governor. Perpetua comments sadly, "I felt
sorry for his pathetic old age."[22] Several days later he appeared again
at the prison, "overwhelmed with sorrow. He started tearing the hairs
from his beard and threw them on the ground; he then threw himself
on the ground and began to curse his old age and to say such words
as would move all creation."[23] Although she resisted his attempts at
dissuasion, nonetheless she felt that his appeals were a ploy of the
devil to enervate her resolve. After one argument, she felt relief at his
departure, describing him as "vanquished along with his diabolical
arguments" (*argumentis diaboli*).[24] Other examples abound of private
drama, away from the gaze of a frenzied crowd of spectators, in which
the martyrs are forced to make an agonizing decision that is even more
agonizing for their being directly confronted with the consequences
for their beloved family or congregation (e.g., the bishop Phileas's wife
and children, and the bishop Irenaeus of Sirmium's family, neighbors,
and friends).[25]

Remembrance

The editorial crafting of material leads into the next historiographical feature evident in the *acta*: *remembrance*. This feature is especially

---

21. *Passion of Perpetua and Felicitas* 3, 5 (Musurillo, 109–11, 113).
22. *Passion of Perpetua and Felicitas* 6 (Musurillo, 115).
23. *Passion of Perpetua and Felicitas* 9 (Musurillo, 117).
24. *Passion of Perpetua and Felicitas* 3 (Musurillo, 109).
25. *Acts of Phileas* 6–7 (Musurillo, 351); *Martyrdom of Saint Irenaeus, Bishop of Sirmium* 3–4 (Musurillo, 297–99).

prominent in hagiography as a primary purpose for recording the stories that have come down to the present: noble people and great deeds should be remembered and not forgotten from the collective memory. In the interest of preserving the memory of people and deeds, the accounts provide significant details that linger in the mind and inspire future generations of Christians, whether they are fighting beasts or fighting sin in their lives.

When he established the Lord's Supper, Jesus requested his followers to remember him by participating in a sacred meal (Luke 22:19; 1 Cor. 11:24–25). The penitent thief requested remembrance as well, by Jesus himself: "Jesus, remember me when you come into your kingdom" (Luke 23:42). Requests for remembrance were repeated by the martyrs as well as those they left behind. Believers remembered Christ, the Master, in a special way in the Eucharist by partaking of his body, remembering his death, proclaiming the gospel, and looking forward to his return (1 Cor. 11:26). Martyrs requested that their witness as sacrifices be remembered; and those left behind asked that the martyrs, their fellow disciples, remember them in the presence of the Lord, interceding from Heaven for them to receive special grace (like endurance under persecution) or to mitigate God's wrath toward their sins.[26] For example, Perpetua's teacher, Saturus, requested of the soldier Pudens, "Good-bye. Remember me, and remember the faith [*memento fidei et mei*]." Saturus then took a ring from Pudens, dipped it in his wound, and returned it to the soldier "as a record of his bloodshed [*memoriam sanguinis*]."[27] The fourth-century martyr Julius the Veteran was asked by a Christian named Isichius (or Hesychius), a fellow soldier imprisoned with him, "Julius, . . . take the crown which the Lord has promised to give to those who believe in him, and remember me [*memoresto mei*], for I too will follow you."[28]

Examples of deeds and people remembered within the centuries of persecution abound, but some can be more directly traced than others. In the three examples that follow, it can be clearly demonstrated how martyrs and their deeds are remembered from one century to the next, even before the legalization of the church. The extant records demonstrate that Christians in the third and fourth centuries looked back to martyrs of the second and third centuries for encouragement, strength, and examples of endurance.

---

26. For examples of references to the martyr's death as a sacrifice, see *Martyrdom of Polycarp* 14 (Musurillo, 13); *Martyrs of Lyons* 2.5 (Musurillo, 83); *Martyrdom of St. Felix the Bishop* (Musurillo, 271); *Acts of Euplus* 2 (Musurillo, 317).

27. *Passion of Perpetua and Felicitas* 21 (Musurillo, 131).

28. *Martyrdom of Julius the Veteran* 4 (Musurillo, 265).

POLYCARP AND PIONIUS

Bishop Polycarp of Smyrna died circa 155. He is memorialized in an early account by Irenaeus (later edited), as well as in the *Martyrdom of Pionius*, who died circa 250.[29] Pionius is himself memorialized in the words of a late third-century editor, who intentionally compared his life and manner of death with Polycarp's. Both men's ordeals also intentionally reflect the passion of Christ. Both accounts emphasize discipleship through suffering, and both include the reasons why the church ought to remember the martyrs and what place the martyrs have in the church's memory and loyalty. The writer of the *Martyrdom of Polycarp* explains that they are admired and imitated for the quality of their discipleship to Jesus: "For him [Christ] we reverence as the Son of God, whereas we love the martyrs as the *disciples* and *imitators* of the Lord, and rightly so because of their unsurpassed loyalty towards their king and master. May we too share with them as fellow *disciples!*"[30]

Recording the events of Polycarp's ordeal was a way to remember him and pass down his example to future generations. The *acta* continued to be read both in churches throughout the empire and in Smyrna at his burial site on the feast day of Polycarp, to remember his noble deeds done out of love and loyalty to his Lord, and to encourage listeners to imitate his fortitude. "Gathering here [perhaps at a church or burial site], so far as we can, in joy and gladness, we will be allowed by the Lord to celebrate the anniversary day of his martyrdom [*martyriou*], both as a *memorial* [*mnēmen*] for those who have already fought the contest, and for the *training* [*askēsin*] and preparation of those who will do so one day."[31]

Approximately a century later (ca. 250), "while the persecution of Decius was still on," Pionius and his fellow believers were preparing to celebrate "the anniversary of the blessed martyr Polycarp."[32] The introduction to the account fully accords with the purposes set out for remembering Polycarp. The emphasis on the importance of remembering is crystal clear, as is the intended result of remembering, which is imitation.

> The Apostle urges us to share [*koinōnein*] in the *remembrances* [*mneiais*] of the saints, fully aware that to *call to mind* [*mnēmēn*] those that have passed their life in the faith wisely with all their hearts gives strength to

29. Timothy Barnes dates the composition of the *Martyrdom of Polycarp* to 157 (*Early Christian Hagiography*, 14–15, 40–49). For subsequent editors of an Irenaean original, see *Martyrdom of Polycarp* 22 (Musurillo, 19–21).

30. *Martyrdom of Polycarp* 17 (Musurillo, 17, emphasis added).

31. *Martyrdom of Polycarp* 18 (Musurillo, 17, emphasis added).

32. *Martyrdom of Pionius* 2 (Musurillo, 137).

those who are striving to *imitate* [*mimeisthai*] the better things. Indeed, more fitting is it that we should *remember* [*memnēsthai*] the martyr Pionius, seeing that this apostolic man, being one of us, kept many from straying while he dwelt in the world, and when he was finally called to the Lord and bore witness [*emartyrēse*], he left us this writing for our instruction that we might have it even to this day as a *memorial* [*mnēmosyna*] of his teaching.[33]

A nice chain of influence is seen here. As Polycarp remembered (and even to some extent reenacted) Christ's passion and imitated his example, Pionius remembered Polycarp and imitated his example, as others would henceforth remember Pionius and imitate his example. Remembering and imitating are inextricably linked, as will also be shown below in the section on *mimēsis*.

MARTYRS OF LYONS

Many more Christians perished in the persecution at Lyons in 177 than are specified in this document. Blandina, Attalus, Maturus, Sanctus, and several others are named because they seemed the most illustrious. They are memorialized in a lengthy epistle that was possibly written close to the time of the actual events, then expanded and circulated in the 250s with the occasion of the Decian persecution, in order to strengthen believers. The final sections cited by Eusebius provide a possible indication of a date. After inserting the dramatic portion of the narrative epistle into his historical work, he selects a few parts to add on at the end. The theme in these final sections is "peace" brought about by the martyrs' "maternal love," joy, harmony, and a conciliatory attitude toward the "fallen," that is, those who had probably lapsed under torture. Apparently the comments reflect a later stern and unforgiving attitude of the church toward the lapsed resulting from the Decian persecution. The writer states, "Let this then be usefully said about the love of these blessed martyrs for their brothers who had fallen, especially in view of the cruel and pitiless attitudes of those who later were so unsparing towards the members of Christ's body."[34]

The martyrs at Lyons were arrested, interrogated, and imprisoned. It seems they were tortured either in prison or before a crowd in the Amphitheater of the Three Gauls, whose ruins remain visible in Lyons. In any case, the imagery of the arena dominates, and the martyrs are pictured as powerful gladiators. The image of "noble athletes" (*gennaious athlētas*) of God receives heavy emphasis. These contestants

---

33. *Martyrdom of Pionius* 1 (Musurillo, 136–37, emphasis added).
34. *Martyrs of Lyons* 2 (Musurillo, 84).

(*agōnistes*) fought for an imperishable crown against the true enemy, the devil, rather than the crowds of people calling for their deaths. Through the descriptions in this account, later readers can commemorate the martyrs' bravery shown in the face of death and can also emphasize an ageless theological truth: our battle in this life is not against flesh and blood but against powers and principalities that war against God (Eph. 6:11–12). By refusing to capitulate to or compromise with idolatry, the martyr was privileged to be called and chosen as an "athlete" through whom Christ continually defeats the devil. As in the editorial prologue to the *Martyrdom of Polycarp*, the martyrs' personal spiritual attachment to Christ is clearly visible. Some further sections of the document selected by Eusebius (who might not have quoted the document in its entirety) indicate the object of the martyrs' utmost loyalty: they were "intensely eager to imitate and emulate Christ [*mimētai Christou*]. . . . For it was their joy to yield the title of martyr [*martyrias*] to Christ alone, who was the true and faithful witness [*martyri*], 'the first-born of the dead,' and the prince of God's life."[35]

PERPETUA AND FELICITAS

These two young North African women died circa 202–3 and were memorialized by a third-century editor, rather close to the actual events. Some think Tertullian is a possible redactor, as the *Passion of Perpetua and Felicitas* bears marked resemblance to his brief exhortation to the martyrs, *Ad Martyras* (*To the Martyrs*); furthermore, Tertullian cited the Perpetua material in his work *De anima* (*On the Soul*).[36] The *Passion* emphasizes many of the same themes as above, as for example, Perpetua's vision of her gladiatorial match with an Egyptian (representing the devil), in which Perpetua appears as a gladiator, rubbed with oil, stripped down, and transformed into a man, ready for the struggle![37] However, the editor has a particular agenda, which he indicates in the prologue and epilogue of the work. He wants to magnify the deeds of the present, which he says are just as worthy of being remembered as deeds of antiquity, since the same Holy Spirit is at work in his own generation, just as he was in the generation of Jesus and the apostles, and the prophets before them (e.g., see Joel 2). Thus he ties the audience both to the martyrs and back to the apostolic church. The emphasis is not so much on imitation but rather on recording and remembering

---

35. *Martyrs of Lyons* 2 (Musurillo, 83).

36. Tertullian, *A Treatise on the Soul* 55 (*ANF* 3:231); Tertullian, *Ad Martyras* (*ANF* 3:693–96). For commentary on dating and textual issues regarding the *Passion of Perpetua and Felicitas*, see Moss, *Ancient Christian Martyrdom*, 129–34. She encourages a healthy skepticism toward accepting the story at face value.

37. *Passion of Perpetua and Felicitas* 10 (Musurillo, 119).

these noble deeds as potent works of the Spirit through the church, as a witness to unbelievers and an encouragement to believers that they are not alone and can be vessels of the Spirit's power during the persecution.

The redactor of the *Passion* evinces a telling historical understanding. Whereas the contemporary bias against history reflects a snobbery that favors the present as more important than the past (Timothy George brands this attitude "the heresy of contemporaneity or, in less theological terms, the imperialism of the present"), in antiquity the case was just the opposite, as evidenced above in Christian apologetic material (chap. 3).[38] The redactor readily admits that ancient deeds of the faith (*fidei exempla*) both demonstrated "God's favour" and "achieved . . . spiritual strengthening" (*aedificationem hominis*); therefore, they were valuable and worth writing down for others to read later. "They were set forth in writing [*documenta*] precisely that honour might be rendered to God and comfort to men by the recollection of the past through the written word."[39] The redactor then claims the same honor for more recent events, which, despite their lack of a "prior claim of antiquity," show continuity with the noble past.[40] The same Holy Spirit was at work just as potently in antiquity as in the writer's own day. In the future, contemporary events will also constitute "ancient history." He shows an awareness that he records (or at least intends to record) the events he has witnessed for the spiritual benefit of future generations. The story he records is the "history" of the Holy Spirit's powerful work through human agents, specifically the church's martyrs. The stories need to be written down and passed along for the twofold purpose of glorifying God and edifying those of "weak or despairing faith," probably referring to those in danger of lapsing under torture.[41] The account that follows illustrates the author's several points. First, God's Spirit is as much at work now as at the time of Joel's prophecy and its fulfillment at Pentecost. Second, the Holy Spirit strengthens the church via prophecies and visions (*revelationum*) and even the "grace of martyrdom."[42] Third, the martyrs' ordeals and their privileged visions from God testify to the truth of the Christian message before unbelievers (such as Pudens, a prison guard who eventually converted), and serve as a "blessing to the faithful."[43] Finally, the redactor

---

38. Timothy George, *Reading Scripture with the Reformers* (Downers Grove, IL: IVP Academic, 2011), 23.

39. *Passion of Perpetua and Felicitas* 1.1–1.2 (Musurillo, 106–7).

40. *Passion of Perpetua and Felicitas* 1.2 (Musurillo, 106–7).

41. *Passion of Perpetua and Felicitas* 1 (Musurillo, 107).

42. *Passion of Perpetua and Felicitas* 1 (Musurillo, 107).

43. Pudens is mentioned at *Passion of Perpetua and Felicitas* 9, 16, and 21 (Musurillo, 117, 125, and 130–31).

concludes the extensive prologue with a desire to help the reader bond somehow with the events described. He knows that some readers will have been eyewitnesses to the events, and these are encouraged to recall and dwell upon (*rememoremini*) the significance of the events, while those who "now learn of it through hearing" might have "fellowship [*communionem*] with the holy martyrs, and through them, with the Lord Christ Jesus."[44]

Bearing in mind the assessment of Musurillo concerning the authenticity of the *Martyrdom of Saints Montanus and Lucius* (who died ca. 259), it becomes apparent due to numerous textual similarities that this account was crafted to resemble the *Passion of Perpetua and Felicitas*.[45] The former document apparently originates in Carthage, so the story of Perpetua would have been well known there. The account also shows a possible influence from the *Martyrdom of Cyprian*, since the bishop had died the year before. The themes found in the document are consistent with authentic accounts mentioned above and could be understood as a further communal affirmation by the church, expressing the importance of inscribing the events of martyrdoms. The author states that "love and a sense of obligation have urged us to write this account, that we might leave to all future brethren [*ut fratribus post futuris*] a loyal witness to the grandeur of God and a historical record [*memoriae*] of our labors and our sufferings for the Lord."[46] The emphasis that writing down the events of "recent times" is just as edifying as "the ancient writings" also appears in the epilogue, as does the connection between memorializing and imitation of the examples offered. "Duly have these been written down to be preserved for those to come, that just as we have taken examples and learnt from the ancient writings, so too we may derive some profit from those of recent times."[47]

As is generally known, persecutions were mostly localized and sporadic. There were only two major empire-wide, government-sponsored persecutions, and these took place in the mid-third century under the emperor Decius (r. 249–51) and under the Tetrarchy (286–311) devised by the emperor Diocletian (r. 285–305) in the late third and early fourth centuries. Therefore what the documents indicate is that the deeds of the martyrs were recorded, remembered, reiterated, and used to strengthen and embolden those who might be called and chosen to

44. *Passion of Perpetua and Felicitas* 1 (Musurillo, 107–9).

45. "Of all this (material) the author, clearly a disciple of Cyprian, attempts to create a *passio* that will rival the story of Perpetua and Felicitas; for this reason, if for no other, the degree of historicity will always remain difficult to determine" (Musurillo, *Acts of the Christian Martyrs*, xxxv).

46. *Martyrdom of Saints Montanus and Lucius* 1 (Musurillo, 214–15).

47. *Martyrdom of Saints Montanus and Lucius* 23 (Musurillo, 238–39).

suffer later. Those undergoing persecution under Decius would have looked back to earlier martyrs, and those suffering under Diocletian would be looking back to the accounts preserved from the Decian persecution and earlier.

Mimēsis

A third historiographical feature is tied to the classical education system known as *paideia* (see the expanded description in chap. 2). Just as in its classical counterpart, the Christian *paideia* consists of moral pedagogy, in which examples of virtue are offered with the aim that the audience will take note of noble deeds and examples, remember them, and model themselves accordingly via imitation (*mimēsis*). Readers (or listeners) are expected to imitate the subjects' virtues of courage, steadfastness, and sound doctrine, as well as their values and expressions of self-identity.

EXAMPLES OF INTENTIONAL MIMETIC EXEMPLARS

What follows are several examples of intentional efforts by the narrators or editors of particular martyrdom accounts to set forth examples for imitation by others and to clearly connect commemoration and attention to narrative detail with imitation.

In the prologue to the *Martyrdom of Pionius the Presbyter* (cited more fully above), the link between *mimēsis* (imitation) and *mnēmē* (remembrance) can be clearly seen. "The Apostle urges us to share in the remembrances [*mneiais*] of the saints, fully aware that to call to mind [*mnēmēn*]; those that have passed their life in the faith wisely . . . gives strength to those who are striving to imitate [*mimeisthai*] the better things."[48] The Smyrnaean editor of the document narrating the martyrdom of Polycarp wrote to the church in Philomelium and other churches (perhaps of Asia Minor) for much the same reasons, that the church might imitate this kind of discipleship. Polycarp's ordeal "took place that the Lord might show us from Heaven a witness in accordance with the gospel. Just as the Lord did, he too waited that he might be delivered up, that we might become his imitators [*mimētai*]."[49] The narrator ends with the summary statement, "This, then, was the story of the blessed Polycarp, who, counting those from Philadelphia, was the twelfth to be martyred [*martyrēsas*] in Smyrna; yet he alone is especially remembered [*mnēmoneuetai*] by everyone, and is everywhere mentioned, even by the pagans. He was not only a great teacher but also

---

48. *Martyrdom of Pionius* 1 (Musurillo, 136–37).
49. *Martyrdom of Polycarp* 1.2 (Musurillo, 2–3).

a conspicuous martyr [*martys*], whose testimony [*martyrion*], following the Gospel of Christ, everyone desires to imitate [*mimeisthai*]."[50]
The concluding portion states, "And may it be granted to us to come
into the kingdom of Jesus Christ following his [Polycarp's] footsteps,"
indicating the document's purpose to lay out a paradigmatic martyrdom
from beginning to end.[51]

Several examples from less historically reliable accounts follow, but
I offer them nonetheless because, although their historical authenticity
is in question, they demonstrate similar concerns for remembrance and
imitation in diverse Christian communities. The martyrdom of Apollonius Sakkeas (possibly meaning "the ascetic") reflects a time (likely the
fifth century) when commemoration of the martyrs and their ordeals
was a well-established practice. In Musurillo's rendering, the phrase
"Lord, have mercy" immediately follows the title.[52] This phrase suggests
that the *acta* are being used in a liturgical context or some other type
of commemorative context, such as the anniversary of Apollonius's
death. As Apollonius goes to execution, the author concludes,

> Such was the glorious end of martyrdom endured by this most holy
> victor called Sakkeas with sober mind and generous heart. *Today* was
> the day established on which he was to obtain his victory over the Evil
> One. So then, because of his heroic deeds, brothers, strengthening our
> own souls in the faith, let us show ourselves lovers of the same grace,
> through the mercy and favour of Jesus Christ, with whom to God the
> Father together with the Holy Spirit is glory and power for ever. Amen.[53]

By his words we are given the impression that the author's community
remembers Apollonius's death and "heroic deeds" and thereby draws
strength to continue their own striving against the "Evil One."

The account of the ordeals of Montanus and Lucius should also be
considered with caution, but it reflects the same concerns for remembrance and an understanding that dwelling on those memories forms
collective Christian character in a context of persecution. Purportedly
composed by imprisoned martyrs who have directed a letter to the
church at Carthage, the writer of this text insists on the critical necessity of love, harmony, and peace within the church, as the martyrs
offer themselves as worthy examples of this kind of fraternal love and

50. *Martyrdom of Polycarp* 19 (Musurillo, 16–17).
51. *Martyrdom of Polycarp* 22 (Musurillo, 19).
52. *The Martyrdom of the Saintly and Blessed Apostle Apollonius, also Called Sakkeas*
(Musurillo, 91).
53. *The Martyrdom of the Saintly and Blessed Apostle Apollonius, also Called Sakkeas* 47
(Musurillo, 103, emphasis added).

concord. "Wherefore, dearest brothers, let us all cling to harmony, peace, and unanimity in every virtue. Let us imitate here what we shall be there. . . . If we long to live and reign with Christ, then let us do those things that lead to Christ and to his kingdom."[54] As the martyrs imitate Christ in this respect, so is the church exhorted to imitate him (and them).

Furthermore, the martyrs themselves are presented as worthy paradigms of courage and sound doctrine. As the martyrs (including Lucius) were led to the place of idolatrous sacrifice, a crowd of pagans and Christians came out to watch. "There they could see the martyrs of Christ witnessing to their glorious joy by the cheerfulness of their faces so that even without a word they would have drawn the rest to imitate their courage, . . . but by exhortation each one continued to strengthen the people."[55] Montanus also exhorted the Christians and admonished them against the worship of idols, while criticizing heretics and apostates. To the faithful he urged, "Hold your ground courageously, my brothers, and fight perseveringly. You have good models [*exempla*]; let not the treachery of apostates [*perfidia lapsorum*] lead you to ruin, but rather let our own endurance strengthen you for the crown."[56] The martyrs' continual call for mutual love within the church intentionally echoes Jesus's command to his disciples in John 15:12.[57] The author(s), then, presented the martyrs as models of humility, abiding love, harmony, courage for future martyrs, and orthodoxy.[58]

In a final example, Phileas, the respected fourth-century bishop of Thmuis in Egypt, writes of the Diocletianic persecution, which he himself witnessed when imprisoned in Alexandria, and under which he himself became a martyr. In a letter to his congregation, he presents the martyrs of Alexandria as following the examples of suffering they found in the Scriptures, as well as other martyrs' endurance to the death; but above all they looked to Christ, who had "taught us to resist sin unto death," citing Christ's incarnation, abasement, and atoning death in Philippians 2:6–8. Therefore, "following his example, the

54. *The Martyrdom of Saints Montanus and Lucius* 11 (Musurillo, 225).

55. *The Martyrdom of Saints Montanus and Lucius* 13 (Musurillo, 227).

56. *The Martyrdom of Saints Montanus and Lucius* 14 (Musurillo, 227).

57. *The Martyrdom of Saints Montanus and Lucius* 23 (Musurillo, 237).

58. See also the *Acts of Euplus*, whose offense had to do with owning and refusing to surrender Scriptures that were outlawed by an imperial edict under the emperor Diocletian. The martyrdom of Euplus occurred in the late third or early fourth century, and the text was possibly edited to reflect doctrinal controversies of the fourth century; Musurillo labels these *acta* "somewhat questionable" (*Acts of the Christian Martyrs*, xlv). In any case, the Greek recension of his *acta* mentions that he was ultimately rewarded with the "crown of orthodox belief" (*Acts of Euplus* 2 [Musurillo, 313]).

blessed martyrs endured all sorts of tortures and penalties."[59] Eventually Phileas himself was remanded, tried, and tortured. After multiple hearings and interrogations, Phileas was beheaded, and in his final words he presented himself in his suffering as an example of discipleship, in words similar to the martyr-bishop Ignatius of Antioch from roughly a century and a half earlier: "Before, we did not suffer; but now we begin to suffer; now we begin to become disciples of Christ."[60]

The later use of these accounts demonstrates how subsequent generations of Christians who were called upon to give their lives drew inspiration from the examples of previous generations. These narratives continued to be read during subsequent persecutions as well as after the Peace of the Church because believers continued to commemorate these martyrs' noble deeds and to strive to imitate their virtues in the Christian life. The imagery of the martyrs' battles continued into later hagiography in stories of ascetics who perceived themselves as living according to the martyr's ideal.

EXPRESSIONS OF SELF-IDENTITY

Martyrs expressed their identity in many ways, which can be broadly classified into five main descriptors. They were *cosufferers* with Christ, imitating him (*imitatio Christi*) and participating in his passion. Because of Christ, they had a *new family*, made up of others who had been redeemed by Christ's sacrifice. In their suffering, they were not passive victims but rather active victors, powerful combatants, *athletes and soldiers* under the training and leadership of Christ. Christians were not only members of a new family but also *citizens of another kingdom*, meaning that they acknowledged Christ alone as Lord and King, placing themselves dangerously at odds with the earthly powers to which they were subject.

First and foremost, the martyrs felt a powerful personal identification with Christ, as shown by two mystical Pauline themes in the *acta martyrum*: (1) intimate union with Christ ("Christ in you"), and (2) knowing Christ in such a way as to experience the "fellowship [*koinōnian*] of His sufferings, being conformed to His death," and holding out for the "resurrection from among the dead" (Phil. 3:10–11). This feature is known in martyrological (and later devotional) literature as *imitatio Christi*, and several examples have already appeared above; indeed, this is a thematic feature in virtually every

---

59. *Letter of Phileas* B (Musurillo, 325).

60. *Acts of Phileas* B.9 (Musurillo, 353). Cf. Ignatius of Antioch, *Letter to the Ephesians* 3, in *The Apostolic Fathers*, trans. J. B. Lightfoot and J. R. Harmer, ed. and rev. Michael W. Holmes (Grand Rapids: Baker, 1989), 87; Ignatius of Antioch, *Letter to the Romans* 4–5 (Holmes, 103–4).

account, but a few notable examples will suffice. Ignatius comes to
the fore again as he begs the congregation in Rome not to interfere
with his trial and desired execution: "Do not give to the world one
who wants to belong to God. . . . Allow me to be an imitator of the
suffering of my God."[61] Perpetua's servant girl, Felicitas, expressed her
solidarity with Christ through suffering in terms of her own situation
as a woman in labor. As she was not quite to term in her pregnancy,
she was in danger of being remanded until delivery, to be executed
later with "common criminals" rather than together with her fellow
Christians.[62] Her companions prayed for her, and she went into labor
two days before their scheduled execution. As she was enduring labor
pains, one of the guards sneered that labor pains are minor compared
with the agony of being devoured or mauled by beasts. Felicitas replied that she suffered the pangs of labor (*laborans doleret*) alone,
but in the arena "another will be inside me who will suffer for me,
just as I shall be suffering for him."[63] The imagery of giving birth is
rich with spiritual meaning in Scripture (John 16:21; Gal. 4:19) and
takes on multiple meanings in this context, which is both physical/
maternal and spiritual. The baby being born causes her suffering and
does not ease the labor pains at all; but in the contest, Christ will be
inside her, and he will bring assistance as a cosufferer with her. Felicitas's statement also accords well with Perpetua's earlier vision, in
which the deacon Pomponius seems to represent Christ. He walked
Perpetua to the middle of a packed gladiatorial arena and left her
with the words, "Do not be afraid. I am here, struggling [*conlaboro*]
with you."[64] A graphic example actually pictures *imitatio Christi* in
the person of the venerable slave Blandina. As one of a number of
Christians being tortured in the amphitheater, the account relates the
following about her:

> [She was] hung on a post and exposed as bait for wild animals. . . . She
> seemed to hang there in the form of a cross [so that those suffering were
> encouraged], for in their torment with their physical eyes they saw in
> the person of their sister him who was crucified for them, . . . for she
> had put on Christ, that mighty and invincible athlete, and had overcome
> the Adversary in many contests [*agōnos*].[65]

61. Ignatius of Antioch, *Letter to the Romans* 6 (Holmes, 104).
62. *Passion of Perpetua and Felicitas* 15 (Musurillo, 123). The account explains that it was
illegal to execute pregnant women. See also *The Martyrdom of Saints Agapē, Irēnē, and Chionē
at Saloniki* 3 (Musurillo, 285), in which Eutychia is kept in prison and not executed with Agape
and Irene because she is seven months pregnant.
63. *Passion of Perpetua and Felicitas* 15 (Musurillo, 122–25).
64. *Passion of Perpetua and Felicitas* 10 (Musurillo, 116–17).
65. *Martyrs of Lyons* 1.41 (Musurillo, 74–75).

One final, particularly poignant example comes from the martyrdom of the Spanish bishop Fructuosus and his two deacons, who were all sentenced to be burned at the stake. The three had been bound, and the sight of them brought to mind the story of Daniel's three friends in the fiery furnace (Dan. 3:19–27), a deliverance narrative widely known and beloved during this period. As their bonds were burned by the flames, Fructuosus and the two deacons knelt down, "and stretching out their arms in memory of the Lord's cross, they prayed to the Lord until together they gave up their souls."[66]

In addition to identifying with Christ as their Master, the martyrs also clung to one another as family members. Numerous examples testify to this, but several clearly stand out. The *Testament of the Forty Holy and Glorious Martyrs of Christ Who Died at Sebaste* (henceforth *Forty Martyrs of Sebaste*) purports to be a letter written to Christian communities everywhere, but it was probably circulated mostly in Armenia, where these men died.[67] Traditionally, these martyrs were Christian soldiers sentenced to die of exposure in the winter, sometime between 308 and 324.[68] As in many other accounts, the context is one of urging the Christian community to pursue love among the brotherhood, for the church is one large family bound by fraternal ties of faith rather than bloodline.

> For the invisible God is revered in our brother whom we see; and though this saying refers to our true brothers, the meaning is extended to all those who love Christ. For our God and holy Saviour declared to be brothers not those who shared a common nature, but rather those who were bound together in the faith by good deeds and who fulfil the will of our Father who is in heaven.[69]

In other accounts, Blandina is called "a noble mother encouraging her children," while Irene, Chione, Agape, and the other women martyred at Thessalonica are consistently called "sisters."[70] About Bishop Phileas we are told that "all of Phileas' relatives . . . embraced his feet and begged him to have regard for his wife and concern for his children. But it was like water wearing away a rock. He rejected what they said, claiming that the apostles and martyrs were his kin."[71] In the

---

66. *The Martyrdom of Bishop Fructuosus and His Deacons, Augurius and Eulogius* 4 (Musurillo, 181–83).

67. See Musurillo, *Acts of the Christian Martyrs*, xlix.

68. Sozomen, *Church History* 9.2 (NPNF[2] 2:420).

69. *Forty Martyrs of Sebaste* 2 (Musurillo, 359).

70. *Martyrs of Lyons* 1.55 (Musurillo, 79); *Martyrdom of Saints Agapē, Irēnē, and Chionē at Saloniki* 5, 6, 7 (Musurillo, 289, 293).

71. *Acts of Phileas* 6.4 (Musurillo, 350–51).

introduction to the *acta* of Justin Martyr and his companions, identity is also expressed in familial terms: "Now the saints did not have the same native city, for they came from different countries. But the favor of the Spirit bound them together, and taught them to have fraternal thoughts and to have but one head, Christ."[72]

Christians identified with Christ and with one another even ahead of their own identification with geographical and family provenance. For example, when "the proconsul asked [the bishop] Carpus, 'What is your name?'" he received the reply, "My first and most distinctive name is that of Christian; but if you want my name in the world, it is Carpus."[73] Similarly, the soldier-martyr Dasius answered, "I am a soldier by rank. Of my name I shall tell you that I have the excellent one of Christian. But the name given me by my parents is Dasius."[74] Other martyrs refused to give any other information concerning themselves, but stated repeatedly, "I am a Christian," as did Sanctus of Vienne (*Christianos eimi*) and Blandina of Lyons (*Christianē eimi*), as well as the soldier-martyr Maximilian (*Christianus sum*).[75]

The martyrs saw themselves as athletes whose trainer was Christ, and as soldiers in Christ's army. Athletic imagery abounds in these accounts, especially when spectacle in an arena is the mode and locus of execution. Clearly the Christians considered themselves victors through Christ rather than victims of the state. Descriptions of the martyr under torture present the physical body as the locus of the conflict between the devil and Christ. At times the bodies are exhausted from torture, mangled, shapeless, and unrecognizable, yet some were later physically restored and strengthened for further combat. Sanctus of Vienne's body was "all one bruise and one wound," but "Christ suffering in him achieved great glory, overwhelming the Adversary."[76] At other times when perhaps death was imminent, the martyrs' bodies began to take on a heavenly aura, as if they were already living a heavenly life and had been made fit for heaven. As Pionius undressed before his execution, he "realized the holiness and dignity of his own body."[77] Polycarp appeared no longer as a man but as an "angel," while the souls of the young women who had fled their persecutors to a mountain with Agape and Irene "lived in heaven" although their

---

72. *Acts of Justin and His Companions* 1 (Musurillo, 55).

73. *Martyrdom of Sts. Carpus, Papylus, and Agathonike* 2–3 (Musurillo, 22–23).

74. *Martyrdom of the Saintly Dasius* 6 (Musurillo, 277).

75. *Martyrs of Lyons* 1.19–20 (Musurillo, 66–69); *The Acts of Maximilian* 1 (Musurillo, 244–45). The *Lyons* account says that Sanctus "kept repeating this again and again instead of giving his name, birthplace, nationality, or anything else."

76. *Martyrs of Lyons* 1.23 (Musurillo, 69).

77. *Martyrdom of Pionius* 21 (Musurillo, 163).

bodies dwelt on earth.[78] Finally, Perpetua and Pionius are described as having glowing or shining faces, while Saturus and Phileas saw visions of heaven, all reminiscent of the ordeal of Stephen the protomartyr.[79] Combat imagery directly relates to the "causation" section below: the Christians understood that their primary opponent was not the state, nor any earthly authority (not even the beasts), but the devil himself. Although their bodies underwent fearsome agonies, by their resolute refusal to capitulate to pleas and commands to acknowledge the rulers of this world as ultimate lords, the devil continually met resounding defeat.

The documents of this period clearly show that the martyrs (and Christians generally) considered themselves to be citizens of another kingdom whose sovereign is Christ. They felt marginalized by their own society, seeing themselves as "outsiders in the imperial structure" who held an "alien citizenship."[80] Their voicing of this commitment placed them in a politically dangerous position vis-à-vis the empire. They affirmed that Christ reigns *eternally*, unlike their own emperors, and that he holds their highest allegiance as sovereign Lord. For example, Polycarp called Jesus his king or emperor (*basilea*), while the soldier Marcellus (a centurion) declared during a military banquet celebrating the emperor's birthday, "I am a soldier of Jesus Christ, the eternal king. From now, I cease to serve your emperors and I despise the worship of your gods of wood and stone, for they are deaf and dumb images [*idola*]."[81] Similarly offensive was the soldier-martyr Dasius, who proclaimed, "I am a Christian, and I do not fight for any earthly king but for the king of heaven."[82] They were willing to follow the scriptural injunctions to pray for their leaders and rulers, but they would not compromise by sacrificing to the emperor's genius (the *tychē Kaisaros*). *Tychē*, or "genius," referred to the highest spirit of a person, which could be represented by a statue. The ancients saw this kind of veneration as a payment of respect, devotion, and allegiance, but Christians considered it idolatrous. Instead, they prayed to God, acknowledging *him* as supreme, simultaneously denying the emperor's supremacy by not offering

---

78. *Martyrdom of Polycarp* 3 (Musurillo, 5); *Martyrdom of Saints Agapē, Irēnē, and Chionē at Saloniki* 1 (Musurillo, 281).

79. *Passion of Perpetua and Felicitas* 18 (Musurillo, 127: "shining countenance"); *Martyrdom of Pionius* 22 (Musurillo, 165: "his face shone once again"); *Passion of Perpetua and Felicitas* 4, 11–13 (Musurillo, 111–13, 119–23); *Acts of Phileas* 7 (Musurillo, 351–53).

80. Rowan Williams, *Why Study the Past?* (Grand Rapids: Eerdmans, 2005), 34, 47.

81. *Martyrdom of Polycarp* 9 (Musurillo, 9); *The Acts of Marcellus* 1 (Musurillo, 250–51).

82. *Martyrdom of the Saintly Dasius* 7 (Musurillo, 277).

the worship *he* demanded.[83] Speratus of Scilli, who was arraigned in Carthage around 180, unflinchingly voiced this conviction at his trial when ordered to "swear . . . by the Genius of our lord [*genium domni nostri*] the emperor." He replied, "I do not recognize the empire of this world. Rather I serve God whom no man has seen, nor can see with these eyes. . . . I acknowledge my lord [*domnum meum*] who is the emperor of kings and of all nations."[84]

Despite the social and political ramifications of these convictions, the Christians clearly identified obeisance to Caesar as idolatry, and believed (consistent with Paul's teachings in 1 Cor. 8–10) that there was an unambiguous relationship between idolatry and demonic activity, which results in spiritual deception. The bishop Carpus explained to his interrogator that idolatry is demonic and that one becomes what one worships.

> True worshippers . . . take on the image of God's glory and become immortal with Him, sharing in eternal life through the Word, . . . [while idolaters] take on the image of the demons' folly and perish along with them in Gehenna. And justly should they suffer with him who deceived mankind, God's most excellent creation, with the one who out of his native viciousness (I mean the Devil [*diabolou*]) provoked man for this purpose.[85]

Christians viewed God alone as the sovereign God of the universe: Acts 4:24 (God is "the One who made the heaven, the earth, and the sea, and everything in them" [HCSB]) and Jeremiah 10:11 ("You are to say this to them, 'The gods that did not make the heavens and the earth will perish from the earth and from under these heavens'" [HCSB]) emerge consistently in these accounts as, respectively, a statement of monotheism and worship, and a polemic against idolatry. An affirmation of monotheism and praise is found in the prayer of the Christians in Acts 4 after the release of Peter and John, following interrogation and threats in the wake of the healing of the lame man and the apostles' bold proclamation about Jesus. Jeremiah 10:1–16 provides an extended comparison of Yahweh, the true God, and human-made idols, which neither harm nor help. Of course both passages find their origin in the Genesis 1 creation account, a statement of monotheism and God's supremacy in and over the entire cosmos, and this idea is often repeated in the Old Testament as a statement of faith. For example, in Jonah 1:9 (HCSB), Jonah says to the terrified Phoenician

---

83. *Martyrdom of Polycarp* 10 (Musurillo, 11).
84. *Acts of the Scillitan Martyrs* 3, 5 (Musurillo, 86–87).
85. *Martyrdom of Sts. Carpus, Papylus, and Agathonike* 2–3 (Musurillo, 22–23).

sailors, who were likely Baal worshipers, devotees of Baal Shamem: "I'm a Hebrew. I worship Yahweh, the God of the heavens, who made the sea and the dry land." The Acts 4 passage, echoing Genesis 1 and Jonah 1:9, appears in almost every account included by Musurillo in *Acts of the Christian Martyrs*.

An interesting manifestation of this strongly held belief emerges in a tagline that often concludes the accounts: "under the reign of our Lord Jesus Christ," or a slight variation thereof. In the final section, as a particular account is dated by the name of the emperor and other regional rulers pertaining to the location of the persecution, Christ is hailed as ruling over all as the supreme monarch, which is reminiscent of Daniel's vision of the Ancient of Days and the Son of Man, where the point is that God is Lord over all human history, and that at his sovereign behest, kingdoms are raised or toppled (Dan. 7:13–14, 26–27). Indeed, this understanding of God as Lord over history builds up throughout the book of Daniel and is amply illustrated by the events recorded there concerning the Babylonian kingdom under a succession of rulers. Examples of this historical understanding among the early church and the martyrs appear in the accounts of Polycarp, Carpus, Justin, Apollonius, Pionius, Cyprian, Conon ("God the King of the ages"), Marcellus, Dasius, Agape and her companions, Irenaeus, and Crispina. A few examples of this tagline not only demonstrate the Christians' eternal and otherworldly perspective but also point to a certain historical concern for accuracy in dating the ordeals of these holy heroes. The conclusion to the account of Polycarp's martyrdom reads,

> The blessed Polycarp died as a martyr on the second day of the first half of the month Xanthicus (according to the Roman calendar, on 23 February), about two o'clock in the afternoon, on a great Sabbath day. He was arrested under Herod, during the time when Philip of Tralles was high priest and Statius Quadratus was governor—*while Jesus Christ was reigning eternally*.[86]

The redactor of the account of the martyrdom of Irenaeus of Sirmium (Mitrovitsa in the former Yugoslavia) concludes,

> The holy servant of God, Bishop Irenaeus of Sirmium, was martyred on the sixth day of April under the Emperor Diocletian, when Probus was governor, *under the reign of our Lord Jesus Christ, to whom is glory forever*. Amen.[87]

86. *Martyrdom of Polycarp* 21 (Musurillo, 19, emphasis added).
87. *Martyrdom of Saint Irenaeus Bishop of Sirmium* 6 (Musurillo, 301, emphasis added).

The account of the martyrdoms of Agape, Irene, and Chione similarly concludes,

> It was in the ninth consulship of Diocletian Augustus, in the eighth of Maximian Augustus, on the first day of April, *in the kingship of our Lord Jesus Christ, who reigns forever*, with whom there is glory to the Father with the Holy Spirit for ever. Amen.[88]

The martyrs also demonstrated an eschatological concern for their fate on judgment day. Although subjected to *temporal* judgment and condemnation, they would be exempt from *eternal* condemnation and hellfire at the final judgment if they remained resolute without compromising their worship. The day of "the terrible tribunal of Christ" would mean ultimate justice for the martyrs, when their vision of the God who rules all ages and holds all flesh accountable would exonerate and reward firm believers, but condemn their earthly persecutors.[89]

These Christians exemplified lessons that derived from the church's catechetical instruction, its virtues and ethics, and they served as an exhortation to unity, orthodoxy, and spiritual fortitude to bear up under torture without lapsing. Robin Darling Young writes that the inclusion of training for martyrdom—should one be chosen or called to that—was present in the church's catechesis (what we might call "discipleship training") and is especially seen in the writings of Origen and Clement.[90] While in some places it was emphasized that martyrdom was not to be sought out or the magistrates provoked, some still volunteered themselves for punishment (like Euplus).[91] The rewards for steadfastness under persecution were also drawn out: visions of heaven, refreshment, and immediate access to the Lord's presence were granted to the martyrs.

Causation

The fourth historiographical element found in the martyrdom accounts is *causation*. Causation refers to the explanation(s) given by the narrator as to whose influences or what causes drive the action. Explanations of causation tie the narrative together and provide an overarching framework for understanding the events. The martyr ac-

---

88. *Martyrdom of Saints Agapē, Irēnē, and Chionē at Saloniki* 7 (Musurillo, 293, emphasis added).
89. *Martyrdom of Justin* 4 (Musurillo, 59).
90. Young, *In Procession before the World*, 10–11, 13, 37–60.
91. *Martyrdom of Polycarp* 4 (Musurillo, 5); *Acts of Cyprian* 1 (Musurillo, 169–71).

counts are shot through with the vocabulary and metaphors of battle. The cause of persecution was consistently identified as the devil (as Greco-Roman historians referred to Fate, Eris/Envy, or some other malevolent deity), while the One who empowered the Christians was God, who is ultimately the Victor and has already overcome (John 16:33; Rev. 1:12–18).

The imagery, metaphors, and terms used for the devil derive mostly from the Scriptures. In these martyrdom accounts as well as later hagiographical material, he is described as a "roaring lion" who "prowls around, . . . seeking someone to devour" (1 Pet. 5:8), clearly responsible for the suffering of Christians "throughout the world" (5:9); he is the "ancient serpent" and a deadly dragon who wars against God's armies and God's saints, "those who keep the commandments of God and hold to the testimony of Jesus" (Rev. 12:9, 17). The unforgettable image of Perpetua treading the head of the "dragon" (draco) is recorded in her diary. The devil as a dragon and (later) as a vicious gladiatorial opponent ("an Egyptian") are two images merged by the editor of her account in the concluding portions: as she and her companions were brought into the arena, "she was already treading on the head of the Egyptian."[92] He is also depicted as a beast and an enemy/adversary (antikeimenos).[93] A further descriptor used in the martyrdom accounts (as well as later in the vitae and other Christian historical literature), which derives from classical rather than biblical sources, is "envious one" (baskanos).[94] This term recalls the concept of an envious deity who is jealous when affairs in the human world are peaceful and prosperous.

Explanations for the devil's opposition to believers are twofold and interrelated: he knows his end, and he is already vanquished.[95] Revelation 12:9–12 looms large here, as it combines a number of the images listed above.

And the great dragon was thrown down, that ancient serpent, who is called the devil and Satan, the deceiver of the whole world—he was thrown down to the earth, and his angels were thrown down with him. . . . "[The saints] have conquered him by the blood of the Lamb and by the word of their testimony, for they loved not their lives even unto death. . . . Woe to you, O earth and sea, for the devil has come down to you in great wrath, because he knows that his time is short!"

92. *Passion of Perpetua and Felicitas* 4, 10, 18 (Musurillo, 111, 119, 127).
93. *Martyrdom of Carpus* 35 (Musurillo, 27); *Martyrdom of Polycarp* 17 (Musurillo, 15); *Martyrs of Lyons* 2.6 (Musurillo, 84–85, where the devil is described as a "throttled beast").
94. *Martyrdom of Polycarp* 17 (Musurillo, 15).
95. *Martyrdom of Carpus* 17 (Musurillo, 25); *Martyrs of Lyons* 1.5 (Musurillo, 63).

Bearing in mind this selection from Revelation, a celebrated passage that illustrates the causative framework for a martyrdom narrative practically introduces the account of the *Martyrs of Lyons*.

> The Adversary [*antikeimenos*] swooped down with full force, in this way anticipating his final coming. . . . He went to all lengths to train and prepare his minions against God's servants. . . . Arrayed against him was God's grace, which protected the weak, and raised up sturdy pillars that could by their endurance take on themselves all the attacks of the Evil One [*tou ponērou*]. These then charged into battle, holding up under every sort of abuse and torment.[96]

An equally celebrated passage derives from the account of Polycarp's martyrdom and explains how the devil works through the political powers and structures of the empire, through procurators, prefects, emperors, and other officials who are deceived into idolatry under the misguided idea that the idols represent the true and traditional gods who have made Rome great. To this end, they punish the devotees of the true and living God.

> The jealous [*antizelos*] and envious [*baskanos*] Evil One [*ponēros*], who is the adversary [*antikeimenos*] of the race of the just, realizing the greatness of his [Polycarp's] testimony [*martyrias*], . . . prevented us even from taking up the poor body. . . . Hence he got Nicetes, Herod's father and Alce's brother, to petition the governor not to give up his body.[97]

The devil also operated through the (well-intentioned) appeals of family and friends who were unbelievers, like Perpetua's father and Phileas's brother. Through his minions and ministers, Satan fomented unrest among the crowds of onlookers, prodding them to call for torture. He inspired the administrators of punishments to devise various vicious punishments, and he tormented the Christians in jail with discomfort, hunger and thirst, and abuse from the prison guards.[98]

Beyond a Textual *Paideia*

In addition to reading the accounts laid out in the sections above, the church devised other methods for remembrance and building corporate memory through martyrdom accounts. Sacred history, sacred worship,

---

96. *Martyrs of Lyons* 1.5 (Musurillo, 62–63).
97. *Martyrdom of Polycarp* 17 (Musurillo, 15).
98. *Martyrs of Lyons* 1.27, 1.57–61 (Musurillo, 70–71, 81).

sacred art, and sacred remains all served as aids for the commemoration of the martyrs' incredible stories, helping to form collective memory and to solidify a corporate identity.

As we have seen, Christians met together on the anniversary of a martyr's death at the site of death (if possible) or at the burial site. These were probably the earliest annual celebrations in the church, apart from Easter. At these special gatherings, copies of the *acta* or narrative of the martyr's ordeal were read aloud, allowing the hearers to relive in some limited measure the events of that day, to draw strength thereby and inspiration for courageous and virtuous living. These anniversary dates were added to a growing list of dates, thus forming a sacred history of saint days that has come down to us as part of the church calendar.

Second, the church remembered the martyrs in the context of its worship. On martyrs' anniversaries, liturgical *prayers* in memory of the martyr (and even prayers of supplication *to* the martyr) were spoken at the Eucharist. In the context of the early church's sacramental theology (which most Free Church Protestants eschew), the continuity between the living and the departed expressed in terms of the communion of saints was more tightly drawn. It should be admitted that some of the editorial material in the martyrological literature expresses a firm belief in the ability of prayer to bridge the communication divide between the Christian and the departed saints.[99]

Often on their anniversaries, the martyrs were commemorated in the *homily* or sermon. Accounts of their ordeals were read or recapped by the preacher. Augustine was familiar with numerous accounts of North African martyrs such as Perpetua, Felicitas, and Cyprian, and he composed commemorative sermons on these, to encourage the church to imitate the martyrs' virtues.[100] Peter Chrysologus, a fifth-century archbishop of Ravenna, in northern Italy, also offered sermons on the martyrs for their feast days. One particular martyr whose tradition was well known and variously commemorated in Ravenna was Saint Lawrence, a deacon who died in Rome in or around the year 258, roasted on a red-hot iron. In *Sermon* 135, Chrysologus begins, "This day is renowned because of the martyr Lawrence's crown of baptism. . . . His suffering is extraordinary and much to be admired. With the

---

99. This idea appears specifically in the conclusion of recension C of the *Martyrdom of Justin* and his companions, and it is largely to be assumed as a concept in the background of all the accounts. See *Martyrdom of Justin* C.6 (Musurillo, 61).

100. See a helpful thesis by Collin S. Garbarino, "Reclaiming Martyrdom: Augustine's Reconstruction of Martyrdom in Late Antique North Africa" (MA thesis, Louisiana State University and A&M College, 2007), esp. chap. 5.

Lord's help, I shall briefly narrate it."[101] He concludes by calling for remembrance, celebration, and imitation of the martyr's patient suffering, faith, and love: "May prayer be fervent, and let the feast of this martyr be celebrated. But let everyone who celebrates also imitate him, that the celebrating may not be idle."[102] Another particularly striking and apt homiletic example of memorialization of martyrs is Chrysologus's *Sermon* 129 on Saint Cyprian the Martyr. This brief homily is packed with the features discussed throughout this chapter, but it is especially suitable as an example of how the church might (continue to) go about remembering its martyrs and their significance. Several times the preacher attempts to bridge the gap between the fifth-century unpersecuted Christian and the third-century persecuted martyr. Chrysologus explains clearly to his congregation the importance of remembering the event, that the function of feast days is remembering, and that the function of remembering is, in turn, imitation.

> Today we have assembled in the sight of God on the birthday of St. Cyprian the Martyr. *On this date he triumphed over the Devil in an admirable struggle. Moreover, he has left us a glorious example of his virtues.* For these reasons, it is proper for us to exult and rejoice. Dearly beloved, when you hear about the birthday of the saints, do not think that mention is being made of their birth from flesh into life on earth. There is [rather] the question of their birth from earth into heaven; from toil to repose; from temptations to rest; from tortures to delights which are not fleeting, but strong, firm, and everlasting; from worldly hilarity to a crown of glory.
>
> Such birthdays of the martyrs are celebrated in a fitting way. Therefore, when a festival of this kind is being kept, do not think, dearly beloved, that birthdays of the martyrs should be celebrated only by meals and more elegant banquets. Rather, *what you celebrate in memory of a martyr is something proposed for your imitation.* Consequently, dearly beloved, observe the ardor of the congregation which is present. *At one time on this date* a mob of evil men stood by, when, through the tyrant's orders, St. Cyprian was being maltreated. There were crowds of evil-doers and bands of onlookers. *Now*, a devout multitude of the faithful has assembled to rejoice. *Then*, there was a crowd of furious agitators; *now*, one of those who rejoice—*then*, a band of men without hope; *now*, one of the men who are full of it.
>
> It is for a purpose that the birthdays of the martyrs are celebrated every year with joy: *that that which happened in the past should remain in the memory of devout men of every century.* The festival is carried

101. Peter Chrysologus, *Sermon* 135, in *Saint Peter Chrysologus: Selected Sermons; and Saint Valerian: Homilies*, trans. George E. Ganss, FC 17 (New York: Fathers of the Church, 1953), 222.
102. Peter Chrysologus, *Sermon* 135 (FC 17:224).

out, dearly beloved, that you may not say that you do not know about it. *The festivities are celebrated annually to keep you from saying: I forgot. Therefore, animate yourselves to imitate these deeds, dearly beloved.* Desire this grace of magnanimity. Ask that what he merited to obtain may be given you. For all those who desire heavenly goods cannot let themselves be enmeshed by the snares of earthly goods. They have determined that their citizenship is in heaven, after the teaching of the holy Apostle: "But our citizenship is in heaven." Therefore let our hearts direct their desires to the heavenly abode, where your heart will be after you have distributed your treasures to the poor. Christ is the treasure of all good men. May He, with the Father and the Son and the Holy Spirit, deign to heap heavenly gifts upon you and fill you with them, both now and forever.[103]

Chrysologus's contemporary, Bishop Valerian of Cimiez (in modern Nice, France), offered his congregation sermons on the excellence of martyrdom (*Sermons* 15–18), reiterating the same themes. His sermons are replete with the imagery of martyrdom applied to discipleship and virtuous Christian living, as Valerian seeks to make the battles and victories of the martyrs accessible to his congregation.[104] Finally, the famed Cappadocian brothers, Basil of Caesarea and Gregory of Nyssa, both delivered homilies on the Forty Martyrs of Sebaste.[105] Indeed, they had a special connection to these martyrs, as a church in honor of the soldier-martyrs was established in Basil's see of Caesarea, probably one not far from Annisa, where their sister Macrina lived and where she and their parents were buried, and another in the town of Sebaste itself, where their youngest brother Peter eventually became bishop.[106]

Finally, in the context of sacred worship, *songs and poems* were composed and performed in their honor. For example, Aurelius Prudentius Clemens (ca. 385–424), a Spanish composer of hymns and lyrical verse, was inspired by the festal celebrations of the martyrs, especially the liturgies commemorating their lives and heroic feats. In his hymns he combined material from the *passiones* that were recounted as part of the homily, from documentation accessible to him (some of the same sources that have come down to us), and from local traditions

103. Peter Chrysologus, *Sermon* 129, on Saint Cyprian the Martyr (FC 17:213–14, emphasis added).

104. Valerian, *Homilies and Letter to the Monks* (FC 17:397–420).

105. Basil of Caesarea, *Homily* 19, in *"Let Us Die That We May Live": Greek Homilies on Christian Martyrs from Asia Minor, Palestine and Syria c. 350–c. 450 AD*, trans. Pauline Allen, ed. Johan Leemans, Wendy Mayer, Pauline Allen, and Boudewijn Dehandschutter (New York: Routledge, 2003), 67–77.

106. Joan Petersen, ed. and trans., *Handmaids of the Lord: Holy Women in Late Antiquity and the Early Middle Ages* (Kalamazoo, MI: Cistercian, 1996), 62, 78.

surrounding martyr shrines he visited.[107] Although he probably did not intend his verses to be used liturgically, four of his hymns on the martyrs were eventually incorporated into the Old Spanish Liturgy (Mozarabic Rite), as were portions of four additional hymns. Their inclusion in the liturgy ensured regular commemoration of the martyrs—for example, the Spanish bishop Fructuosus and his deacons.[108]

Sacred art offers an additional method of commemoration. Martyrs are enshrined in countless mosaics and confront our gaze via numerous frescoes and icons. Several examples include the processions of martyrs at Ravenna's Saint Apollinare Nuovo Church, in which Perpetua and Felicitas are featured; a colorful and excellently preserved mosaic of Saint Lawrence at the mausoleum of Galla Placidia, also in Ravenna; mosaic representations of Perpetua and Felicitas (among other holy women and martyrs) at the bishop's palace in Ravenna; a catacomb fresco of Cyprian in the Roman catacombs of Saint Callistus; and myriads of other examples throughout the Mediterranean basin.

A final method of recalling historical persons and events has to do with sacred material remains, even though we cannot be at all certain about the provenance of the majority of relics. The martyrdom accounts above indicate that the martyrs' remains (bodies, bones, ashes, clothing) were exceedingly precious to those left behind, just as Stephen's (Acts 8:2) and John the Baptist's (Mark 6:29) remains were lovingly collected and laid to rest by their friends and disciples. Sometimes entire churches/ basilicas consisted of their reliquaries, for example, the Church of the Holy Martyrs of Sebaste or the remains of San Vitale in the Church of San Vitale at Ravenna. Of course there are inherent dangers involved in sacramental and material methods of memorialization, and this danger was manifest no less in Israel's experience than in the church's. Israel became presumptuous about their status in God's eyes and took for granted God's protection and provision as long as the temple and the ark of the covenant were intact. The nation's shock is palpable in the book of Lamentations as the mourners surveyed the temple ruins (Lam. 1:10; 2:6–7) following the devastating Babylonian siege and exile. They had relied on a mediating object rather than on a personal God for protection. Likewise, by the time Martin Luther nailed his Ninety-Five Theses to the door of Wittenberg Castle Church, the cult of saints and a brisk and burgeoning trade in relics ensured theological aberrations and spiritual abuses aplenty. Early on, however, the power of a martyr's

107. Sister M. Clement Eagan, trans., *Prudentius: Peristephanon*, FC 43 (Washington, DC: Catholic University of America Press, 1962), xiii.
108. *The Martyrdom of Bishop Fructuosus and His Deacons, Augurius and Eulogius* 1–7 (Musurillo, 176–85).

remains functioned as a concrete link to an exceptionally significant event in the life of a holy community, a kind of souvenir (which literally means "remembrance") of an identity-shaping past. The problem arose the moment the token became a totem.

Perhaps more intentional focus on memorials such as these can provoke questions about their meaning from our own children. As the Israelite children asked, "What do these stones mean to you?" perhaps ours will ask, "What do these bones mean to you? What does this church mean? This pilgrimage site? This ceremony? This holiday?" We can explain that real men and women made of flesh and bone shed real blood, felt real pain, and bore real witness before crowds and officials. They followed in the footsteps of the Master in self-denying, cross-bearing discipleship, and so must we in whatever ways we are called upon to serve in our current society. Stories of men and women, young and old, from all classes show that Christians in all life situations can victoriously bear a powerful witness. We ought to answer mindfully as we consider our children's own spiritual pilgrimage and their search for identity, and also consider what ought to be *our* part in the consolidation, edification, and practice of their faith. By doing so, we can better help them (and ourselves) find locatedness, rootedness, and belonging in the centuries-old family of faith.

HAGIOGRAPHY

Martyrdom as Discipleship
in Early Christian Biographies

Toleration and Its Import for the Church

As far as the persecuted church was concerned, a miracle of Providence took place in the year AD 312/313. Over the course of that year, the newly converted future emperor Constantine and his ally in the East (and future brother-in-law), the general Licinius, met several times for talks regarding the state of the empire, especially the plight of the persecuted church. Out of these talks emerged an "edict" that brought to a decisive end the era of violence against the church by the Roman Empire. Some scholars point out that the church had been tolerated since the reign of the emperor Gallienus (r. 260–68), whose father Valerian had been a persecutor.[1] Eusebius's account indicates that the church had experienced about forty-three years of peace and official recognition, for it was in those decades of respite that a number of heterodox ideas arose in the church. Despite the peace, however, it seems that Christians were still not accepted as a mainstream group, nor so integrated into the empire that the emperors of the early fourth century would hesitate to victimize them again on a wide scale.

Constantine's declaration of toleration is known as the Edict of Milan—a contested title for this document in the form of a letter—of which there are two versions: one recorded by Eusebius of Caesarea, and the other by Lactantius.[2] The Edict of Milan actually reinforced a previous Edict of Toleration promulgated on April, 30, 311, by the Caesar Galerius, who released it virtually on his deathbed, after having instigated an almost decade-long anti-Christian persecution, which raged most intensely in the East.[3] His son Maximinus Daia renewed the persecution in 311/312 by issuing a rescript, which resulted in many more martyrdoms.[4] Eventually he himself also issued a proclamation of toleration in 313 (echoing that of Constantine and Licinius at Milan), but he did not live long afterward, having made the declaration as an act of capitulation.[5] Constantine and Licinius came against him

---

1. Timothy Barnes, *Early Christian Hagiography and Roman History* (Tübingen: Mohr Siebeck, 2010), 97–99, 111–14, 148–55. Barnes makes a solid case for the Diocletianic edict of 303 being rescinded in the West relatively quickly in Gaul, Britain, Spain, and Italy (after about one to two years). Those provinces received toleration and restitution under Constantine. However, Barnes still shows by the evidence that in Africa, Egypt, Asia Minor, Syria, and the Balkans—a sizable territory—conditions of persecution persisted until 311 and in some places till 313. He also estimates that in the decade of persecution in the East, "several, perhaps many thousands" of Christians were killed, "more than 660 for the city of Alexandria alone" up to the year 311, when the persecutions there had not yet ceased. Despite these figures, Barnes still refers to that period as "the so-called 'Great Persecution'" (111).

2. The two versions are found in Eusebius, *Church History* 10.5.2–14; and Lactantius, *On the Deaths of the Persecutors* 48.2–12, both cited in James Stevenson, ed., *A New Eusebius: Documents Illustrating the History of the Church to AD 337*, revised by W. H. C. Frend (London: SPCK, 1987), 284–86. The portrayal of the "edict" as a new official policy initiated by Constantine, guaranteeing the church's freedom and legal status, has been contested in recent scholarship. For example, Timothy Barnes asserts, "Incalculable damage has been done to modern understanding of both Constantine himself and the whole 'age of Constantine' by the widespread use of the bogus, improper and dangerously misleading term 'Edict of Milan,' which encapsulates an entirely false historical perspective" (*Early Christian Hagiography and Roman History*, 98).

3. Lactantius, *Deaths of the Persecutors* 34; Eusebius, *Church History* 8.17.

4. G. S. R. Thomas, "Maximin Daia's Policy and the Edicts of Toleration," *L'Antiquité Classique* 37, no. 1 (1968): 179. Among these were several illustrious men: Peter, bishop of Alexandria; Silvanus, bishop of Emesa; and Lucian, a presbyter at Antioch.

5. Ibid., 185.

in a "war to the death," provoked by Maximinus.[6] Once Maximinus "the tyrant" had met his death painfully and ignominiously, Eusebius explains that the way was open for the other two allies to establish a permanent policy. The policy set forth by Constantine and Licinius sought to "grant both to the Christians and to all others full authority to follow whatever worship each man has desired," so that "no man whatever should be refused complete toleration."[7] Further, they directed that "every one of those who have a common wish to follow the religion of the Christians may from this moment freely and unconditionally proceed to observe the same without any annoyance or disquiet," and that "every man may have complete toleration in the practice of whatever worship he has chosen."[8]

This chapter explores several questions related to the church's identity in light of its new status in the empire—that is, as not only tolerated but also favored—and will progressively treat the major historiographical ideas traced thus far through the martyrologies. First, we will want to know how the identity shaped by the era of persecution and martyrdom continued to operate in the post-persecution church. That is, how did the martyr ideal continue to manifest itself? Second, we will investigate the documents themselves and the biographical and thematic material contained therein. Why were they such wildly popular "best sellers" in their day? Who were the Christians described in them, and what themes characterized such historical accounts? Next we will examine three biographical accounts from the fourth and fifth centuries, noticing the specific hagiographical features used to illuminate the portrait of a holy person. The lives to be examined are those of Antony (ca. 251–356), an Egyptian who is traditionally hailed as the father of desert monasticism; Macrina (d. 380), a celibate virgin from Cappadocia, and sister of two of the great Cappadocian bishop-theologians, Basil of Caesarea and Gregory of Nyssa; and Melania the Younger (ca. 383–439), a wealthy Roman aristocrat who negotiated her life situation and its expectations to pursue a fervent discipleship as she understood it. These three great saints had several commonalities: all came from wealthy families but renounced (or were prepared to renounce) their fortunes, and all three were laypersons whose biographies were written by bishops who knew them personally. Finally, we will want to note similarities and dissimilarities between these ancient believers and our own practice of discipleship and seek to draw out possibilities for fruitful retrieval of their examples.

6. Eusebius, *Church History* 9.10 (trans. G. A. Williamson, rev. and ed. Andrew Louth [New York: Penguin, 1989], 297).

7. Lactantius, *On the Deaths of the Persecutors* 48.2–3, in Stevenson, *New Eusebius*, 284–85.

8. Lactantius, *On the Deaths of the Persecutors* 48.4–6, in Stevenson, *New Eusebius*, 285.

Historiographical features in the *vitae* show continuity with those in the martyrologies and include (1) *narrative*, involving the subject's biography as told through a biblical framework, and showing the influence of philosophical *Lives* in various literary motifs (known as *topoi*), as well as the genre of the ancient novel; (2) *remembrance*, which is present in the *Lives* just as in the martyrological literature and directly connected with the purpose of remembering, imitation (*mimēsis*); (3) *mimēsis*, involving the author's didactic purpose to provide an example of the pursuit of virtue via asceticism, as the holy person strives to imitate martyr ideals as well as the life of Jesus; and (4) *causation*, which involves both the natural and the supernatural. Under this last feature, the devil appears again (as in the martyr accounts), knowing that he will ultimately fail. Through various methods, he fiercely opposes a saint's wish to pursue holiness and shun worldliness, and together with his demons, he constantly seeks to impede a saint's spiritual progress. Today we label this aspect of the literature "spiritual warfare." At times the description of causation is presented in biblical terms, while at other times it appears more in Hellenistic terms. Along with the devil and his "schemes" (Eph. 6:11), God's grace is also apparent, working in and through the saint, as even Paul expressed throughout his ministry: although the grace of God works in him, nevertheless he is clothed in the armor of God, and he himself puts forth effort to accomplish the work of God in the proclamation of Christ to every person (Col. 1:28–29). Clearly, the saint's free will and personal effort/desire to persevere are also involved as causes, as the three texts examined below amply illustrate.

The Rise of Holy Biographies

Hagiographical biographies arose among Christians as a wildly popular literary genre toward the end of persecution, and therefore the end of the era of "the blessed martyrs." In retrospect believers regarded this era as a kind of golden age when the church was strong and uncompromising, flourishing and experiencing rapid expansion. Whether this perspective was accurate or not seemed irrelevant. An excellent example of such a sentiment may be found in a letter to a certain Ascholius written by the fourth-century bishop Basil of Caesarea. As he thought about the "good old times" of persecution and martyrdom, Basil remembered that period, "the blessedness of old," as a time when the church was united "by the peace which the Lord bequeathed us." Christians were strong and faithful, living together harmoniously. The "blood of the martyrs" was "watering the churches" and inspiring future generations of "athletes," or as he called them, "champions of true religion, each generation stripping for the struggle with the zeal of those that had gone before." In his own day, the church was torn by schism, by the heresy of Arianism, and by other theological aberrations regarding the doctrine of the Trinity. He strongly desired that God should reconcile himself to his churches and "restore them to their ancient peace."[9]

How, then, were people to prove the dedication of their discipleship and their devotion to their Master when no one was hunting them down and hauling them into court? To be sure, even after the so-called Edict of Toleration, there were still some groups (such as the Donatist Christians in North Africa) who experienced religious persecution under Constantine and his successors. These victims continued to produce accounts of their own martyrs.[10] In large measure, though, the era of throwing Christians into arenas at the mercy of wild animals or armed gladiators was past.

In literary terms, the continuity between the struggles of the persecuted church's martyrs and the struggles of the liberated church's faithful was expressed by adopting the *ascetic* lifestyle. It is important to recognize that asceticism did not *originate* at this time, for various strains of philosophical adherents had advocated rigorous living for centuries before Christianity, and therefore Christian asceticism already existed among, for example, students of Origen and Clement of Alexandria. But the yoke of an ascetic life seemed to be taken on more broadly than before in the church, by persons in all walks of life. Writers transferred to hagiographical accounts the same vocabulary that had described the martyrs' ordeals; terms such as *athlētēs*, *agōn*, *martyria* (and their cognates), along with causal indicators of demonic opposition, were now used to describe the spiritual struggles of the faithful.[11] Biblical, devotional, and cultural elements were synthesized and poured into the mold of classical literary conventions of philosophical or social biographies, resulting in the sacred biographies that have come down to us. The chief purposes of these *Lives* were to preserve the memory and spread the fame of the historical subject treated, to

9. Basil of Caesarea, *Letter 164* (*NPNF*[2] 8:215–16). In reality, the church had encountered heresy from the time of Paul's and John's Epistles. Marcionites, Montanists, Manichaeans, and other heterodox believers also sometimes appeared in martyr accounts, so the early times of complete theological harmony in the church were a rhetorical (not to mention wishful) construct on Basil's part. An additional blow to his reminiscence comes from the martyr accounts themselves, from which strongly emerges the theme of the martyrs' and confessors' urgent exhortation to reconciliation within congregations and among clergy (see, e.g., *Passion of Perpetua and Felicitas* 13).

10. See Barnes, *Early Christian Hagiography*, 151–53.

11. See John E. Bamberger, trans., *Evagrius Ponticus: Praktikos and Chapters on Prayer* (Kalamazoo, MI: Cistercian, 1981), 5–6.

instruct the reader(s) in holy living (the daily struggle of self-denying discipleship), and to provide a useful example to imitate in one's striving for spiritual progress.

Martyrdom and Asceticism

In addition to subtler literary overtones adapted from the martyrological narratives, the hagiographical authors sometimes drew very forthright comparisons between their subject and the martyrs. Such acute comparison should evoke little surprise because the church had wrestled with the definition of true martyrdom even during the centuries of persecution. This discussion can be clearly observed in the writing of Clement of Alexandria on the subject. "If the confession to God is martyrdom [*martyria*]," he begins, "each soul which has lived purely in the knowledge of God, which has obeyed the commandments, is a witness [*martys*] both by life and word, in whatever way it [the soul] may be released from the body."[12] Here Clement means that whether dying by martyrdom or natural causes, the believer is a witness to Christ in both word and deed. He further compares the martyrs' shed blood to the faith of the believer who lives out life to its natural end. This latter kind of Christian soul sheds "*faith* as blood along its whole life till its departure."[13]

Clement distinguishes two kinds of martyrdom: a "simple martyrdom" in which a person witnesses by his death, and what he calls a "gnostic martyrdom" (meaning a true Christian, not a heretical Gnostic) in which a person witnesses by his life. This latter person "has conducted himself according to the rule of the Gospel, in love to the Lord . . . so as to leave . . . worldly kindred, and wealth, and every possession, in order to lead a life free from passion."[14] Such a believer truly knows the Lord, understands the gospel, and fulfills it.[15] G. W. Bowersock explains that Clement's point here is important in the context of persecution and death—or exemption from death—in the Christian community, "because he wants to establish that martyrdom in the true sense does not necessarily involve death at all. It is rather an expression of one's commitment to the Christian God."[16] This second-century discussion concerning the meaning of true martyrdom allows the later church to

---

12. Clement of Alexandria, *Miscellanies* 4.4 (*ANF* 2:412).
13. Clement of Alexandria, *Miscellanies* 4.4 (*ANF* 2:412, emphasis added).
14. Clement of Alexandria, *Miscellanies* 4.4 (*ANF* 2:412).
15. Clement of Alexandria, *Miscellanies* 4.4 (*ANF* 2:412).
16. G. W. Bowersock, *Martyrdom and Rome* (Cambridge: Cambridge University Press, 2002), 67.

extend the appellation of "martyr" to those in its ranks who exhibit a disciplined and faithful witness even after Christianity is no longer outlawed. As a case in point, in the *Life of Antony*, the comparison between Antony and the martyrs occurs about two-thirds of the way through the narrative, where Antony's rigorous asceticism is considered on a par with the suffering endured by the martyrs who died in Maximinus's persecution (e.g., Peter, the bishop of Alexandria).[17] Athanasius describes Antony as having achieved "a daily martyrdom of faith and conscience."[18] This aspect will be further elaborated below in the section on Antony's life.

Some examination of asceticism seems in order. The Greek term *askēsis* indicates physical training, as in a gymnasium or other training facility (*askētērion*), while the athlete is referred to as an *askētēs*, one who trains, exercises, and practices.[19] "Asceticism" simply refers to spiritual exercise, fulfilling Jesus's requirements for his disciples to deny themselves, take up their cross daily, and follow him (Luke 9:23–24). This type of discipleship can be accomplished via the Christian spiritual disciplines, which involve a daily spiritual regimen of prayer, service to one another in humility, regular fasting, and study of and meditation upon the Scriptures. By the faithful and consistent practice (exercise) of the disciplines, the Christian strengthens the soul to withstand the onslaughts of various *passions*, or temptations to sin. Early Christians contextualized this idea by integrating it with Greco-Roman virtue theory. Four major passions appear in classical literature: grief, delight, lust, and fear, with their various derivations. The late fourth-century spiritual master Evagrius of Pontus insightfully nuanced this set and added a few more, positing "eight evil thoughts," which in later Christian tradition earned the label "seven deadly sins."[20] As the martyrs had fulfilled their discipleship by enduring physical suffering, later Christians denied themselves and died to themselves daily. Asceticism's chief concern, therefore, was spiritual formation, and it was intended for every Christian who wished to persevere in the virtuous life.

17. Athanasius, *Life of Antony* 46, in *Early Christian Lives*, trans. Carolinne White (New York: Penguin, 1998), 37.

18. Athanasius, *Life of Antony* 47 (White, 38). Additional witness comes from Jerome's *Life of Paula the Elder*, in which he writes to her daughter, Eustochium: "Your mother has now after a long martyrdom won her crown. It is not only the shedding of blood that is accounted a confession; the spotless service of a devout mind is itself a daily martyrdom. Both alike are crowned" (*Handmaids of the Lord: Holy Women in Late Antiquity and the Early Middle Ages*, ed. and trans. Joan M. Petersen [Kalamazoo, MI: Cistercian, 1996], 159).

19. See articles on *askeō*, *askēsis*, *askētērion*, and *askētēs*, in *A Patristic Greek Lexicon*, ed. G. W. H. Lampe (Oxford: Oxford University Press, 1961), 243–45.

20. Evagrius Ponticus, *Praktikos* 6–14 (Bamberger, 16–20).

Eventually asceticism came to be inextricably associated with the monastic movement, but it never lost its association with martyrdom. It was sometimes called the "bloodless martyrdom," as Clement of Alexandria had explained it. The monastery became known as an *askētērion*, while its residents were called *askētikoi*. The practice of asceticism came to mean a rigorous spiritual training resulting in a fruitful devotional life, such as that undertaken by desert solitaries or monastic dwellers; but the ascetic life was not only for those who had the luxury of withdrawing to the desert and could make it a permanent or full-time vocation. The ascetic life was one of discipleship, and discipleship is for every Christian alike, not just "professionals." A chief aim of hagiographies was to inspire typical Christians by offering an example of holy living that they could emulate themselves, whether male or female, young or old, cleric or congregant, urbanite or rustic, married or celibate.

Asceticism constitutes more than merely "monkish virtues."[21] The writer of Hebrews beautifully draws out the relationship between discipline and sanctification, declaring that discipline bears fruit in righteousness and holiness (Heb. 12:4–11). Paul advised Timothy to "train" (*gymnaze*) himself for piety (1 Tim. 4:7) (using a term from which our word "gymnasium" derives), and believers from the first century to the twenty-first have been obediently and dedicatedly doing so. At times, though, contemporary promoters of asceticism find that the concept needs explaining (and defending) to current evangelicals, who remain skittish about the term and its medieval baggage. Richard Foster seems to equivocate on the issue because he wants to distinguish between asceticism and the Quaker discipline of simplicity. He admits that he is conflicted on the issue of asceticism but cites Dietrich Bonhoeffer's affirmation that "if there is no element of asceticism in our lives, if we give free rein to the desires of the flesh, . . . we shall find it hard to train for the service of Christ."[22] The late Dallas Willard is less ambivalent. While he roundly decries misguided spiritual practices (those subscribing to a theology of meritorious works), and also physical abuse and "body hatred" under the guise of spiritual practice, he also asserts, "Somehow, the fact that 'mortification'—self-denial, the disciplining of

---

21. David Hume used this phrase to describe ascetic practices and intimates that only "a gloomy, hare-brained enthusiast" practices spiritual disciplines. See Dallas Willard, *The Spirit of the Disciplines: Understanding How God Changes Lives* (San Francisco: HarperSanFrancisco, 1988), 132.

22. Richard Foster, *Celebration of Discipline: The Path to Spiritual Growth* (San Francisco: HarperSanFrancisco, 1998), 133–34. A more strongly worded distinction between asceticism (which he alleges makes an unbiblical distinction between "an evil material world and a good spiritual world") and simplicity appears on 84–85.

one's natural impulses—happens to be a central teaching of the New Testament is conveniently ignored" by many Protestants.[23] He affirms that according to his definition of asceticism, once it is divested of historical and theological misunderstanding, the lives of Jesus as well as his disciples fit the model of "sensible asceticism."[24] Gerald Sittser also explains and defines asceticism, calling it a means rather than an end in itself. Asceticism is self-denial for the purpose of obeying God, weaning oneself from worldliness, building up strength to resist temptation, and achieving inner spiritual transformation. For ancient Christians, the ultimate goal of asceticism was humility and love, issuing forth in sacrificial service.[25]

Moreover, when one approaches the ancient texts open-mindedly, it becomes plain that even those who may have desired to live exclusively in solitude (like Antony, for whom solitude is described as his dearest friend) actually spent a good deal of time with devoted followers and caregivers, investing time and wisdom into communities of disciples.[26] It also emerges that withdrawal from the world can be a state of mind rather than an actual place, so that those who live in this world and use its trappings may act according to otherworldly priorities. This perspective appears also in the writings of Paul, as he advised the Corinthian church about issues in marital relationships: "Let . . . those who deal with the world [live] as though they had no dealings with it. For the present form of this world is passing away" (1 Cor. 7:31).

Popularity of Hagiographies

In addition to the end of persecution, two major factors catalyzed the publication of lives and practices of ascetics for public consumption: a flourishing literary culture that had always enjoyed biographies, and the wildly successful exportation of Egyptian desert monasticism to the West by Athanasius and others. Of course, one must never underestimate the power of human curiosity to know more about these holy men and women who shunned publicity and desired to live a Godward life in seclusion, or who renounced fabulous wealth and potentially high worldly status and culinary delicacies in exchange for obscurity, poverty, coarse and raggedy dress, and equally coarse and meager cuisine, just

23. Willard, *Spirit of the Disciplines*, 133.
24. Ibid., 138.
25. Gerald Sittser, *Water from a Deep Well* (Downers Grove, IL: InterVarsity, 2007), 73–95, esp. 85, 89, 91.
26. Philip Rousseau, "Christian Asceticism and the Early Monks," in *Early Christianity: Origins and Evolution to A.D. 600*, ed. Ian Hazlett (Nashville: Abingdon, 1991), 112.

barely enough to sustain life. There is something compelling about such a move, perhaps because it seems counterintuitive.

Biographies in general were not new in this era, having had classical precursors in philosophical biographies such as *Lives of the Philosophers and Sophists* written by Eunapius (ca. AD 347–420) and a similar work by Philostratus (ca. AD 170–205), who also authored the *Life of Apollonius of Tyana*. Some features of the romantic novella are also evident in hagiographical literature, even the martyrdom retellings—for example, the *Passion of Perpetua and Felicitas* or the *Martyrdom of Montanus and Lucius*. A novella is an oral or written narrative that is "short and entertaining, set in the real world instead of the make-believe world of the fairy tale, and focused on a single unexpected turn of events."[27] Some of the themes expressed in these works include "emotional intensity and introspection, alienation and separation from old civic structures, individualism," and a familial setting, many of which appeared in the martyr narratives.[28] Some political and social historians also composed lives of famous statesmen, in both Greek and Latin, as for example *Parallel Lives* by Plutarch (ca. AD 45–120) and *Lives of the Twelve Caesars* by Suetonius (ca. AD 60–140).[29]

The purposes of this literature varied, but in general authors were rather more interested in instructing in moral virtue and illustrating certain moral themes than in setting forth an ample historical account. By drawing attention to the manifestation of vices and virtues (and their respective consequences) in the arenas of politics, warfare, society, and so on, they urged readers to root out vices and imitate virtues. As an example, Plutarch's biographies of prominent Greeks and Romans follow this tack. In the *Life of Coriolanus* (originally named Marcius), the hero receives praise for his courage and military service to his country.[30] Having grown up fatherless, he serves as a wonderful example that parental disadvantage should be no hindrance to virtue. Also in this vein, Plutarch praises Marcius's mother, Volumnia, a noble and respectable matron held in the highest esteem by her son. Marcius also showed himself to be a dispassionate and impartial judge, at times making decisions even to his own detriment. Despite these many virtues, however, he allowed himself to be overcome by anger, a cardinal

27. Lawrence Mitchell Wills, *The Jewish Novel in the Ancient World* (Ithaca, NY: Cornell University Press, 1995), 7. See also Sophie Trenkner, *The Greek Novella in the Classical Period* (Cambridge: Cambridge University Press, 1958).

28. Wills, *Jewish Novel*, 19.

29. Plutarch, *Makers of Rome* [*Moralia*], trans. Ian Scott-Kilvert (London: Penguin, 1965); Suetonius, *Lives of the Twelve Caesars*, trans. Robert Graves and Michael Grant (London: Penguin, 1979).

30. Plutarch, *Life of Coriolanus* 4 (Scott-Kilvert, 18).

vice. The Romans had tried him, found him guilty of attempting to set himself up as a tyrant, and sentenced him to perpetual banishment. Although his feelings of outrage and betrayal might be considered justifiable, his anger led him to a basically treasonous situation in which he was prepared to lead enemy tribes against the Romans.[31] Plutarch thus demonstrates that even a person possessed of so many admirable virtues (which should be emulated) can nevertheless succumb to the vices of pride and anger such that it can result in his downfall.

A second major influence on the popularity of Christian biographies was the burgeoning monastic movement, which had originated in the harsh Egyptian desert and was well under way before Constantine's final legalization of Christianity and unification of church and state. There already existed solitaries who, to practice the ascetic life, had withdrawn to the edge of town, where it met the desert.[32] The monastic movement was both embodied in and catalyzed by the best-selling ascetic biography of Antony, ostensibly composed by his protégé, the great bishop Athanasius of Alexandria (297–373).[33] Athanasius had probably exported the ideals and practices of Egyptian monasticism to the West during some of his time in exile there. In his preface he indicates that monks in distant Western provinces of the empire, possibly in cities like Treves in Gaul (modern Trier, Germany) and Milan, Italy, requested that he write a life of Antony, thus indicating the widespread interest in and popularity of the movement.[34]

Identity Building: Continuity and Transformation

Before moving on to a closer examination of three saintly biographies, we should identify several themes from the martyrologies that find continuity in the hagiographical material. At least four of the major identity-building themes carry over, though in a slightly transformed mode. First, the reality of *physical death* through martyrdom is transformed into the idea of *dying to self* in a spiritual kind of martyrdom. Battling the devil via beasts in the arena gave way to ideas of fighting

31. Plutarch, *Life of Coriolanus* 23–31 (Scott-Kilvert, 36–44).

32. Antony, for example, chose as his mentor one of these men living on the outskirts of his own town.

33. There is some debate over authorship of the *Life of Antony* (*Vita Antonii*), and alternative authors have been suggested, such as Serapion (of Thmuis?), who had intimate and extensive personal and experiential knowledge of Antony, having lived with him in the desert (which Athanasius had not), and to whom Antony left two of his relics or personal effects. See Barnes, *Early Christian Hagiography*, 168–69.

34. Athanasius, *Life of Antony*, preface, 2, in *Athanase d'Alexandrie: Vie d'Antoine* [*Life of Antony*], trans. G. J. M. Bartelink, SC 400 (Paris: Cerf, 1994), 127.

the devil's onslaughts via temptations to sin in the arousal of the passions. Since the desert was often seen as the domain of demons and wild beasts (as in Jesus's temptation episode [Mark 1:13]), occupying that territory and training in holiness were in some sense storming the devil's fortress. This kind of spiritual warfare parallels the imagery found in the martyrologies, in which the body of the martyr functions as the battleground between God and demonic forces. Similarly, in later accounts the body of the holy man or woman (virgin) functions as the locus of spiritual warfare between Jesus and Satan. The strength of the Christian's own will plays a vital role: some fall away from the faith in the face of impending martyrdom (the threat of physical death), and later believers are discouraged by temptations to fall away from practicing a life of virtue. Conversely, other believers persevere through torture and through temptations to emerge victorious in the struggle (*agōn*, a term used in both kinds of narratives).

A second theme, *imitatio Christi*, has to do mainly with picturing the death of Christ in one's own death. Imitating Christ in his *passion* (suffering and death) gradually gave way to imitating Christ in his *life* of victory over sin and demonic temptations. This notion is linked to a third theme, that of *citizenship in another world*. The martyrs had felt themselves alienated from their idolatrous culture and a political regime that branded them traitors and mandated their deaths. For later Christians, this feeling of alienation became more acute and generalized in its spiritual orientation: devout believers became estranged from a culture of worldliness. Ascetics withdrew from the cities representing the world and populated the desert (after having dislodged the demons), seeking citizenship in the kingdom of God through self-denial. Indeed, Athanasius wrote that the Egyptian monastic dwellers had made the desert into a "heavenly city!"[35]

A fourth and final theme, that of *identifying with a new family* whose members share a common spiritual orientation, also overlaps with the previous three. For ascetics living in monasteries, their community was their new family. For example, many treated Antony as a son and brother, and later as a father; Macrina treated her community of virgins as sisters, while they looked to her as a mother, teacher, and spiritual nurse; and Melania also humbled herself beneath the women in her religious communities, throwing off class distinctions (although she herself was the founder of the institution) and refusing to place herself at the head of the community as abbess. In this new family (as

---

35. Athanasius, *Life of Antony* 14.7 (cf. Bartelink, 175; White, 18–19). See also Athanasius, *St. Antony of the Desert by St. Athanasius*, trans. J. B. McLaughlin (Rockford, IL: TAN Books, 1995), 19.

among the martyrs), many walks of life were represented, but all had to serve equally in love and humility. These aristocratic and wealthy women abased themselves and served their slaves and other lower-class members of the household as equals.[36] The development of these themes illustrates how collective identity building was still a priority for the authors, who found themselves in a somewhat paradoxical situation. While they were well aware of the church's new status as legitimate and favored, they still wanted to leverage the identity forged in the era of the martyrs. Writers in the earlier centuries had concerned themselves with *dying* for Christ—which actually resulted in true life—while later writers concerned themselves with *living* for Christ but, as Antony taught his disciples, "as dying daily."

Narrative Topoi

Hagiography contains multiple narrative features and themes known as *topoi*. These emerge from a stock of such items, and they contribute to the impression of a stylized rather than realistic biography. Occasionally it is difficult to fully retrieve the flesh-and-blood Christian described by these *topoi*, so caution should be exercised in drawing firm conclusions about the subject's historical realities. However, these are works of *hagiography*, after all, not strictly historical biographies, in the sense that both the author and the audience are more interested in the subject as *saint* rather than sinner. In pagan philosophical biographies, *topoi* might include wisdom and perspicacity, calmness of soul (probably in the sense of a Stoic fatalism or sense of resignation) regarding oneself and one's future, a lack of care for the body, and a concomitant prioritization of the health of the soul. In Christian works, some of these same features intrude and are adapted to conform to the overriding idea of sanctity and its resulting characteristics. Thematic continuities with the martyr accounts also appear: the narratives share some *topoi* in common.

Holiness served as a foundational characteristic of these spiritual heroes and manifested itself in various ways. The saint was said to lead an "angelic life," and descriptions of their luminous beauty, youth, moral purity or chastity, and robust physical appearance abounded. The association of holiness and light appears in depictions of both martyrs and saints as having faces or bodies that appeared radiant, glowing, or outright dazzling, reminding readers of biblical examples like Jesus and the prophets at the transfiguration (Luke 9:28–36; Moses

---

36. Gregory of Nyssa, *Life of Macrina*, in Petersen, *Handmaids of the Lord*, 59–60; *Life of Melania*, in Petersen, *Handmaids of the Lord*, 336.

experienced the same in Exod. 34:29–35) and Stephen the protomartyr at his death (Acts 6:8–7:60). These depictions indicated the special spiritual power that saints possessed as a result of holiness: Perpetua was like a bride of Christ, Pionius realized the beauty of his own body and his face glowed, Polycarp was like an angel, and Irene and her companions lived on earth, but their souls were already acceptable in the company of angels because of their dedication to protecting the Sacred Scriptures.[37]

Holy people also possessed *wisdom*, which resulted in a lifestyle resembling the Christian version of a sage. This quality was sometimes expressed by the phrase "philosophy of Christ," or the saint was said to live out the "true philosophy" and inspired others to do so as well. The attribute of wisdom was not necessarily of an intellectual nature, based on a fine secular education (although some ascetics were the beneficiaries of such an education). Instead, the "true philosophy" mentioned by Justin Martyr, Clement of Alexandria, and Origen consisted of saturation with the Scriptures, memorizing and reciting them throughout the day, and chanting them as songs. The Christian "philosopher" would teach disciples and model for them Christlike virtues of purity, humility, service, and love. The wise holy person also sometimes possessed discernment and keen intellectual ability as supernatural gifts, in spite of illiteracy or lack of formal education.

Another attribute of holy persons was their *power against demonic forces*, especially evident in narratives of the desert ascetics. In addition to fervent prayer, making the *sign of the cross* appeared particularly effective, as did appeal to the *name of Jesus*. The sign of the cross carried special meaning, for it was a reminder of two things: (1) the devil's defeat and (2) baptism, in which the believer renounced the devil in a ceremony of exorcism and was signed on the forehead with special oil. Claiming these two weapons, many holy men and women were credited with working miracles and physical healings. Although the miraculous element in medieval hagiographies gradually developed into unbelievably fantastic tales, at this early stage the miraculous works are more modest (and perhaps even believable!). Antony was credited with many healings and miraculous works, but the narrative of his life emphasizes that he always rejected people's praise and admiration, insisting that God was the real miracle worker; he was

---

37. *Passion of Perpetua and Felicitas* 18, in *The Acts of the Christian Martyrs*, vol. 2, ed. and trans. Herbert Musurillo (Oxford: Clarendon, 1972), 127; *Martyrdom of Pionius* 21, 22 (Musurillo, 163, 165); *Martyrdom of Polycarp* 3 (Musurillo, 5); *The Martyrdom of Saints Agapē, Irēnē, and Chionē at Saloniki* 1 (Musurillo, 281).

but a vessel who was willing to pray for them.[38] His attitude indicates a related *topos*, that of *humility*. He encouraged those who brought their petitions to pray as well, not to rely on Antony himself, but to leave the results to the Lord.[39]

The accounts make readily apparent the ideological currents of their time and describe the saint as *devout* and *doctrinally orthodox*. The martyrdom accounts had mentioned tensions between the Christian and Jewish communities, as well as hinting at conflicts with Marcionites and Montanists. Later hagiographies mention Arians, Meletians, Manichaeans, and Nestorians and portray the saint as refuting their teachings or just repudiating those communities, refusing to associate with them. They thus offer an example of the wise orthodox response to heresy. The *devotion* of the holy man or woman is expressed through regular (practically unceasing) worship, scriptural study and meditation, service toward the destitute, pilgrimage, and donations to the church for the foundation of monasteries and the building of holy places and commemorative shrines.

A final feature is *asceticism*, which has already received some attention above. Asceticism was practiced in a variety of ways, which included (but was not limited to) extensive times of prayer and various bodily deprivations from food (fasting), sleep (vigils), sex (chastity), human company (solitude), and bodily comforts such as bathing or sleeping on a bed. The goal of ascetic practices, paired with devotional practices of engagement like worship and service, was to strengthen the soul so it could withstand the assaults of the passions, thereby achieving what Athanasius called "calmness of soul" (*ataraxia*) and the Cappadocians called "passionlessness" (*apatheia*). This achievement meant that a person could make decisions and react to spiritual challenges based on reason's control of the passions or bodily desires. These passions might include physical appetites like lust, but could also include psychological or emotional tendencies like grief (manifest in mourning, sadness, or depression), anger, or envy. One who is perfectly guided by reason has a balanced and tranquil soul, so that any news is received calmly; both good and bad are borne with equanimity. The one controlled by reason is also characterized by the cardinal virtues (prudence, justice/righteousness, temperance/self-control, and fortitude/strength), which liberate the believer from entanglement with the passions, allowing

---

38. Athanasius is consistent throughout in his insistence that the Lord, not Antony, was the primary agent in miraculous healings: Antony heals only through God's power, and in humility shuns the attention of crowds. Bartelink comments that this virtue posed a contrast with other wonder-workers who attracted crowds and claimed to work miracles by their own strength. See Athanasius, *Life of Antony* 83–84 (Bartelink, 350–53, esp. 353n1).

39. Athanasius, *Life of Antony* 48, 49, 56 (Bartelink, 265–69, 286–88; White, 38–39, 44).

growth toward the ideal of *apatheia*.[40] The term *apatheia* draws attention to the *imago Dei* in the Christian, since while living a life in which passions are controlled and overridden (as far as humanly possible in a sinful body), the believer more clearly reflects the perfection of the divine nature, which is impassible. Striving for *apatheia*, therefore, allowed one to share in union with the divine, to some extent, even in this life.[41] The soul's progress in its pursuit of virtue (*aretē*) and eschewing of passions (*pathos, pathēma*) led it to the eventual attainment of *apatheia*, resulting in a more perfect reflection of God.[42]

Three Lives

Saint Antony, Desert Father

NARRATIVE

Antony was born around AD 251 into a relatively well-off Coptic Christian family. He apparently had a rudimentary education but did not pursue advanced studies.[43] Interestingly, his biographer redeems this deficit by using it to make the point that this holy man was a precocious child and was given a supernatural gift of discernment (the *topos* of wisdom), evincing startling rhetorical skills that later proved capable of confounding learned Greeks.[44] At the age of twenty, he and his sibling—a sister—were orphaned. Antony felt the call of God initially through Jesus's words to the rich young ruler (Matt. 19:21–22) and later through his exhortation to the crowds following him to "not be anxious about tomorrow" (Matt. 6:34). He accordingly placed his sister with a community of older women, sought out an older ascetic mentor to whom he could apprentice himself, and withdrew to the solitary life. First he practiced asceticism near home, at the edge of his village, with other solitaries. Later, around the age of thirty-five,

40. Jaroslav Pelikan, *Christianity and Classical Culture: The Metamorphosis of Natural Theology in the Christian Encounter with Hellenism* (New Haven: Yale University Press, 1993), 145.
   41. Ibid., 145–46.
   42. This idea is characteristic of the Cappadocian theological concept of *theōsis*, imperfectly translated into English as "deification" or "divinization." It implies progress in sanctification and thereby an increasing participation in the divine life. The Cappadocians nonetheless acknowledge that full union with the divine is impossible until the final transformation and glorification of the body in the resurrection.
   43. Athanasius, *Life of Antony* 1. So Athanasius leads the reader to believe, but see Susan Ashbrook Harvey, "Martyr Passions and Hagiography," in *The Oxford Handbook of Early Christian Studies*, ed. Susan Ashbrook Harvey and David Hunter (Oxford: Oxford University Press, 2008), 610.
   44. Athanasius, *Life of Antony* 72–80 (White, 53–59).

he moved farther into the desert and lived in a tomb, eating sparsely.[45] As his fame spread on account of his friends and curious visitors, he moved even farther into the desert, shunning attention as an intrusion on his solitude. He set up his dwelling in a deserted fortress at the foot of a mountain, where he remained for twenty years.[46] In that place he experienced a fruitful ministry of practicing the spiritual life, traveling occasionally to teach groups of monks, and strengthening communities that had begun to establish themselves and build monastic dwellings in the desert.[47] A significant portion of Athanasius's work contains Antony's various teachings to his disciples on asceticism and the spiritual life.[48] The persecution of Maximinus Daia (ca. 311/312) brought him to Alexandria to strengthen and support the confessors/martyrs; Antony would have been approximately sixty years old then. His fame spread like wildfire, and people increasingly sought him out, specifically for his prayers, power to heal, and counsels on the spiritual life. At that point the Lord spoke to him, as to Elijah, and led him even farther into the desert to a spot at the foot of a mountain, a remote place that became known as the Inner Mountain. There Antony made his home for the rest of his life (approximately forty-five more years), leaving it occasionally to visit and encourage the monks in the "Outer Hills," and once to counter Arian allegations that Antony endorsed their doctrines. After a lifetime of practicing *askēsis*, receiving and encouraging and ministering in various ways to visitors, and teaching disciples by sharing his wisdom and visions, he felt his time was at an end, having reached 105 years of age. His thoughts turned to the manner of his death and the import of a particular Egyptian burial custom, which he rejected. The author's emphasis on issues surrounding this burial custom indicates its importance for that context and for his specific hagiographical concerns.[49] In great humility, Antony insisted that he be buried in the ground and not be embalmed and kept in a house to have his body venerated, as was the Egyptian custom for holy men and "especially . . . the holy martyrs."[50] He died circa 356.

TOPOI

After detailing Antony's family life and conversion, the narrator describes his early steps into spirituality and his sojourn into the desert and gradual conquest of the devil in his life through asceticism. Antony

45. Athanasius, *Life of Antony* 3, 11.
46. Athanasius, *Life of Antony* 14 (McLaughlin, 18; White, 18).
47. Athanasius, *Life of Antony* 14 (McLaughlin, 19, cf. 23; White, 19).
48. Athanasius, *Life of Antony* 15–45 (Bartelink, 177–259; McLaughlin, 23–51; White, 19–54).
49. Athanasius, *Life of Antony* 90 (McLaughlin, 101).
50. Athanasius, *Life of Antony* 90 (McLaughlin, 102–4).

is on a journey to virtue via the desert (*erēmon*). The narrative's chief concern is his progress in sanctification and how it was accomplished, and numerous *topoi* bolster this idea throughout. Antony's holiness manifests itself in his physical appearance: his rigorous asceticism leaves his body healthy rather than wasted, and his countenance glowing and radiant, demonstrating the purity of his soul.[51] After twenty years of living and eating sparsely and dwelling in a tomb in the desert, Antony emerged from solitude "as from a holy of holies, filled with heavenly secrets, and possessed by the Spirit of God. . . . His body kept its former state, being neither grown heavy from want of exercise, nor shrunken from fastings and strivings against demons."[52] The text more literally has overtones of a mystical initiate who carries about himself "an aura of holiness" and inspires others to imitate him.[53] Antony's asceticism consisted of frequent fasting, constant prayer, scriptural meditation, vigils (periods of abstaining from sleep), singing the psalms, and all kinds of spiritual exercises that trained him to keep his mind and body under control so as to remain strong before the attacks of the devil.

Paralleling his physical health, the narrative emphasizes his spiritual health: "the light of his soul, too, was absolutely pure," and the glow of holiness radiated from his soul through his countenance until the day of his death.[54] The prioritization of the soul over the body appears regularly as an ideal in philosophical literature. Lack of care for the body—bathing only when absolutely necessary—was not only an ascetic virtue, but in hagiographies that virtue also took on pious rather than Platonic or Cynic overtones (although the latter are not completely absent): the saints wished to keep their bodies covered and not exposed (as bathing would require) to practice the virtue of modesty.

The health of the soul achieved by ascetic practice also put the holy man in a position to dispense wisdom to others. Antony's wisdom and spiritual discernment was such that he mentored groups of disciples and also confounded the pagan philosophers who challenged him with their worldly wisdom.[55] Holy wisdom leads to right belief, and Athanasius highlights Antony's doctrinal orthodoxy, as the latter strongly and consistently warned against association and fellowship with the schismatic Meletians, the Christologically heretical Arians,

---

51. Athanasius, *Life of Antony* 14.3 (Bartelink, 172–73; McLaughlin, 18–19).

52. Athanasius, *Life of Antony* 14.3 (McLaughlin, 18–19; cf. Bartelink, 172). This description is reminiscent of Daniel and his friends, who abstained from culinary delicacies received from the king's table (Dan. 1:8–21).

53. Athanasius, *Life of Antony* 14 (White, 18).

54. Athanasius, *Life of Antony* 14 (McLaughlin, 19). See also section 59: "His countenance glowed as he lay [dying]" (McLaughlin, 104).

55. Athanasius, *Life of Antony* 43–49 (Bartelink, 320–41; White, 53–59).

the Manichaeans, and the idolatrous pagans.[56] The great discipline of his body and the strength of his soul also meant that he was armed against the devil's schemes. He taught his disciples that asceticism (a "right life," not just "right belief") was the key to defeating the devil and demonic forces:

> The great weapon against them is a right life [*bios orthos*] and confidence in God. For they dread the ascetics' fasting, watching, prayers, meekness, peacefulness, their scorn of wealth and of vainglory, their humility, love of the poor, alms-deeds, their mildness, and most of all, their devotion to Christ. This is why they do all they can that there may be no one to trample on them: for they know the grace that the Saviour gave to His faithful against them when He said, "Behold I have given you power to trample on serpents and scorpions and on all the strength of the enemy."[57]

The power possessed by a holy person was exercised against demonic opposition by means of calling on the name of Jesus, signing oneself with the cross, and singing the psalms. Antony's life is probably best known for his constant struggle against demons, and he is often pictured surrounded by beastly, contorted creatures who claw and glower fiercely at him. In one particular didactic passage, Antony describes his warfare tactics against Satan and his hosts.

> How many times did they threaten me like armed soldiers and surround me with scorpions, horses, huge beasts, . . . but I countered by *singing*, "Some are proud of their chariots and some of their horses, but we take pride in the name of the Lord our God," and at once Christ's compassion put them to flight. On one occasion they appeared with a great light and said, "Antony, we have come to bestow our brightness on you," but I closed my eyes because I refused to look upon the devil's light; I *prayed*, . . . and the light of those wicked creatures had gone out.[58]

In another passage, Antony relates an episode very much reminiscent of Christ's temptation in the wilderness.

> Once I saw the devil standing very tall. He dared to claim that he was the power and the providence of God, and he said to me, "What do you want me to give you, Antony?" But I spat hard in his face and attacked

---

56. Athanasius, *Life of Antony* 82, 91 (Bartelink, 345–49, 366–71; McLaughlin, 82–83).

57. Athanasius, *Life of Antony* 30 (McLaughlin, 37–38; cf. Bartelink, 218–21). The knowledge that demonic forces have already been defeated is a *topos* throughout the biography (e.g., Athanasius, *Life of Antony* 42 [White, 33–35]).

58. Athanasius, *Life of Antony* 39 (White, 33, emphasis added), citing Ps. 20:7.

him, protecting my whole self against him with the *name of Christ*: at
once this tall figure of his disappeared.[59]

In yet another representative passage, Antony reiterates to the monks
the effectiveness of the sign of the cross.

> [Demons] often come at night, pretending to be angels of God, and
> praising the monks' dedication, admiring their perseverance and prom-
> ising future rewards. When you see them, protect yourselves and your
> dwellings with the *sign of the cross* and immediately they will dissolve
> into nothing for they fear that sign of victory by which the Saviour,
> depriving them of their powers of the air, has shown them up.[60]

His journey to virtue results in calmness or tranquility (*ataraxia*) of
the mind and soul, a common theme in philosophical biographies as
an ideal of the ascetic life, appearing often in Cynic works. Antony's
success in achieving this spiritual equanimity and control is evident to
all in his face and manner; anyone meeting Antony for the first time
would recognize him even in a crowd. Athanasius explains, "He could
recognize Antony's spiritual purity from his face, and through the mirror of Antony's body he would perceive the grace of his holy mind."[61]
     The biography proceeds very much like pagan accounts of eccentric
philosophers who have withdrawn into ascetic seclusion (e.g., *Life
of Socrates*, *Life of Plotinus*, *Life of Pythagoras*); yet while the form
of the biography approximates works familiar to its fourth-century
audience, the narrative also paints a picture of Christ's resistance to
and defeat of the devil, for Antony's life reads like an extended temptation narrative, seeming to expand on the temptation of Christ. In
a very real sense, just as Jesus encountered the devil in some measure
throughout his ministry after having dealt him an initial critical blow,
so also Antony battled the demonic forces in lesser ways after having
powerfully resisted the devil and his minions in the first twenty years
of his solitude.[62]
     The narrative basically recounts a journey from the comforts of
home to living with God at the base of the Inner Mountain. Antony's
journey and tenure at the mountain recall elements of the lives of such
biblical figures as Moses and Elijah, both of whom received revelations
from God on a mountain, a traditional symbol of divine revelation.
Like Moses and Elijah, Antony was considered a prophet, a "man of

---

59. Athanasius, *Life of Antony* 40 (White, 33, emphasis added).
60. Athanasius, *Life of Antony* 35 (White, 30–31, emphasis added), citing Col. 2:15.
61. Athanasius, *Life of Antony* 67 (White, 51).
62. Athanasius, *Life of Antony* 10 (Bartelink, 165; White, 16).

God" (*theou anthrōpon*) to be sought out for prayer, advice, healings, or other miracles.[63] As people looked to him for inspiration, the monastic movement grew and monastic zeal spread into the desert, in a very real sense encroaching on the devil's and his demons' territory.[64] Monastic foundations colonized the demonic sphere, transforming it into a heavenly and harmonious community, reminiscent of the description of Israel spread out and encamped on the plain of Moab as they received the Lord's blessing through Balaam (Num. 24:5–6).[65]

REMEMBRANCE

By the very act of writing Antony's life, Athanasius remembers him and his example, and also helps others (whether lay Christians, monks, or pagans) to remember him. Athanasius's literary tribute perpetuates Antony's memory in the church. In the introductory preface, Athanasius mentions that remembering (*mnēmoneuein*) Antony leads to imitating his "purpose," and he can thus serve as "a guide [*charaktēr*] to religious life."[66] Clearly, remembrance is a primary purpose of recording the account and is intertwined with the purpose of remembrance, which is imitation, whose purpose, in turn, is spiritual growth and mature discipleship. Antony's example is one of perseverance to the very end of a lengthy life, an end that is itself worth imitating: "The manner of the end of his life I ought also to tell [*mnēmoneusai*], and you to hear eagerly, for this also is a pattern to imitate [*zēlōton*]."[67] Antony also commended to his disciples throughout his ministry the remembrance and imitation of biblical predecessors: "Remember [*mnēmoneuein*] the deeds done by each of the saints so that the memory of their example will inspire your soul to virtue and restrain it from vices" as "[you] meditate on the commands of the Scriptures."[68] On his deathbed, Antony specifically urged his disciples to remember his example of orthodoxy and avoid schismatics and heretics.[69]

Beyond the text, there remained for the church concrete souvenirs of holiness: Antony left his cloak, hair shirt, and two sheepskins to Athanasius, Serapion, and a few of Antony's devoted disciples. Athanasius reports, "They who received the sheepskins of the blessed Antony and the cloak that he wore out, each guard them as some great treasure. For to look on them is like looking on Antony, and to wear

63. Athanasius, *Life of Antony* 70.2 (White, 52).
64. Athanasius, *Life of Antony* 41.2 (Bartelink, 246–47; White, 34).
65. Athanasius, *Life of Antony* 44 (Bartelink, 253–55; White, 36).
66. Athanasius, *Life of Antony*, preface, 3 (McLaughlin, ix; cf. Bartelink, 127).
67. Athanasius, *Life of Antony* 89 (McLaughlin, 101; cf. Bartelink, 362–63).
68. Athanasius, *Life of Antony* 55 (White, 43).
69. Athanasius, *Life of Antony* 58 (White, 67).

them is like joyfully taking on us his teachings."[70] In other words, to see Antony's effects and to read his biography is to see him and remember his teachings. They are powerful reminders of Antony's life, yet there is no hint of veneration of the saint or his relics, and indeed such a reaction would be entirely opposed to Antony's own expressly stated wishes.

As a historical piece, the *Life of Antony* reflects one of the major objectives of historians, to write a narrative that is useful to the audience. Within Athanasius's general purpose expressed in the introduction's opening lines, the *Life of Antony* was intended to encourage monks who had embarked on an ascetic lifestyle and were striving toward virtue (*kat' aretēn hymōn askēsei*).[71] The *Life of Antony* also served as an encouragement to any believer wishing to live a life of self-denial in service to God, as beautifully illustrated in the concluding section: "Though they themselves [God's own people] act in secret and wish to be unnoticed, yet the Lord shows them as lanterns to all, that even from this the hearers may know that the Commandments are able to be fulfilled, and so may take courage on the path of virtue."[72] Finally, Athanasius intended the biography as a convicting and somewhat polemical/apologetic work against pagans (and possibly heretics) to demonstrate the deity of Christ as "God and the Son of God," through whom Christians trample on and drive out "the demons whom the Greeks think gods" but "are no gods."[73]

MIMĒSIS

In the reception of this account of Antony's life, *mimēsis* is clearly evident in two ways, personal and literary. First, readers who had already followed Jesus and had striven to grow in perfection drew strength from imitating Antony's personal example of holy living. Seekers after a life of significance were also drawn to the account because of Antony's clear sense of vocation and high ethical standard, which drew admiration even among secular audiences due to their respect for their own ascetics. Thus the *Life of Antony* seems to have served an evangelistic purpose as well, leading many to personal conversion to Christ, as the example of Augustine and his friends will show. The literary aspect of *mimēsis* has to do with the models used by the author to make his subject more vivid to readers, and Athanasius's use of prophetic biblical figures achieves this aim particularly well.

70. Athanasius, *Life of Antony* 92 (McLaughlin, 104; cf. Bartelink, 373).
71. Athanasius, *Life of Antony* 1.1 (Bartelink, 131).
72. Athanasius, *Life of Antony* 93 (McLaughlin, 105).
73. Athanasius, *Life of Antony* 94 (McLaughlin, 105–6).

As Athanasius reiterates throughout the narrative, the purpose of remembering Antony is to imitate his life. Athanasius intended the *Life* as an example of how to be a monk, for monks wishing to practice the severity of desert eremitism. Antony consistently and self-consciously imitated Christ and ascribed all credit for anything he did or accomplished to God working through him, constantly pointing people to Jesus. In addition to the *topoi* throughout the narrative that construct a portrait of the ideal monk, Athanasius offers a few additional lessons to imitate. Throughout the *Life*, there appears a thinly veiled critique of self-proclaimed "holy men" who desired flashy gifts such as prophecy (more in the sense of foretelling the future than preaching), or the performance of miraculous healings and dramatic exorcisms. Perhaps some self-styled holy men reveled superciliously in their spiritual status and disdained the clergy. Antony, by contrast, modeled for his disciples humility, graciousness, deference to ordained clergy (even deacons!), and above all, love for Jesus, following him in daily, self-denying discipleship.[74] Each monk should regularly examine the quality of his own commitment to Jesus, with the help of accountability from his fellow monks.[75]

Augustine's classic spiritual autobiography, the *Confessions*, testifies to the evangelistic effect of the *Life of Antony*. Augustine first encountered Antony's biography through an acquaintance named Ponticianus, who recounted the story of how some young friends of his had sought career advancement in the emperor's service, but they grew dissatisfied with their spiritual state (as "seekers"). Augustine and his close friend, Alypius, listened intently as Ponticianus spoke. Augustine describes the effect of the *Life* on these friends, who encountered and read it while "off duty" in Trier.

> [Ponticianus] began to tell us the story of Antony, the Egyptian monk, whose name was held in high honor by your servants, although Alypius and I had never heard it until then. When Ponticianus realized this, he went into greater detail, wishing to instill some knowledge of this great man into our ignorant minds, for he was very surprised that we had not heard of him. For our part, we too were astonished to hear of the wonders you had worked so recently, almost in our own times, and witnessed by so many, in the true faith and in the Catholic Church.[76]

Two of Ponticianus's friends were wandering around in Trier, waiting for the emperor to finish some business. As they walked around, they encountered a monastic community,

---

74. Athanasius, *Life of Antony* 67 (Bartelink, 310–11; White, 51).
75. Athanasius, *Life of Antony* 55 (Bartelink, 282–87; White, 43–44).
76. Augustine, *Confessions* 8 (trans. R. S. Pine-Coffin [London: Penguin, 1961], 167).

servants of Yours, men poor in spirit, to whom the kingdom of heaven belongs. In the house they found a book containing the *Life of Antony*. One of them began to read it and was so fascinated and thrilled by the story that even before he had finished reading he conceived the idea of taking upon himself the same kind of life and abandoning his career in the world—both he and his friend were officials in the service of the State—in order to become Your servant. All at once he was filled with the love of holiness. Angry with himself and full of remorse, . . . he said, 'What do we hope to gain by all the efforts we make? What are we looking for? What is our purpose in serving the State? Can we hope for anything better at Court than to be the Emperor's friends? . . . And how long is it to be before we reach it? But if I wish, I can become the friend of God at this very moment.'

After saying this he turned back to the book, laboring under the pain of the new life that was taking birth in him. He read on and in his heart, where You alone could see, a change was taking place. His mind was being divested of the world, as could presently be seen. For while he was reading, his heart leaping and turning in his breast, a cry broke from him as he saw the better course and determined to take it.[77]

With this, the young man told his friend, and both became Christians. Augustine continued, "So these two, now Your servants, built their tower at the cost which had to be paid, that is, at the cost of giving up all they possessed and following You" (Luke 14:28–33).[78]

The story profoundly affected Augustine, who had been journeying as a seeker himself and was nearing the point of conversion. This narrative, he wrote, forced him to confront the ugly and inescapable truth about his personal sin and catalyzed him toward conversion: "In this way You brought me face to face with myself once more, forcing me upon my own sight so that I should see my wickedness and loathe it. I had known it all along, but I had always pretended that it was something different. I had turned a blind eye and forgotten it."[79] The holy example of Antony propelled Augustine toward conversion (as it had attracted the two friends of Ponticianus as well), after which there was no looking back for this future bishop who would so profoundly influence Christian theology.

As the literary device of *mimēsis* helps readers consider Antony as a role model of holiness, the story's unfolding leads the audience to ponder Antony's own role models, the martyrs and the biblical prophets. While the author associates Antony with the holy martyrs and confessors of his own time and highlights Antony's *askēsis* as an

---

77. Augustine, *Confessions* 8 (Pine-Coffin, 168).
78. Augustine, *Confessions* 8 (Pine-Coffin, 168).
79. Augustine, *Confessions* 8 (Pine-Coffin, 169).

endeavor equal in holiness to their calling to the ultimate sacrifice, the author also points to biblical models of holy men upon whom Antony's character and reputation are patterned. Antony went forward to Alexandria to be martyred, "that we may suffer if we are called," but he was passed over for martyrdom.[80] He did not wish to "give himself up" (indicating the policy evident in the martyrdom of Polycarp and others), so he contributed to Christian solidarity with the martyrs and with persecuted confessors by ministering to those "in the mines and in the prisons."[81] His zeal for the Lord and his willingness to die were channeled into another avenue of service. The author writes,

> [Antony] mourned because he was not martyred, but God was keeping him to help us and others, that to many he might be a teacher of the strict life that he had himself learned from the Scriptures. For simply at seeing his behavior many were eager to become followers [zēlōtai, "imitators"] of his way of life.[82]

Rather than being chosen to witness with his death during the persecution, he demonstrated how to live as a "daily martyr to conscience, fighting [agōnizomenos] the fights [athloi] of the faith."[83] Clearly through the language of martyrdom and association with the martyrs in the narrative, the author indicates that Antony's stringent asceticism served favorably as an equivalent to martyrdom, and it gave hope to monks living in an era of toleration, that they could fulfill the martyr ideal via lifelong service to Christ in ministry and a disciplined life.

Throughout the account, Antony's scriptural models show Jesus acknowledged as Antony's Lord, Savior, and Master; aspects of the lives of Moses and Elijah also figure prominently, even from the very outset. In the preface the author mentions that he knew some things about Antony from personal experience but had learned other details from one who had served him for a long time, one who had "poured water on his hands," citing 2 Kings 3:11, a phrase describing Elisha's service to Elijah.[84] Like Moses and Elijah, Antony was widely acknowledged as a "man of God" (Deut. 33; 1 Kings 17–18; 2 Kings 1). He was humble like Moses (Num. 12:3), and like him, he died at an advanced age (Moses was 120 years old, according to Deut. 34:7).

80. Athanasius, *Life of Antony* 46 (McLaughlin, 57).
81. Athanasius, *Life of Antony* 46 (McLaughlin, 57).
82. Athanasius, *Life of Antony* 46.7 (McLaughlin, 57; cf. Bartelink, 262).
83. Athanasius, *Life of Antony* 47.1 (McLaughlin, 58; cf. Bartelink, 262).
84. Athanasius, *Life of Antony*, preface.

The author adds that although Antony had reached 105 years, his eyesight was undiminished and his body remained vigorous, again like Moses (Deut. 34:7). At his death, Antony was unconcerned about his body and wished it to be buried in obscurity;[85] similarly, Elijah and Moses both were taken by the Lord, and their graves' locations are unknown (Deut. 34:6; 2 Kings 2:16–18, noting that the notion of Elijah's "grave" is somewhat problematic; the point is that his body was not found). Each man had passed on a legacy of a sort to successors: Moses to Joshua, Elijah to Elisha, and Antony to his disciples and, ostensibly, to Athanasius. As Antony had passed on personal tokens from his ministry, we find that Moses had laid hands on Joshua and bestowed "the spirit of wisdom" on him (Deut. 34:9), which was acknowledged by the people who then obeyed Joshua. More similarly to Antony, Elijah had bequeathed to Elisha his cloak and a "double portion" of his spirit (2 Kings 2:9), which was acknowledged by the sons of the prophets (2:15). Elijah's cloak is particularly significant for our examination of the *Life of Antony*, as the miracle performed by both Elijah and Elisha through the cloak (the parting of the Jordan) hearkens back to Moses's parting of the Red Sea, as well as to the later parting of the Jordan under Joshua's leadership just before the conquest of Canaan. Several times in the narrative of Antony's life, a parting of the waters occurs—or some other miraculous event, like a translation—allowing the holy man Amun (or Ammon) to cross the river without getting wet, and Antony to cross a canal full of crocodiles unharmed.[86]

CAUSATION

In this aspect of Christian historical works, the devil figures highly, yet he is neither the only nor the primary causative agent. Hagiography (as well as classical histories) involves at least two causative factors: human striving (for virtue and against vice) and the occasional intervention of the gods or Fortune. For the author of the *Life of Antony*, three factors are involved in the dramatic narrative progression: God's call and sustenance, Antony's heeding of the call and desire to undertake training for the life of spiritual combat, and the devil, who occupies the role of the malignant, envious force that cannot bear to witness progress in virtue. Moreover, he especially cannot bear the fact that Antony is encroaching on his domain, the desert, and bringing other ascetics with him. His temptations to sin are being overthrown in his own territory.

85. Athanasius, *Life of Antony* 91 (McLaughlin, 103–4).
86. Athanasius, *Life of Antony* 15, 60 (White, 19, 46).

Moving the story forward in the first instance is God's call to Antony: he hears the scriptural injunction ("If you want to be perfect") to divest himself of his wealth and follow Jesus. He accepts the gospel call to sacrificial discipleship together with the entailed cost: in earthly terms, he must leave his sister in the care of others, effectively bestowing his inheritance to the community; and in spiritual terms, he embarks on a challenging journey in which he finds both God's powerful grace and the devil's opposition looming large. God calls him to self-denying discipleship (*askēsis*) while the devil attempts to thwart any spiritual progress or influence Antony might have. Between these two forces, he finds himself exercising his free will to humbly obey God and to fiercely oppose the devil, teaching his disciples repeatedly to "resist the devil, and he will flee from you" (James 4:7). At the beginning of his ascetic life, the devil tested him fiercely. In vocabulary reminiscent of the secular historiographers, the devil is described variously as "the hater and envier [*phthoneros*] of good" and "the enemy of all good," while in biblical terms he is described as a serpent/dragon, a lion, the enemy or adversary, the devil, and Satan.[87] After Antony's initiatory trials, the Lord made his presence known by a ray of light descending into the tomb where Antony dwelt after having been maliciously assaulted by demons. When Antony inquired why Christ had not aided him from the beginning, he received the reply, "'I was here, Antony, but I waited to see thy resistance [*agōnismon*]. Therefore, since thou hast endured and not yielded, I will always be thy Helper, and I will make thee renowned everywhere.' Hearing this, Antony arose and prayed, and he was so strengthened that he perceived that he had more power in his body than formerly."[88] The account bears unmistakable similarities to the temptation of Christ in the wilderness. Even though in this instance as well as in later encounters Antony bested the devil, the latter remained a force to reckon with. Throughout Antony's career, the devil still tempted, threatened, and tried to intimidate the holy man, who taught his disciples to "draw inspiration from Jesus and set your faith in His name firmly in your minds: then all the demons will be put to flight by the sure faith." Even on his deathbed Antony reminded his disciples that the demons' "attacks are savage, but . . . their strength has been rendered powerless."[89] As in the martyrologies, the devil who tempted the martyrs to recant their faith likewise tempted monks embarking upon the ascetic life, urging them to renege on their commitment via sensual temptations and discouragement of their pursuit of holiness.

87. Athanasius, *Life of Antony* 4 (McLaughlin, 7).
88. Athanasius, *Life of Antony* 10.3 (McLaughlin, 14–15; cf. Bartelink, 162–65).
89. Athanasius, *Life of Antony* 91.3 (White, 67; cf. Bartelink, 368).

Saint Macrina, Domestic Mother

NARRATIVE

Another account composed to memorialize a holy person is the *Life of Macrina*. This beautifully moving biography was authored by Gregory of Nyssa, Macrina's brother, about the year AD 382. In effect, he wrote not only a biography of Macrina but also the story of their entire illustrious family. The account is an incredibly rich and layered literary gem, playing on formats and images derived from philosophical biographies—especially the prototypical dialogues on the death of Socrates in Plato's *Crito* and *Phaedo*—and martyrdom literature.[90] Macrina is therefore intentionally constructed as both saint and sage. The *Life* is in epistolary format, but Gregory readily admits it is lengthier than a letter and is practically a history of her life.[91] He relates her early life as well as subsequent life events in a way that emphasizes her growth in virtue, a common philosophical theme; as a result some chronological difficulties and lapses of strictly historical or biographical information exist in the account.

Macrina was likely born in Cappadocia (modern Turkey) around 327, the first child of Basil and Emmelia, a wealthy Christian couple. Gregory leads the reader to believe that Macrina received no formal education but was homeschooled by her mother and instructed in the Scriptures rather than a classical curriculum. The secular curriculum would have included the Greek corpus of tragedies and comedies, to which her mother objected, as they were indecent and would pollute her mind.[92] At the marriageable age of twelve, her parents chose a husband for her out of the "swarm of suitors" who "besieged her parents."[93] Her father chose a young man of integrity who was possibly a newly minted lawyer and had already distinguished himself in the law courts by taking up the cause of "the wronged."[94] Shortly afterward, however, the man died, and Macrina decided to continue in a life of chastity, refusing her parents' recommendations of other suitors. In language typical of consolatory literature, Macrina insisted that her groom was not dead but "was on a journey" and was "living

---

90. A particularly helpful and well-written piece on this topic is by Ellen Muehlberger, "Salvage: Macrina and the Christian Project of Cultural Reclamation," *Church History* 82, no. 2 (2012): 273–97.

91. This format is not unlike Jerome's biographies of women in his life, which are also in the form of lengthy letters.

92. Gregory of Nyssa, *Life of Macrina* 3 (Petersen, 53). She was probably also taught by her father, who was a noted rhetorician; Gregory's emphasis, however, remains on the pious Emmelia.

93. Gregory of Nyssa, *Life of Macrina* 4 (Petersen, 54).

94. Gregory of Nyssa, *Life of Macrina* 4 (Petersen, 54).

in God."[95] Macrina then threw herself into the work of the family's household and property management, becoming her mother's partner, since her father passed away at some unspecified point in the narrative. As Gregory explains these years of partnership in running the household, Macrina's main thought was to remain with and serve her mother in order to continue under her mother's spiritual influence (and doubtless also to beg off from marriage), but Gregory also describes a gradual role reversal between the two women: Macrina became the spiritual trainer, and her mother became the student.[96] Her mother had educated her in the ways of the Lord by providing her education (training), and in turn, Macrina shared with her mother a higher kind of education, "the ideal of philosophy" by which Emmelia was led to greater detachment from worldliness.[97] She also imparted this ideal to her brother Basil, a recent "Ivy League" graduate, who had studied rhetoric abroad in Constantinople and Athens and was puffed up by his superior oratorical skill.[98] He had returned to his family estate at Annisa between 355 and 358, and under Macrina's spiritual influence, he divested himself of pride in worldly accolades and began practicing the ascetic life within his family.

Gregory next describes three heavy blows that Macrina sustained, by which he intended to demonstrate her progress in virtue and spiritual strength. Five or more years after Basil's return and the conversion of the household at Annisa into a domestic monastery (later to become a double monastery administered jointly by herself and her youngest brother, Peter), Macrina's younger brother Naucratius perished in a fishing accident, causing their mother profound grief. Macrina, as her mother's spiritual "trainer," comforted her in her grief and ultimately brought "healing to her soul" through her ministrations.[99] Sometime later, possibly 370, Emmelia herself died, expiring in the arms of both Macrina and Peter, who lived at home. Macrina and Peter had grown up in a relationship of teacher (*didaskalos*) and student, and upon their bereavement of their mother, they practiced together the "philosophy" to which they both subscribed. Fighting against the waves of human emotion, they strictly reined in their grief, as Macrina had taught him, since she was his "trainer" (*paidagōgos*) in virtue.[100] Finally, "over eight

---

95. Gregory of Nyssa, *Life of Macrina* 5 (Petersen, 55).
96. Gregory of Nyssa, *Life of Macrina* 6 (Petersen, 56).
97. Gregory of Nyssa, *Life of Macrina* 5 (Petersen, 56).
98. Frederick Norris, "Basil of Caesarea," *EEC*, 170.
99. Gregory of Nyssa, *Life of Macrina* 10 (Petersen, 59).
100. Gregory of Nyssa, *Life of Macrina* 12, 13 (Maraval, 182, 186; cf. Petersen, 61). This Peter was consecrated as a priest by Basil and later (perhaps after Macrina's death) ordained bishop of nearby Sebaste.

years later" (around 379), Basil passed away after an illustrious and influential theological career, ministering and teaching in the church.[101] This time it seems that Macrina might have borne her grief alone, adhering to her own "philosophy" of battling the passion of grief that attempts to overturn human nature.[102]

Roughly the second half of the narrative concerns Gregory's own experience of the harsh blow *he* endured in the death of his sister, whom he calls the "great Macrina." Slightly less than a year after Basil's death, Gregory decided to visit Macrina, having been informed by an acquaintance that she was ill (although Gregory does not include this detail in the narrative). Basil's death was still fresh in his mind, and he thought that he and his sister would reminisce about their brother, especially since Gregory and their mutual family friend Gregory of Nazianzus were embroiled in the fallout of the Neo-Arian controversy, in the midst of which Basil had died. Gregory arrived at Annisa only to find that Macrina herself was not well, consumed by fever, and was in fact dying.[103] She and Gregory conversed at length several times in her final two days, exchanging memories of their parents and their brother Basil. Around sunset on her final day, Macrina seemed to lapse into a semiconscious state and subsequently spoke only in prayer, with her strength gradually ebbing until she ceased to breathe.[104] She died about the year 379 or 380. The remainder of Gregory's account narrates his own emotional turmoil, the funeral rites performed for Macrina, and the funeral itself. Toward the end of the narrative and also in a brief epilogue, he very restrainedly shares two examples of Macrina's miracles, one worked for herself and one for the child of a high-ranking military official.[105]

TOPOI

Gregory's narrative themes in this piece include holiness, wisdom, beauty, and asceticism. As with the *Life of Antony*, holiness is the chief virtue, out of which the others flow. Gregory not only constructs a portrait of a saint but also takes great pains literarily to portray his sister as a true martyr. By associating her with martyrs and the terminology

101. Gregory of Nyssa, *Life of Macrina* 14 (Petersen, 62).

102. Gregory of Nyssa, *Life of Macrina* 14 (Petersen, 62–63). Peter is unmentioned in the passage, but later, when Gregory came to visit, he clearly expected to see Peter, who was still head of the men's side of the double monastery at Annisa. Peter had either set out by a different route to meet and welcome him, or he had set out on his own initiative to possibly inform Gregory of Macrina's rapid physical deterioration.

103. Gregory of Nyssa, *Life of Macrina* 16–17 (Petersen, 64–65).

104. Gregory of Nyssa, *Life of Macrina* 23–25 (Petersen, 70–72).

105. Gregory of Nyssa, *Life of Macrina* 31 (Petersen, 76), 36–38 (Petersen, 80–82).

of martyrdom from first to last throughout the account, Gregory neatly situates his family within the stream of victorious Christian heroes who have overcome death and its "sting," sin (1 Cor. 15:56).[106]

Gregory wrote reverentially about Macrina; he was awed by his sister's holiness and spoke of her life as "angelic," by which he indicates her lifelong chastity and detachment from the trappings and concerns of the physical realm. Her way of life served as a pattern for all those dwelling at the double monastery, and their "angelic life" even transcended this world, as it refers to the state of people in the resurrection. Gregory's description of life in the monastery at Annisa depicts a heavenly microcosm, essentially heaven on earth:[107]

> All differences of rank were removed from their way of life. Indeed such was the ordering of their lives and so sublime their philosophy and so noble the principles underlying their way of living that no words can describe them. [Their life] was lived apart from all worldly trivialities and was brought into harmony with the life of the angels.[108]

Gregory continues to list the many heavenly virtues they shared and the many worldly vices they spurned, committing themselves to humility, poverty, manual labor, prayer, and singing the psalms. He adds even more strikingly,

> What human words could bring before our eyes a picture of such a way of life? . . . On the one hand, the liberation of their nature from human passions was something which made them superhuman; on the other, their appearance in a body, their confinement within a human form, . . . made them into beings lower than those whose nature is angelic and incorporeal. Perhaps one might dare to say that the difference between them and the angels was rather slight, because though living in the flesh, the virgins . . . were not weighed down by the burden of the body. On the contrary, their life was elevated above the earth, and they walked on high with the heavenly beings. . . . Their philosophy advanced ceaselessly towards greater purity.[109]

Macrina has even transcended her gender, so that Gregory speaks of her at times as masculine. In his opening segment Gregory writes, "A woman was the starting-point of our story, if indeed one may call her

---

106. Toward the conclusion of his funeral oration for Basil, Gregory of Nazianzus refers to Basil's body carried in the funeral procession as "holy," and speaks of him as a "martyr [added] to the martyrs" (*Oration* 43.80 [*NPNF²* 7:422]).

107. This description is similar to Athanasius's description of monastic desert communities.

108. Gregory of Nyssa, *Life of Macrina* 11 (Petersen, 59).

109. Gregory of Nyssa, *Life of Macrina* 11 (Petersen, 60).

a woman, for I do not know whether it is appropriate to call someone a woman who was by nature a woman, but who, in fact, was far above nature."[110] This rhetoric may reflect several facets of Gregory's thinking. First, it reflects a particular understanding of Jesus's teaching on angels, who are understood to be neither masculine nor feminine, neither marrying nor being given in marriage (Matt. 22:30; Mark 12:25). Second, it was a countercultural way of speaking in Gregory's patriarchal context, even if somewhat of a traditional *topos* in hagiographical literature. The idea of holy women transcending gender or nature harks back to Perpetua and other female martyrs such as Blandina, Agape, Chione, and Irene, and is often subsequently applied to construct an image of a spiritually strong ("manly") woman.[111] Third, for this community of virgins, transcending gender also meant transcending sexuality (as with the angels), and virginity is a concept or state that Gregory ties closely to one's ability to progress in godliness and one's capacity to attain to various divine attributes such as holiness, *apatheia*, goodness, and beauty.[112]

Despite her apparent lack of a formal education, Macrina is characterized by wisdom. Her education as a young girl was based on the Scriptures, notably on the Wisdom literature ascribed to Solomon. Gregory's description foreshadows Macrina's later role: she became a venerable teacher in her family, with respect to both her siblings and her mother. She imparted the "true philosophy" in her household and later in her monastic house; she trained her brother Peter, and he in turn implemented this philosophical way of life in the men's monastery. Gregory writes concerning Peter's upbringing that Macrina "immediately snatched him from his wet-nurse and looked after him herself," training him from childhood in "the sacred branches of learning" to keep him from falling into vanity.[113] "She became everything for the little boy: father, teacher [*didaskalos*], tutor [*paidagōgos*], mother, counselor in all that was good; thus, even before he left the age of childhood, he . . . was being raised up towards the high goal of philosophy."[114] The notion of a "trainer" (*paidagōgos*) is often used throughout the text and holds particular significance in terms of the martyrs. The latter were perceived as athletes, while encouragers or teachers in the church

110. Gregory of Nyssa, *Life of Macrina* 1 (Petersen, 51).

111. This *topos* will recur in Gerontius's description of Melania the Younger below, as well as in Palladius of Helenopolis's description of the life of Melania the Elder (Petersen, 299 and 311).

112. As in Gregory's earlier work *On Virginity*; see also V. K. McCarty, "Beauty for the Rest of Us: Re-considering Gregory of Nyssa's *On Virginity*" (paper presented at the Fourth Annual Conference of the Sophia Institute, Union Theological Seminary, New York City, 2012).

113. Gregory of Nyssa, *Life of Macrina* 12 (Petersen, 61).

114. Gregory of Nyssa, *Life of Macrina* 12 (Petersen, 61).

(like catechists) were seen as athletic trainers. Macrina, then, is herself an athlete who became a trainer, a narrative similar to Antony's in this respect. Although Antony lived in the historical era of persecution while Macrina did not, the literary connections make it clear that Macrina identified with and followed in the securely established spiritual tradition of the noble and intrepid martyr-athlete.

A further prominent *topos* is physical beauty (*kalos*). Beauty is both a traditional theme in saintly portraiture, as well as a philosophical theme of particular interest to the Cappadocians. Descriptions of Macrina's beauty are symmetrical: she is harmoniously beautiful in life as well as in death, in youth as in old age.[115] As the skilled painters' art could not do her beauty justice in the flower of her youth, so human hands were unnecessary to lay out her body's final resting state. "Her whole body had, of its own accord, assumed an harmonious posture and did not need any hand to lay it out," Gregory wrote.[116] Gazing at his sister as she lay dressed and prepared for public viewing, Gregory intertwines the notions of beauty, virginity, holiness, and radiance, remarking, "She was radiant; the divine power, I think, added this further grace to her body, so that her beautiful form seemed to throw out rays of light, exactly as I had seen in the vision which occurred in my dream."[117] Looking back to the martyrologies, Perpetua was described as a beautiful bride/spouse of Christ, and the martyr/confessor Thecla was also praised for her beauty.[118] For the Cappadocians, however, beauty was also a philosophically loaded concept, since beauty (like impassibility, the attribute related to *apatheia*) was considered an attribute of the divine. Macrina possessed not only a physical attractiveness, but she was also in some sense cosmically beautiful, reflecting (and superseding) the harmony of the heavenly elements, the "sun and planets."[119]

A final *topos*, asceticism, overlaps with the theme of wisdom and involves the Stoic idea of control over the passions by the use of reason—that is, living out the "Christian philosophy" and imparting it to others. Antony was tested and tempted in all kinds of ways, thereby illustrating the same theme, but admittedly we are further from the demonology of desert asceticism in this document and closer to a Platonic or Stoic

---

115. See Gregory of Nyssa, *Life of Macrina* 4.4–14 (Petersen, 54), for her beauty in youth, inimitable by painters or sculptors; *Life of Macrina* 25.20–28 (Petersen, 72), for her harmonious beauty in death, needing no human assistance.

116. Gregory of Nyssa, *Life of Macrina* 24 (Petersen, 72).

117. Gregory of Nyssa, *Life of Macrina* 32 (Petersen, 77).

118. *Passion of Perpetua and Felicitas* 18 (Musurillo, 127); *Acts of Paul and Thecla* 25, 34, in *New Testament Apocrypha*, vol. 2, *Writings Related to the Apostles*, ed. Wilhelm Schneemelcher, English trans. ed. Robert McL. Wilson (Philadelphia: Westminster, 1964), 243, 245.

119. Gregory of Nyssa, *Life of Macrina* 4 (Petersen, 54).

worldview. Something of a synthesis, however, appears in this document, and in the Cappadocian writings generally.[120] Warring against
the passions was akin to battling the beasts in the arena, yet fighting
the beasts lasted a few minutes, hours, or days, while mastering the
passions required an arduous and lifelong effort, facing down whatever
eventualities may arise, such as sudden and unexpected death. In this
narrative, the passion that seems to pervade the narrative is grief *(lypē)*.
In a beautifully crafted description of the tragic death of Macrina's
younger brother Naucratius, Gregory pulls together several overlapping themes, as he contrasts Emmelia's and Macrina's reactions to
Naucratius's death. His purpose is to demonstrate Macrina's consistent
progress in virtue and how she trained others to progress along with
her, which is reminiscent of the arena in which the martyrs encouraged
one another as fellow athletes of Christ. Although Emmelia had progressed well in her training in virtue, nonetheless the news of her son's
demise overcame her completely. Gregory writes that "her soul was cut
down, and she was immediately deprived of breath and the power of
speech. Her sorrow *[pathei]* overcame her reason *[logismou]*. There
she lay, prostrated by the shock of the terrible news, like a well-trained
athlete *[athlētēs gennaios]* who is laid low by an unexpected blow."[121]
    By contrast "the great Macrina" mastered "her sorrow with her
reason, she bore herself without flinching; she became the support of
her mother in her weakness and aroused her again from her depths of
grief *[lypēs]*."[122] Here Gregory follows with an interesting gendered
comparison of the proper, respectable, and virtuous reaction to death.
He writes that "through her own unyielding firmness, [Macrina] trained
her mother to be stout-hearted *[andreian,* literally, "manly"]. Thus her
mother was not carried away by her sorrow *[pathos]*, nor did she give
way to any base or womanish *[gynaikeion]* sentiment."[123] This sentiment
would include the loud wailing, lamentations, and frequent rending of
garments that accompanied death dirges, as mourning was practiced
in the ancient world, which considered this ritual (for the most part)
the women's responsibility. Gregory considers this kind of behavior
to be weak and a concession to the passion of grief, which ought to be
opposed by the virtue of fortitude. Instead of this "womanly" behavior,
then, Macrina and her mother must strive to be "manly" or brave and
courageous, the proper virtuous reaction to the onslaughts of grief
that can overwhelm the soul. While Gregory makes it clear that both

---

120. See Pelikan, *Christianity and Classical Culture.*
121. Gregory of Nyssa, *Life of Macrina* 9 (Petersen, 58; cf. Maraval, 170–72).
122. Gregory of Nyssa, *Life of Macrina* 10 (Petersen, 58; cf. Maraval, 172).
123. Gregory of Nyssa, *Life of Macrina* 10 (Petersen, 58–59; cf. Maraval, 172).

women were suffering inwardly (they still possessed a human nature, after all), nonetheless their virtue was both demonstrated and enhanced by this tragedy, and each found in it an opportunity for further progress. Emmelia "endured the onslaughts of human nature," but she "thrust them from herself through her own thoughts [*logismois*] and those suggested by her daughter, to bring healing [*therapeian*] to her soul."[124] As for Macrina, "her own life . . . was always rising to greater heights of excellence": by training her mother in patience and fortitude (again the term *andreian*), she "provided her mother with an opportunity not so much for grieving over the son and brother who had left them as for rejoicing in the goodness which she could see."[125]

REMEMBRANCE

As Gregory commemorates Macrina, he cites a conventional reason for writing his historical piece: keeping the memory of her life from falling into oblivion. Of course, his reasons go far beyond the conventional and are both deeply personal and more broadly corporate. Remembering her is important to his immediate family as well as to their extended spiritual family, the church. When she died, he wept despondently but also remembered with gratitude "all the goodness [*agathou*]" that had gone out of his life.[126] When he commemorated her, he also commemorated many more members of his family, as she had such a powerful spiritual impact within her household, upon him, his brothers Basil, Naucratius, and Peter, and their mother, Emmelia. She had a fundamental and lasting influence in the ecclesiastical legacy of the Cappadocians. Beyond their immediate family, though, others reminisced with Gregory, remembering Macrina's hospitality and generosity and her miraculous deeds. A number of the women in her monastic community referred to her as "mother" and "nurse," as she had taken them into her home and given them a family at a time when they were wandering destitute "at the time of the famine" (368/369), as Gregory explains. These women Macrina "cared for and brought up and directed towards a pure and incorrupt life."[127] Remembering Macrina meant remembering her teachings and her virtues, and apart from her holiness and other attributes, these women (and the broader community of surrounding villages that were affected by the famine) remembered Macrina's *philanthrōpia*, her generosity. Indeed, as Macrina recounts the lives and legacy of their parents in conversation with

124. Gregory of Nyssa, *Life of Macrina* 10 (Petersen, 59; cf. Maraval, 172–74).
125. Gregory of Nyssa, *Life of Macrina* 10 (Petersen, 59).
126. Gregory of Nyssa, *Life of Macrina* 36 (Petersen, 80; cf. Maraval, 256).
127. Gregory of Nyssa, *Life of Macrina* 26 (Petersen, 73).

Gregory, she locates herself squarely in a family tradition of compassionate generosity and hospitality, both of which are expressed through the virtue of *philanthrōpia*, another divine attribute.

MIMĒSIS (ROLE MODELS)

"Look at her and remember her teachings, through which she trained you," Gregory admonished the virgins who wept upon Macrina's passing.[128] Throughout her life, Macrina had called upon her mother and the rest of the community to imitate her life and priorities and incessant progress in sanctity, her virtuous example of humility, generosity (*philanthrōpia*), hospitality, detachment from materialism, and control of the passions through the exercise of reason, particularly in the face of death and tragic loss. While the women in her convent imitated her hospitality and humility—serving one another as equals, practicing manual labor, and erasing class distinctions—none were able to imitate her *apatheia* as she bore up under death with such equanimity and virtual stoicism. Neither Emmelia nor Gregory could match her example; it seemed an unattainable goal, though no less desirable.

Macrina's own role models were both biblical and traditional. Her ascetic practices constituted a form of *imitatio Christi*. This imitation is reflected in her deathbed prayer, as she lifts up the petition of a penitent. Comparing herself with the thief on the cross (Luke 23:42), Macrina pleads with Christ, "Remember me too in your kingdom, because I too have been crucified with you."[129] She asserts that she has "nailed down [her] flesh . . . in fear of [his] judgements." She offered up her life as a sacrifice at the time of Vespers, thus ending "her life and her prayers at the same moment."[130] Her life of renunciation and withdrawal from the world reiterates some themes of desert asceticism. For example, Macrina placed great emphasis on the power of the cross, which figured prominently in her theology of atonement and her devotional life. As noted above, she had "nailed [her] flesh" to the cross, and she wore a cross pendant and a cross-engraved signet ring containing a relic of the true cross ("Tree of Life").[131] On one occasion, Macrina performed (or was granted) a healing through the efficaciousness of the sign of the cross. In Gregory's description (as the story was told to him), she experienced healing from a cancerous lump in her breast by making a salve from her tears and the dirt on the floor of the sanctuary (chapel) where she had spent a night in intense supplication. Asking her mother

---

128. Gregory of Nyssa, *Life of Macrina* 27 (Petersen, 73).
129. Gregory of Nyssa, *Life of Macrina* 24 (Petersen, 71).
130. Gregory of Nyssa, *Life of Macrina* 24–25 (Petersen, 71–72).
131. Gregory of Nyssa, *Life of Macrina* 30 (Petersen, 75).

to put her hand on the growth and sign it with the cross, Macrina found herself healed. The growth had receded, leaving but a slight scar as a reminder of a "divine visitation."[132]

In her pursuit of chastity, Macrina imitated not only Jesus but also the so-called protomartyr Thecla, a role model for young women, whose *cultus* was widespread in Cappadocia at that time.[133] In fact, a connection to the martyrs appears in the portrait of Macrina probably more than in either of the other two biographies in this chapter. Gregory takes up the martyrdom/asceticism theme throughout the piece, commemorating her as a martyr, athlete, model of virtue, and spiritual trainer. Gregory explains that Macrina was named after her paternal grandmother. "At the time of the persecutions [probably of Maximinus Daia, 306–12], she took part in the struggle [*enathlēsasa*] by confessing Christ on more than one occasion. The child was named after her by our parents."[134] Macrina also had a secret name, revealed to her mother in a dream while she was pregnant with Macrina. An immortal (possibly Christ or an angelic being) "addressed the child whom she was carrying as Thecla" three times, "to foretell what the life of the virgin would be and to show, through the identical character of the name, that she would choose the same way of life as Thecla did."[135] So Macrina the elder was a confessor during an era of persecution, while Thecla was a virgin who spurned marriage, desiring instead the virtuous life of celibacy and suffering thereby. The connection to martyrdom, therefore, emerges from the very beginning of the account, and Macrina's lot in life would be a lifelong struggle against sin, a struggle in which, as Gregory indicates, she was victorious upon her death, citing traditional relevant passages (2 Tim. 4:7–8).

A little further into the narrative, Gregory relates a premonitory dream about his sister on his way to visiting her. In his dream, he felt as though he were in a sacred procession, "carrying the relics of a martyr."[136] The remains glowed blindingly, like a bright flash, and the vision "appeared to me three times" that night.[137] He later reflected, "What I saw lying before me was really the remains of a holy martyr, who lay dead to sin, but shone with the grace of the Holy Spirit."[138] The "hidden meaning" (*ainigma*) of the vision was clearly revealed upon her

132. Gregory of Nyssa, *Life of Macrina* 31 (Petersen, 77).

133. See chap. 4; see also Stephen Davis, *The Cult of St. Thecla* (Oxford: Oxford University Press, 2001).

134. Gregory of Nyssa, *Life of Macrina* 2 (Petersen, 52). See also Maraval, 144–45.

135. Gregory of Nyssa, *Life of Macrina* 2 (Petersen, 53; Maraval, 146–49).

136. Gregory of Nyssa, *Life of Macrina* 15 (Petersen, 63).

137. Gregory of Nyssa, *Life of Macrina* 15 (Petersen, 63).

138. Gregory of Nyssa, *Life of Macrina* 19 (Petersen, 66).

death shortly thereafter, and Gregory recalled his dream as he observed Macrina's glowing body prepared for burial. In contrast to Antony's directions concerning the lack of ceremony surrounding his death and the obscurity of his final resting place, Macrina's bier was escorted by throngs of people who had "passed the whole night around her, singing hymns just as they would have done for the feasts of the martyrs."[139] Her destination was also quite deliberate and worked together nicely with Gregory's purpose to associate his sister with the holy martyrs. Not only would she be buried with her saintly parents, but the actual chapel (on their estate) was also a shrine to the memory of the Forty Martyrs of Sebaste (or at least contained some of their remains).[140]

CAUSATION

In this narrative Gregory indicates a threefold causation, much the same way it appears in the *Life of Antony*: the divine call of God, the freely undertaken vow of the saint, and the fierce opposition and even persecution of the devil, whose mission it became to hinder the saint's spiritual progress. The supernatural events surrounding her birth (essentially prophesying the manner of her life) indicate that this life of virginity, "the angelic life," was not randomly chosen but constituted a divine invitation to a vocation.[141] This invitation she freely and eagerly accepted, and once her earthly betrothed had passed away prematurely, she dedicated herself to her eternal spouse alone. Once she had "made up her mind," Gregory states, her resolve was unshakable.[142] The free will and unflinching steadfastness of the saint are highlighted throughout the narrative in conflict with demonic opposition, an opposition that actually provides opportunity for spiritual growth. In this regard, Gregory intrepidly used the vocabulary of the classic (pagan) historiographical tradition as well as biblical terms and imagery. For the death of Macrina's fiancé, Gregory blamed "Envy" (*Phthonos*), which "cut off these promising hopes by snatching him from life at an age to arouse our pity."[143] Naucratius's death was "due, in my opinion, to the plotting of our Adversary" (*antikeimenou*, "enemy").[144] Each disaster or misfortune (*symphoran*) Macrina encountered constituted

---

139. Gregory of Nyssa, *Life of Macrina* 33 (Petersen, 77).
140. Gregory of Nyssa, *Life of Macrina* 34 (Petersen, 78).
141. In her deathbed prayer Macrina expresses her own belief that her lifelong chastity was a divine vocation to which she was called, saying that for God she was "snatched from my mother's womb" (Gregory of Nyssa, *Life of Macrina* 24 [Petersen, 71]).
142. Gregory of Nyssa, *Life of Macrina* 5 (Petersen, 54).
143. Gregory of Nyssa, *Life of Macrina* 4.18 (Petersen, 54; cf. Maraval, 154).
144. Gregory of Nyssa, *Life of Macrina* 9 (Petersen, 58; cf. Maraval, 170). The "image of the cross" is given to "destroy the adversary" (*Life of Macrina* 9.6 [Petersen, 58], 24.19 [Petersen, 71]).

a temptation to wither, collapse, or regress spiritually; the saint must prove victorious by resisting the urge to react in a natural, human way. Virtue requires that loss be borne with strength, overcoming by reason the sorrow that leads to an overwhelming grief that could plunge one into unmitigated depression. Narrating the close sequence of deaths (Naucratius, Emmelia, Basil), Gregory compares Macrina to gold in the smelter. As gold is purified by being tested on three different occasions, so was Macrina thrice tested and purified as gold. "The lofty nature of her thought was tried from every direction by successive blows of fortune [*symphoran*], but she displayed purity and steadfastness of soul . . . [and] remained firm, like an athlete who could not be defeated [*athlētēs akatagōnistos*], and never flinched at the blows of fortune [*symphorōn*]."[145] In this imagery, the story of Job comes to the fore, and Gregory probably has in mind a verse like Job 23:10, as Job was also tested by God through the agency of the devil. Finally, as Macrina faced the final stages of death, she called the devil both the biblical *drakontos* (serpent, dragon) and *Baskanos* (the Jealous one), a classically derived designation for evil causes, similar in function and meaning to "envy."[146]

Saint Melania, Pilgrim Ascetic

NARRATIVE

Our third and final narrative illustration concerns Melania the Younger, a high-born Roman aristocrat, in whose blood pulsed a fervent desire for poverty, chastity, and humble, hidden service to the Lord and his church. Little is known of Gerontius the priest, Melania's most thorough biographer. It appears that he knew her personally and witnessed her deeds and benefited from her teachings in person. She possibly sponsored and mentored him, and he felt indebted to her for that, as well as crediting her prayers and godly influence for his salvation. Melania lived in a historically turbulent period for the Roman Empire, when the nomadic tribes in the North were pressing in on the empire's borders, resulting in frequent military clashes, incursions, and outright invasions, as when Alaric and the Visigoths burned Rome in 410. The church experienced its own internal turbulence as the Christological controversies of the 420s and 430s escalated, and

---

145. Gregory of Nyssa, *Life of Macrina* 14.11, 14.28 (Petersen, 63; cf. Maraval, 188–90). In using *symphoran*, Gregory is at once conventional but also true to theological commitments in avoiding the term *tychē*.

146. Gregory of Nyssa, *Life of Macrina* 24.13, 24.37 (Maraval, 224). Petersen translates this as "the malignant Enemy" (71).

the likes of Cyril of Alexandria and Nestorius roiled the theological waters. This turmoil on various fronts is well reflected in Gerontius's biographical presentation. Although the struggles of the martyrs were in the distant historical past, they were still very much alive in the hagiographical tradition and ingrained in the church's collective identity. From beginning to end, Melania's life is depicted as a struggle (*agōn*), against her family, her in-laws and extended relatives, the Senate, and the devil. Gerontius feels inadequate to "describe such mighty contests [*agōnōn*]."[147] Throughout the narrative, her life is framed in the language of the martyrs' struggles and victories.

Melania was born in Rome around 383 (a few years after the death of Macrina) to Publicola and Albina, members of the highly esteemed senatorial class and a venerable Roman family, the Valerii. The fortunate marriage between Melania's grandparents, Valerius Maximus Basilius and Melania the Elder (the latter came from an extraordinarily wealthy Spanish family), created for the family fabulous wealth spanning multiple provinces, including Italy, Sicily, Africa, Brittany, Mauretania, Numidia, and Spain.[148] Having heard stories of her venerable grandmother, Melania the Elder, who became a very famous ascetic and traveled widely throughout Egypt and Palestine founding monastic houses and learning from holy men, Melania felt a fervor for the chaste and ascetic life. Her parents desired grandchildren, though, and therefore determined that Melania should marry. At age fourteen, she was married to a distant seventeen-year-old cousin, Pinian, a union that produced two children: a girl dedicated into a life of virginity, who seems to have died as a toddler or small child; and a prematurely born son, who died at birth. After that, Melania concluded that a conventional family life was not meant for her and that she was free to withdraw from the world and consecrate herself to the Lord, along with Pinian, who agreed to a celibate marriage henceforth. Gradually they eased their way into "the angelic life," all the while encountering family opposition.[149] Eventually their parents relented, and the pair finally withdrew at the ages of twenty and twenty-four. They first moved to the outskirts of Rome, to a family-owned villa on the Via Appia, and demonstrated their new commitment by wearing dark, cheap clothing, a way of showing outwardly their break from worldly extravagance (an act akin to taking on the monastic habit). They also ministered to the sick, provided for beggars, practiced hospitality to

---

147. Gerontius, *Life of Melania*, prologue, in *Vie de sainte Mélanie* [*Life of Saint Melania*], ed. and trans. Denys Gorce, SC 90 (Paris: Cerf, 1962), 124–25 (cf. Petersen, 311).

148. Gerontius, *Life of Melania* 11, 20 (Petersen, 318, 326).

149. Gerontius, *Life of Melania* 8 (Petersen, 316).

visitors, and ransomed many who were in exile for debt.[150] Desiring to be "perfect" (Matt. 19:21), they began selling their possessions (meaning great tracts of real estate, including many homes and servants), for which once again they encountered family opposition, this time from Pinian's side of the family. The kind of disbursement and divestment of property that Melania and Pinian proposed was considered an act of insanity by their social circle, so the family was understandably perturbed.[151] In order to resolve the dispute, it became necessary for them to appeal to "Empress" Serena, a member of the royal family. In the end, the lavish and expensive disputed property was burned by the Visigoths in 410, and the property became worth "less than nothing."[152] On another occasion when they sold substantial tracts of real estate, they were vindicated by later events. The developed land that they sold for an excellent profit was later devastated by foreign invaders and would have been worthless. As it turned out, Melania and Pinian were able to use that money for their travels, for ransoming captives on an unfortunate island overtaken by barbarians, and for endowing monasteries and hermitages everywhere they traveled. Through their many benefactions, they showed themselves to be able and trustworthy stewards, and other donors were encouraged to entrust their money to the pair to distribute as they determined best.[153]

After they had sold their properties in Italy, Melania and Pinian used their money to help the church and the monastic movement in various ways, distributing money to endow monastic houses, donating silver to make holy liturgical vessels, and offering their own silk garments to make liturgical altar cloths for churches and monasteries.[154] Once they were "freed" of their vast wealth, they began a pilgrimage to fulfill their desire to meet with and learn from holy men, to visit monastic communities, to practice the austere asceticism they had begun, and to venerate shrines (*martyria*) and sites in the Holy Land. Their pilgrimage spanned from Italy to Sicily, then Africa (after Alaric's invasion and attack on Rome), where they spent seven years in Thagaste, the bishopric of Augustine's close friend Alypius. There they established and endowed two monastic houses, practiced asceticism, and Melania carried on a ministry of teaching and encouragement to virtue. In about 417, they

150. Gerontius, *Life of Melania* 9 (Petersen, 317).

151. Gerontius, *Life of Melania* 9–10 (Petersen, 290, 317–18).

152. Gerontius, *Life of Melania* 11–19, esp. 14 (see Petersen, 318–25, for the entire account of their efforts at complete disbursement and generous distribution. Gerontius intends this extensive narrative to show that Melania has overcome the diabolical enslavement to wealth: "the enemy . . . was not getting the better of her" but was instead soundly trounced).

153. Gerontius, *Life of Melania* 19 (Petersen, 325–26, 330).

154. Gerontius, *Life of Melania* 19 (Petersen, 324).

set out for Jerusalem and lived there about two years until they received (unexpectedly) a sum of money from the sale of their properties in Spain. With this money, then, they funded a pilgrimage to the desert fathers in Egypt. In 419 or so, they returned to Jerusalem. In 420, her mother Albina died, and Melania entered a period of seclusion in her cell within the women's monastery she built on the Mount of Olives. That monastery housed around ninety virgins and also contained a chapel that served as a *martyrium*, since she had deposited in it "relics of the holy martyrs."[155] Melania lived with this community for fourteen years, Gerontius writes, but was not their mother superior; instead, "she was so excessively humble" that she had appointed another woman to direct the convent, while she herself served the virgins and practiced her own rigorous asceticism.[156] She lived and worshiped with them, teaching and exhorting them to pursue the virtues, especially love and humility; they in turn loved her dearly as a mother. Around 432, Pinian died, driving Melania into a second period of seclusion, during which, Gerontius laments, "she became excessively thin, being wasted away through fasting, vigils, and incessant mourning."[157] Two more building projects awaited her, the construction of a men's monastery and another shrine nearby, which would house other relics. Two personal matters occupied her as well: namely, witnessing to Volusianus, an uncle of hers who was yet a pagan and who eventually received baptism on his deathbed; and strengthening a friendship with the Western empress Eudocia (wife of Theodosius the Younger) and "the imperial ladies who loved Christ."[158] Eudocia journeyed back to Jerusalem with Melania to visit the Holy Land and Melania's community, celebrating with them the deposition of relics into the new *martyrium* near the men's monastery. About the year 439, Melania grew ill around Christmastime, but she still eked out sufficient strength to celebrate the feast day of Stephen the protomartyr at her own shrine, which contained some of his relics. Several days later, possibly December 31, surrounded by her community of holy men and virgins, and clad in various garments belonging to other holy men and women, Melania "departed for heaven, clad in her virtues, as in a cloak."[159]

TOPOI

Many themes in the narrative overlap with ones appearing in the previous two biographies—in fact, too many to reiterate and tease out.

155. Gerontius, *Life of Melania* 48 (Petersen, 340).
156. Gerontius, *Life of Melania* 41 (Petersen, 336).
157. Gerontius, *Life of Melania* 49 (Petersen, 341).
158. Gerontius, *Life of Melania* 56 (Petersen, 346).
159. Gerontius, *Life of Melania* 70 (Petersen, 358).

Melania's holiness (*tēs hagias*, "the holy one") and physical beauty are highlighted, as are her desire for virginity and chastity as a vocation, her many virtues, and her rigorous ascetic practices. She and Pinian embarked on the "angelic life" (as did the previous saints), and both cultivated humility and extreme generosity. Their humility in dress, voluntary poverty, and generosity to the church via endowment of monastic houses both signaled their detachment from the priorities of the world and in some sense cut them off from the possibilities accorded to them by wealth, which was their birthright.

Another familiar theme that emerges is Melania's "masculinity." In his prologue, Gerontius praised "her truly masculine acts [*andragathemata*]."[160] Her detachment and ascetic practices gave her such a reputation that, according to Gerontius, when she had occasion to visit the desert fathers,

> the saintly fathers [*hagiōtatoi pateres*] received Melania as though she were a man [*andra*]. It can be truthfully said that she was a woman of more than average feminine ability ["she surpassed the measure of a woman" (*gynaikeion metron*)] and that she had acquired a masculine [*phronēma andreion*, "masculine mind-set"], or rather, a heavenly cast of thought. They were therefore at one with the holy fathers.[161]

Normally women were perceived not only as spiritually inferior but also as a temptation to male ascetics. Denys Gorce explains that this passage highlights the classical contrast, which we have observed elsewhere, between masculinity associated with reason and therefore virtue, and femininity associated with the passions and therefore vice.[162] It is a contrast leveraged for hagiographical effect by both Gerontius and Gregory of Nyssa above.

Pilgrimage is a feature absent from the prior accounts. The couple expressed a desire to see and venerate holy sites, especially those associated with Jesus.[163] As they moved around, they overnighted at shrines of various martyr-saints, including Phocas, Euphemia, and Leontius. As a wonderful outcome, these two pilgrims actually spread their wealth to these places, facilitating their continued existence as hospitality stops along the way for other pilgrims. Melania held theological *orthodoxy* in the highest regard and made it her business not only to read the Scriptures diligently but also to be a student of the church's teachers, such as Augustine and Alypius. Gerontius gives examples of Melania's

---

160. Gerontius, *Life of Melania*, prologue (Petersen, 311; cf. Gorce, 126).
161. Gerontius, *Life of Melania* 39 (Petersen, 334–35; cf. Gorce, 201–3).
162. Gerontius, *Life of Melania* 39 (Gorce, 202n1).
163. Gerontius, *Life of Melania* 34 (Petersen, 331).

active promotion of sound doctrine and repudiation of heresy (in her day, Nestorianism), even as Antony had repudiated the Arians and Meletians.[164]

REMEMBRANCE

The church commemorates each of the three saints discussed in this chapter through written accounts as well as the liturgy and feast days on the Christian calendar. All three biographies were produced at someone's request: a community, a close friend, or a cleric. In distinction from the other two narratives, Gerontius's prologue shows evidence that his account was read aloud in church on Melania's feast day (December 31), as he begins with the phrase "Bless me, Father" and continues to address himself to the presiding cleric.[165] Her life and the incidents Gerontius selected are those that proved most useful (in his opinion) to a person's spiritual growth. She had lived a life worth remembering, full of "outstanding virtues" and "mighty contests," and he believed that his account would "arouse in [the listeners] a zeal for virtue," especially for those wanting to dedicate themselves to God.[166] Through the memorial shrines, Melania in turn facilitated remembrance of martyrs who had fought bravely under persecution and thereby (unintentionally) memorialized herself as well.

MIMĒSIS

Gerontius wrote that when he remembered Melania's teachings, it spurred him to dwell on "her very great virtues," and he wrote about her life so that his audience would imitate her devotion and spiritual zeal, her ascetic practice, generosity, and humility.[167] Her own role models included biblical and traditional figures, plus members of her own family. Biblical examples included Mary and Martha: she patterned her endowment and care for the monastic houses after Martha, and her rigorous Bible study and asceticism after Mary. Effectively, she had followed one as a model of the active life and the other as a model of the contemplative life. After her Bible study, in which she took copious notes in little notebooks, Melania "went through the lives of the Fathers as if she were eating a cake."[168] Presumably these were the lives of the desert fathers, but they probably included some martyrs and great teachers as well. As for her family heritage, she seems a person of

164. Gerontius, *Life of Melania* 27–28 (Petersen, 328–29), 54 (344–45).

165. Gerontius, *Life of Melania*, prologue (Petersen, 311).

166. Gerontius, *Life of Melania*, prologue (Petersen, 312), 29 (Petersen, 329–30).

167. Gerontius, *Life of Melania*, prologue (Petersen, 312).

168. Gerontius, *Life of Melania* 22–23 (Petersen, 327).

great spiritual intensity like her grandmother and namesake, Melania the Elder. Probably the example of Paula the Elder influenced her as well, and we learn through the *Life* that she and Melania were cousins, and that Melania in turn influenced Paula's granddaughter of the same name to leave her aristocratic Roman life and descend "to the depths of humility," reminiscent of Macrina's influence on Basil or on their mother, Emmelia.[169] Additional evidence tells us that the ascetic bishop Paulinus of Nola was related on her father's side, and the virgin Asella was her aunt, her mother Albina's cousin.[170]

CAUSATION

Melania's entire narrative is framed by her struggle with the devil, who appears almost on every other page. As a causative force, the devil primarily functions as an agent of hindrance to spiritual progress. The devil placed barriers in her path to virtue via the temptation of worldly wealth and status, parental denial of the vocation of virginity, illness and physical pain, heresy in the church, and strife among fellow Christians. The traditional terms for an evil cause appear in Gerontius's history as well. The devil is "the enemy of truth" and of "the good," who was "envious [*phthonēsas*] of the young people's ardour for God," and later he was envious of the results of Melania's orthodox teaching, threatening her with bodily affliction; but he is soundly defeated by love and humility.[171]

In many ways, Melania is portrayed via elements derived from accounts like the two treated above, although the language and themes of Neoplatonism are largely absent here, showing a return to the language and themes of desert asceticism. Upholding Melania and propelling her forward into increasingly difficult "contests" and projects was not only her free will—that is, her own desire to follow God in the footsteps of her role models—but also something that did not appear in the prior accounts: the "wound of love [*erōti*]" that fueled her desire for "bodily chastity" and for visiting and venerating places made holy by Jesus and saints who had died for him.[172] This "wound" was divinely given and constituted her calling by God, by which she set herself apart for him and progressed to even greater heights of virtue.[173] Her burning

169. Gerontius, *Life of Melania* 40 (Petersen, 335).

170. The correspondence of these relatives with Jerome provides many clues to the relationships among this extended aristocratic family. Gorce (SC 90:27) provides a helpful family tree. It was to the estate owned by Paulinus that Melania and Pinian first withdrew (Petersen, *Handmaids of the Lord*, 325).

171. Gerontius, *Life of Melania* 10 (Petersen, 317–18; cf. Gorce, 144). For the devil's defeat through love and humility, see Gerontius, *Life of Melania* 42–43, 54 (Petersen, 337, 345).

172. Gerontius, *Life of Melania* 1 (Petersen, 313).

173. Gerontius, *Life of Melania* 32 (Petersen, 330).

love and zeal for God and his saints consumed her and inspired her to undertake pilgrimages and monastic building projects, thereby memorializing holy people and places more permanently. As she loved God ardently, she also loved and revered the saints and martyrs, honoring them as a kind of extended family, associating with them through their relics that she collected and preserved, addressing them as the "Athletes of the Lord," and communicating with them through prayer. This account, composed later than the previous two, shows clear evidence of the development of the *cultus* of the martyrs; remembrance fueled by love has progressed to veneration and intercession, definite markers that point to the devotional practices of the medieval church.

Maintaining Continuity and Constructing Identity through Hagiography

The hagiographers drew subtle and explicit parallels between their own time and the era of the martyrs. These intentional links construct identity as they acknowledge that the Christian life is one of combat against the devil via passions of the mind and body as believers strive toward sanctification. Christians also saw themselves as *victors* in the fight, conscious *successors* of the martyrs, having taken up their mantle, and *continuators* of their struggle against invisible powers and principalities in high places, thus fulfilling the apostle Paul's vision of the Christian life as one of warfare (Eph. 6:11–17). We saw above that although Antony had a desire for martyrdom under Maximinus's persecution, he was not called to such, and therefore he returned to his ascetic life in the desert. Athanasius says he was preserved by God "for us." He became a catalyst for the monastic movement, a spiritual example, teacher, trainer, and doctor of souls. While Antony's life spanned both times of persecution and times of peace for the church, the two women here considered were at about two or three generations' remove from the persecutions. The narratives, then, must intentionally find ways to connect these women with the martyrs. Macrina is connected by her family lineage and is a martyr as a role model, while Melania appears connected to the martyrs through her devotional practice of veneration at the shrines of the martyrs on their feast days and by her service to their memory. These women are "athletes" in that they struggle with the passions and with opposition from various quarters—especially the envious devil—to their desire to live a life pleasing to their heavenly Bridegroom, and they are "trainers" in that they motivate others to holiness and cultivate virtue among communities of Christians.

In a very real sense, these biographies may strike us as foreign to our ways of thinking about being Christian. How are these figures of the early church along with their values alien to us? All three accounts seem to communicate an unhealthy disdain for the body and personal hygiene, possibly due to the encroachment of Neoplatonic dualistic anthropology, which is exemplified in the *vitae* of philosophical men. Antony and Melania refused to bathe so as not to be immodest (the latter bribed the servants not to tell her mother), Melania wore herself out with unnecessarily rigorous fasting, and Macrina refused to visit the doctor even when she was gravely ill (again, for the sake of modesty). Indeed, in denying the body, they were all trying to point out the value of asceticism for the soul: vice can penetrate to the soul through the body; therefore, subduing the desires of the flesh yields the immeasurable spiritual benefit of a beautiful soul. From a biblical perspective, the apostle Paul also indicated that the members of his body lead him into sin, evincing "another law" that works against the Spirit (Rom. 7:23). Paul is complemented by James, who clearly identifies the source of sin as "[one's] own desire," through which a person is lured into committing sin, resulting in death (James 1:13–15). Ascetic training, therefore, can produce discipline in body, mind, and soul. In addition, the writers portrayed their subjects as setting an example not necessarily attainable by mere mortals (despite what they claim in their editorial comments), but rather challenging the reader to a higher standard of virtue.[174]

Despite their sometimes peculiar and era-bound ideas and practices, these ancient Christians left a legacy for the church, including several valuable elements evangelicals can (and ought to) embrace. Ideas of the Christian life as a life of discipline, rather than of ease and leisure, emphasize the necessity of putting on the armor of God for *spiritual combat*. Understanding that the way to spiritual growth is not easy negates "easy believism" and casual, leisurely Christianity. It also guards against disappointment, discouragement, and confusion on the part of new believers when they cannot meet the standard of Christlike perfection and are tempted to slip back into the habits of the "old nature." Additionally, the church misleads believers to our collective detriment when it fails to explain the very real dynamics between the physical and spiritual world. The typical evangelical believer lives very much in the cultural mainstream, and with so many distractions and attractions demanding the believer's attention, it is easy to lose sight of spiritual truths that lie behind the visible. Surely we do new believers a disservice by not warning them up front, presenting the

174. Robert Wilken, *Remembering the Christian Past* (Grand Rapids: Eerdmans, 1995), 143.

Christian life as only something pleasant and easy because Jesus has prevailed against the powers of evil. We need to distinguish between calling on Jesus as Savior (in which it is certainly true that "Jesus paid it all"), and following Jesus as Lord, in which we are responsible for striving to live a victorious Christian life in the power of the Spirit sent by Jesus. In the life we live in the flesh, we are to be holy, striving for virtue, doctrinal orthodoxy, humility, and respect for church leaders. We must be morally and spiritually vigilant, powerful prayers, and acutely aware of the dual nature of the world as fleshly and tempting, and yet simultaneously the arena and proving ground of our spiritual commitment to a heavenly citizenship. In other words, believers must recognize that the nature of the combat is both internal and external. Temptations arise in the mind as well as the heart, as temptations to sin arose for the desert ascetics even when they had barely any material possessions!

The original intended audience would not have needed convincing of the benefits of *withdrawal* or retreat, but our culture can learn from these early Christians the idea of the desert and the importance of retreat. For Antony this was literal; for Macrina it was figurative, as her retreat was within the walls of her home; for Melania there were periods of both travel and seclusion, and through her benefactions she was able to arrange withdrawal as an experience for others within monastic communities. For all three, their seclusion was voluntary, and for Antony and Macrina it was permanent. The ascetics' ideal of withdrawal and desire for obscurity and hiddenness are a rebuke against human ambition and greed for power, position, prestige, and a taste for fame and luxurious living within and without the church. In the thinking of the desert ascetics, these things would be classed as "the desires of the flesh and the desires of the eyes and pride of life" (1 John 2:16), fleeting and deceptive worldly desires that will pass away along with the world itself. Withdrawal from the world breeds detachment and fosters this mind-set in every area of life vis-à-vis the world. In the *Life of Melania*, the desire for detachment from wealth is a constant theme, engendering struggle and demonic temptation, but in the end Melania feels it has been a burden from which she had been freed. She did not throw her wealth to the winds, however; detachment from money enabled her to freely and gladly invest it in God's work and for kingdom priorities. The ascetics strove for the eternal kingdom, for which they wished to present themselves as "without spot" and "perfect."[175] Of course if everyone remained hidden, where would the

---

175. See Eph. 5:27; 2 Cor. 11:2; Matt. 19:21; Athanasius, *Life of Antony* 2; Gregory of Nyssa, *Life of Macrina* 24.44–45; Gerontius, *Life of Melania* 9.

role models be? All three accounts bear testimony that the witness of these Christians was not forgotten and in fact became renowned in the church. Athanasius wrote that God revealed Antony,

> who was almost hidden in another world, set in the midst of such vast areas of solitude. He revealed him to Africa, Spain, Gaul, Italy, Illyria, even to Rome itself, the first city. . . . This occurred because of the Creator's kindness, He who always raises His servants to nobility, even against their will, so that they might learn that virtue is possible and not beyond the bounds of human nature and so that all . . . might thus be impelled . . . to imitate his blessed life.[176]

All three lives indicate that *virtue* is a state to which *all Christians* can attain if they are willing to cling to Christ and to undertake the rigorous training necessary to resist and defeat the devil in their lives.[177] The saints taught their disciples never to weary in the pursuit of pleasing God, and that to defeat the devil one must, in a sense, go back to the basics of discipleship: "live as dying daily," and in this way avoid sin. The "daily" part received heavy emphasis from Antony. If one examines oneself daily, provides daily accountability, and seeks to daily present oneself before God "pure of heart and ready to obey," in effect turning over a new leaf every day or starting fresh every day, one is less likely to fall into grievous and ongoing sin.[178]

Martyrs and saints (Christians whose lives seemed to merit a biography) functioned effectively as Christian *role models*, Christian heroes. These valuable historical examples are in the main forgotten by or unknown to evangelicals. One of the stark truths they convey is that saints are made, not born, and often they are made over a very long period of time. This truth emphasizes the need for consistent and sustained practice in the spiritual life to develop spiritual maturity.[179] In our time, stories of falling from grace seem to abound even in the evangelical community, and lifelong Christian heroes are rare. Practicing the virtues recorded by past generations of Christian disciples and offered up for imitation could inspire a new spate of role models worthy of emulation and perhaps even inscription for the generations to come. Perhaps the narratives above can encourage Christians to look within their own families for examples of a faithfully lived life and to trace a legacy of Christian virtue within their own family tree. These are not martyrs in the conventional sense, except that they bore

176. Athanasius, *Life of Antony* 61 (White, 68–69).
177. See also Wilken, *Remembering the Christian Past*, 144.
178. Athanasius, *Life of Antony* 7 (White, 14).
179. Wilken, *Remembering the Christian Past*, 134.

lifelong testimony to the work of God in their lives by their fasting and prayer and other devotional practices, by their love, hospitality, and charity toward others, by their generous giving to benefit the ongoing work of God through the church, and by the consistency and stability of their Christian walk. The nature of Christian discipleship has to do with dying to self, whether or not one perishes physically. Discipleship that involves "death" is both excruciating and liberating. Denying one's material desires in deference to Christ's desire to make us holy and righteous and to bring about his kingdom gives the disciple both discomfort and joy.

Evangelicals who identify historically with Reformation theology and with the accomplishments of the Reformation might feel an aversion to language of asceticism or any talk of monasteries, perceiving monastics as those who have left the world rather than remaining "in it" as Jesus desired his followers to do (John 17). Paul's admonition against (false and legalistic) "ascetic practices" (Col. 2:18–23 HCSB) may also alienate other readers.[180] Paul reminds the Colossians that they have been spiritually redeemed from bondage to "elemental forces" by the work of the Messiah's atoning death, and he cautions them not to then rely on physical, traditional, and legalistic practices for their salvation, since then they would effectively re-enslave themselves, trying by human doctrines to pay off a debt that has already been paid.

Nonetheless, there does seem to be a revival of interest in monasticism, especially in the more active and evangelistic kinds of orders like the Franciscans or Dominicans. As early as 2005, Rob Moll was using such phrases as "remonking the church" and "ancient-future activism."[181] Although an examination of the size and diverse interests of this movement is beyond the scope of this chapter, its very existence among some sectors of (mostly young and single) evangelicals speaks to the value of retrieving the fruit of the ancient monastic endeavor and the motivation that lay behind it—the active pursuit of holiness and the living out of the martyr ideal, albeit under quite different and newly challenging circumstances.

---

180. Paul does not actually use any version of the term *askēsis* in this passage, using instead the word *tapeinophrosynē*, which means low-mindedness or humble-mindedness.

181. See Rob Moll, "The New Monasticism," *Christianity Today*, September 2, 2005, http://www.christianitytoday.com/ct/2005/september/16.38.html.

ECCLESIASTICAL HISTORY

The Story of the Church

Any man who intends to commit to writing the record of the Church's history is bound to go right back to Christ Himself, whose name we are privileged to share, and to start with the beginning of a dispensation more divine than the world realizes.

—Eusebius, *Church History* 1.1 (Williamson, 2)

Church History Comes into Its Own

With the work of Eusebius of Caesarea (ca. AD 260–339), church history (or ecclesiastical historiography) as a genre came into its own. Although he admitted to using the works of a few predecessors in the field, Eusebius really was the first author of intentional, pointed narrative chronicling the establishment of the church and its various victories and struggles up to his time. He claims as much in his prologue: "I am the first to venture on such a project and to set out on what is indeed a lonely and untrodden path; but I pray that I may have God to guide me and the power of the Lord to assist me."[1] He explains that from the "scattered hints" of previous history writers who had left "partial

1. Eusebius, *Church History* 1.1 (trans. G. A. Williamson, rev. and ed. Andrew Louth [New York: Penguin, 1989], 2).

163

accounts of their own lifetimes,"[2] he has selected material he considered relevant to his task, "plucking like flowers in literary pastures the helpful contributions of earlier writers."[3] Robert Grant explains that "in the church libraries at Caesarea and Jerusalem he and his assistants had found no universal church history but only incomplete accounts by some historians of brief periods. What he did was to provide the first account of the church's life up to the year 302–303."[4] Although his account contains gaps and strong biases toward his agendas of interest, nonetheless his account is invaluable for elucidating the church's situation in its first three centuries, especially in the tumultuous transition leading up to Constantine's sole rule.[5]

Eusebius is hailed as the first church historian, but if one were to look at his *Church History* in the context of his other writings, it would become abundantly clear that he is not *primarily* a historian in the modern sense, but rather an apologist, which provides some clue to a major influence on his narrative history of the church. Johannes Quasten praises Eusebius as the "Father of Ecclesiastical History" and comments enthusiastically that Eusebius "combines with the greatest interest for the past a very active participation in the shaping of the present."[6] Quasten highlights Eusebius's position on the historical stage by calling him "at the same time an historian and a controversialist, a leading figure in the religious struggle of his times, one of the last Apologists and the first chronicler and archivist of the Church."[7] Eusebius's scholarship and research abilities were "simply astonishing" and preserved a wealth of nonextant historical documents.[8] In addition to panegyrics, a chronicle, and a gazetteer (geographical dictionary) of the Holy Land, Eusebius wrote apologetic, polemical, and dogmatic works, as well as exegetical and doctrinal works. It is therefore quite astonishing that this research librarian, apologist, and bishop should have come into the role of "father of church history" and become known by many *exclusively* in that role. Nonetheless, as Quasten writes with some rhetorical flourish, it was the *Church History* "which made Eusebius immortal."[9]

2. Eusebius, *Church History* 1.1 (Williamson, 2).

3. Eusebius, *Church History* 1.1 (Williamson, 2).

4. Robert Grant, "The Uses of History in the Church before Nicaea," *Studia Patristica* 11 (1972): 174–75.

5. Some of these agenda items included possible self-exoneration on charges of Arianism, a vindication of his hero Origen, praise for the emperor Constantine whom he greatly admired, and celebrating the triumph of the church of the martyrs.

6. Johannes Quasten, *The Golden Age of Greek Patristic Literature*, vol. 3 of *Patrology* (Utrecht: Spectrum, 1966), 309.

7. Ibid.

8. Ibid., 311.

9. Ibid., 314.

An intriguing question then follows: What was Eusebius writing, history or apologetic? In truth, Eusebius was doing both. He wrote a history based on apologetic goals and a particular theological vision, which were fleshed out through *pragmata* (deeds) and examples, and through historical causes upon which he expounded. Some modern historians of ancient history chastise Eusebius for his history's limitations as historiography (e.g., Robert Grant and Arnaldo Momigliano).[10] But when considered against an ancient backdrop of heresy, schism, and persecution, it is not difficult to see that Eusebius's endeavor was stamped by an amalgamation of literary influences. Driven by theological apologetics and deeply impressed by the events of his own day, Eusebius was also influenced by Old Testament historiographical themes (as found in Jewish apologetic precursors, whose works strongly leaned on the Septuagint), the history of philosophical schools and their teachers, and classical historiography.[11] His work, then, is recognizably historical in its literary format, which mostly follows classical conventions of historical writing. However, his motivation, themes, and causal explanations are squarely theological and based on traditional Christian apologetic.[12]

In fact, the *Church History* was not Eusebius's first historical work. He had composed an earlier two-volume work called *Chronicle* as well as accompanying *Chronological Tables*. Chronicles were clearly works of history and had a secular historiographical tradition as well.[13] Among Christian chronographers, these works were more apologetically driven and much less elaborate. Usually they contained an account of history from the beginning of the world down to the

10. Robert Grant, Arnaldo Momigliano, Edward Gibbon, and Jacob Burkhardt, among others, accuse Eusebius of various personal agendas that undermined his integrity as a historian. The designation of Eusebius as a church historian seems in dispute among older scholars, but in more recent scholarship, treatment of this bishop seems more nuanced and neutral, acknowledging both his theological biases and his shortcomings as a historian, as also his value as a primary witness of the events described and a preserver of ecclesiastical documents. See, e.g., Michael Hollerich, "Religion and Politics in the Writings of Eusebius: Reassessing the First 'Court Theologian,'" *Church History* 59, no. 3 (1990): 309–25; Devin Singh, "Eusebius as Political Theologian: The Legend Continues," *Harvard Theological Review* 108, no. 9 (January 2015), 129–54.

11. For an excellent study of Eusebius's Jewish apologetic precursors, see Gregory E. Sterling's monograph, *Historiography and Self-Definition: Josephos, Luke-Acts and Apologetic Historiography*, NovTSup 64 (Leiden: Brill, 1992; repr., Atlanta: SBL, 2005).

12. For more information on the chronicle as a literary form born out of apologetic, see William Adler, "Early Christian Historians and Historiography," in *The Oxford Handbook of Early Christian Studies*, ed. Susan Ashbrook Harvey and David Hunter (Oxford: Oxford University Press, 2008), 587; cf. also Sterling, *Historiography and Self-Definition*, on the necessity of defending Christians against various accusations, especially the accusation of novelty.

13. See Ernst Breisach, *Historiography: Ancient, Medieval, and Modern*, 2nd ed. (Chicago: University of Chicago Press, 1994), 60–63.

time of writing, so they are sometimes called a "universal" or "world chronicle."[14] They were quite popular among Christian writers and had two main aims: first, an apologetic aim to show that Christian origins were ancient and not "of late"; and second, to deal with times and days, especially the last days. Their interest in proving the antiquity of Christian origins necessitated going back in history beyond the foundations of Greco-Roman culture, as seen in the apologetic works examined in chapter 3. They needed to show how the Old Testament fit into secular history, and in fact apologists like Justin boasted that the biblical documents had been so well preserved that they could easily prove antiquity, unlike the Greek historians, who could only write about more recent events. They had to relinquish information about primordial human history to the speculations of philosophers and poets.[15] Some chroniclers, like Hippolytus and Julius Africanus, tried to reconcile apocalyptic passages in the Old Testament, like Daniel's seventy weeks, with events in their own time in order to work out when the end would come.[16] Chronicles were unlike classical historical works in that they concerned themselves with apologetic topics—for example, they argued that since Moses was more ancient than Plato, Christianity is more ancient (and more venerable) than Platonism and its respected philosophical ideas. They also had an interest in topics of a decidedly apocalyptic bent, like God's work in the world to bring about the consummation of the ages. Indeed, by Eusebius's time, debate over these topics already had a long tradition since the third century BC, when Hellenistic Jewish apologists unleashed their polemical chronographies against Greeks who had asserted their own cultural superiority over the Jews.[17] The Christian chronographers built upon the Jewish models, addressing topics dear to their own apologetic interests. Eusebius's *Chronicle* began moving away from the usual chronographical themes, preoccupations, and sense of triumphalism. He made a turn toward classical historiography so that his *Chronicle* stands out as a bridge between Christian chronography and classical historiography, which was still being written in his day by pagans like the historians Eunapius and Ammianus.

Other Christian historians followed Eusebius's lead in writing church history and—more or less—his format. Some of the more notable are two laymen from Constantinople, Socrates Scholasticus and Sozomen,

14. Brian Croke, "Origins of the Christian World Chronicle," in *History and Historians in Late Antiquity*, ed. Brian Croke and Alanna M. Emmett (Sydney: Pergamon Press, 1983), 116.

15. Adler, "Early Christian Historians and Historiography," 589–90.

16. Croke, "Origins of the Christian World Chronicle," 121.

17. Ibid., 118–20; see also Sterling, *Historiography and Self-Definition*.

and the bishop Theodoret of Cyrus from Syria.[18] Each historian left an account of the period between the emperors Constantine I (the Great) and Theodosius II (the Younger), roughly spanning the years 320–440. None of these successors are well known to most Christians, evangelical or otherwise, but the accounts they relate and the documents they have preserved help believers today to put together into an understandable, narrative framework "what happened" in our history as perceived and interpreted by Christians of previous centuries. When we value the historical writings of such early Christian historians as Socrates, Sozomen, and Theodoret, we acknowledge the importance of God's outworking in time and space of a providential plan for the cosmos. This plan is accomplished not just through the incarnation of Jesus (although that is a pivotal *kairos* for world history) but also through the testimonies and lives of many believers, only a fraction of whom are represented in the histories that have survived. If not for the narrative material in church histories, we would be faced with quite a fragmented history of Christianity in its early centuries. To Eusebius especially is owed a great debt for knowledge of persons—orthodox and heterodox—and their activities and written works, some of which would otherwise be unknown. While it is true that the accounts are (unavoidably) biased in one direction or another, they still help later believers understand the dynamics of ecclesiastical and theological development, as well as Christianity's development vis-à-vis the state. The biases, while a hindrance in some respects, nonetheless offer glimpses into Christian commitments in a formative and critical time in the church's history; and it is not an exaggeration to say that the principal commitment during the fourth-century doctrinal upheaval was the preservation of the "deposit" Paul urged Timothy to guard (1 Tim. 6:20), the preservation and survival of the truth of the gospel.

Using Eusebius's *Church History* as an example, this chapter will define the ancient understanding of *historia*, the components of a church history, and its usual topics. It is important to notice how Eusebius's product both resembled and differed from the traditional classical histories, and also what elements Eusebius appropriated from the historiographical books of the Old Testament. A brief overview of the church's historical, narrative sources, written by two laypersons and one bishop, gives an idea of how Eusebius's influential model was

---

18. Theresa Urbainczyk argues that Socrates was possibly not a lawyer (based on lack of internal evidence of such training and knowledge) and that the added title "Scholasticus" is of a late dating in the manuscripts. See Urbainczyk, *Theodoret of Cyrrhus: The Bishop and the Holy Man* (Ann Arbor: University of Michigan Press, 2002), 13–14; David Rohrbacher, *The Historians of Late Antiquity* (London: Routledge, 2002), 108; Urbainczyk, *Socrates of Constantinople* (Ann Arbor: University of Michigan Press, 1997), 13–14.

appropriated in the following generations, even under very different historical circumstances. Most attention will focus on the projects of the two bishop-historians, Eusebius and Theodoret, especially on their Christian understanding of historical causation. These bishops' understanding of how and why historical events happen turned on their concept of a sovereign God's wise providence, leaving no room for fate or chance, as their secular contemporaries understood history. As in previous chapters, the four major historiographical features will be traced from the histories of these ancient writers. Finally, the chapter will draw some conclusions with respect to the identity-forming function of reading and writing the church's narrative history.

Ancient History: What Is It?

Chapter 2 delineated some of the ancient views of classical historical writing and provided an overview of the authors' intentions and the audience's expectations. Broadly speaking, histories contained two major parts: a prologue and a narrative body divided into books. The prologue introduced the history, while the narrative body fleshed out the author's historical concept(s). Prologues commonly made some sort of claim to truthfulness, possibly revealed sources to bolster credibility, and set out for the audience the author's overarching plan for the work, sometimes called a *hypothesis*. The prologue also frequently indicated the author's methodology in gathering and organizing information, as well as his access to sources.

Keeping the audience interested required clear writing and a compelling story, which was mainly achieved by skillful *selection* of content. The writer needed to ensure steady and well-paced plot progression and a smoothly flowing narrative. His success in keeping the listener or reader involved turned on knowing what elements and stories to include, as much as what to jettison. Maintaining an audience's attention also required engaging details, which could manifest themselves as *digressions* into the history and customs of other ethnic groups and nations (ethnography); speeches of generals, senators, or emperors; and anecdotes, particularly concerning issues or items that the author deemed of interest to the audience.

Usual topics for a history involved politics, primarily writing about the emperor, the government, and matters of state; natural disasters like earthquakes, droughts, and particularly bad storms or unusual weather; and national military events such as barbarian invasions and conflicts with bordering nations. A history could potentially turn into a hodgepodge of a work, more about the author's own antiquarian or obscure interests rather than the concerns of the audience, and some historical writers did come under criticism because their work was perceived as showing off their writing abilities rather than narrating, inspiring, teaching, and edifying.[19] For this reason, selection and balance of material and topics were essential. Overall, though, the characteristics of classical history are consistent with an audience's expectations of this literary form, since the term *historia* means "research" into the origins and causes of things.

Woven throughout the story, the historian's voice is heard narrating events, describing scenes, commemorating pivotal events and noble people and their deeds for posterity, making moral evaluations and judgments, and explaining the causes of various events, whether good or ill. In many (if not most) histories, inexplicable events were attributed to a divine cause of some kind, even if that attribution sounded conventional rather than truly religious. With the historian's voice emerges a particular, subjective point of view. Historians were driven by their own reasons to write down their stories, and most had not only participated somehow in the events they recorded, but also had some definite opinions about their results. For example, Thucydides had himself participated in the Peloponnesian War as a commander. Tacitus wrote as an experienced senator who despised imperial tyranny and the demise of the republic. The soldier-historian Ammianus Marcellinus fought in military campaigns under Constantine's son, Constantius, and later under the leadership of Julian (the Apostate) after him.[20] Eusebius, Socrates, Sozomen, and Theodoret had all interacted with at least some of those whose deeds they describe in their books.

Historiography functioned well as a vehicle for drawing out lessons from events and their consequences, and it was not uncommon for the writer to mention the audience, to appeal directly to the audience's sympathies or to their sense of moral rectitude, or even to indicate that he anticipated and intended to instruct a future audience many generations later. In addition (and significantly for our purposes), many histories rehearsed well-known national events in order to build a sense of national identity and ethnic pride by inspiring solidarity with the glorious past.

---

19. See Lucian, *How to Write History* 57 (in *Ancient Literary Criticism: The Principal Texts in New Translations*, ed. and trans. D. A. Russell and M. Winterbottom [Oxford: Clarendon, 1972], 547), on limiting flowery descriptions in historical works. Socrates criticizes Philip of Side, who composed a *Christian* history (not an *ecclesiastical* history) in about one thousand volumes. His style was so elaborate and the topics he treated so diverse (history, geography, topography, geometry, astronomy, math, music, etc.) that Socrates's judgment runs thus: "By forcing such irrelevant details into connection with his subject, he has rendered his work . . . useless alike, in my opinion, to the ignorant and the learned" (Socrates Scholasticus, *Church History* 7.27 [NPNF[2] 2:168]).

20. Rohrbacher, *Historians of Late Antiquity*, 18–19; see the entire first chapter on the work of Ammianus (14–41).

Ecclesiastical History: Like and Unlike

The Christian historians followed the classical format so that their works are recognizable as histories. The prologues followed the same pattern, introducing their works and outlining their themes. They treated many of the same topics, but included additional events that they considered material to the development (esp. doctrinal) of the church. Toward the middle of his *Church History*, Eusebius acknowledges the parallels and differences between classical and ecclesiastical concerns. In a brief preface to book 5, he wrote that while "other historians have confined themselves to the recording of victories in war and triumphs over enemies, of the exploits of commanders and the heroism of their men, stained with the blood of the thousands they have slaughtered for the sake of children and country and possessions," Eusebius's history, by contrast, concerns itself with elements that supersede the usual topics in importance.[21] Christian history, Eusebius wrote, is about "*peaceful* wars, fought for the very peace of the soul."[22] Rather than fighting for country and children, Christians fought for "truth" and "true religion."[23] His history is intended to record for posterity the "courage and endurance" of these "champions of true religion" and their "triumphs over demons" and "invisible opponents."[24] His history, in other words, will treat not the perils and glories of earthly warfare but those of spiritual warfare, including the victorious, imperishable "crowns" won by these (martyr) warriors; his account will make them "famous for all time."[25]

Historiography in Light of Eusebius

In the post-Constantinian *Sitz im Leben* of Christendom, Eusebius's almost exclusive focus on the church rather than political or military events would become impossible. When the emperor converted to Christianity, church history could not ignore politics; or to put things another way, politics and military matters again became central concerns of history, even history written by Christians—but with a twist. In the new era, theological disputes among bishops over heresies like Marcionism, Montanism, Manichaeanism, and Arianism took the place of political disputes among senators; and cross-cultural missionary activity among

21. Eusebius, *Church History* 5, preface (Williamson, 138).
22. Eusebius, *Church History* 5 (Williamson, 138, emphasis original).
23. Eusebius, *Church History* 5 (Williamson, 138).
24. Eusebius, *Church History* 5 (Williamson, 138). Here he reflects the mind-set evident in the third- and fourth-century martyrdom accounts as well as the hagiographies.
25. Eusebius, *Church History* 5 (Williamson, 138).

non-Roman nations such as the Persians, Scythians, Goths, and others took the place of historical ethnography. Through various digressions in the narrative—a characteristic feature of historical writing that connects to the audience—Theodoret notes with approval the conversion of the "Indians" (possibly referring to Ethiopia), the "Iberians" (modern Georgia in the Caucasus region), and Constantine's interest in eliminating the persecution of Christians in Persia.[26] Socrates commends the missionary and Bible translation efforts of the bishop Ulfilas (though he was an Arian) among the Goths across the Danube River.[27] He also highlights the embrace of Christianity by the Persians through the ministry of the holy bishop of Mesopotamia, Maruthas, and the conversion of the Germanic Burgundians under the pious emperor Theodosius II.[28]

Another traditional focus of history that the church historians elevated dramatically was the imperial office itself. Eusebius's portrayal of Constantine in both the *Church History* as well as a panegyrical biography called the *Life of Constantine*, set the stage for an imperial theology that would become standard in Byzantine historiography. A host of philosophical virtues stemming from ideas of Hellenistic divine kingship became associated with the imperial office based on Plato's maxim that rulers should be philosophers or vice versa.[29] The kingship became invested not just with cardinal moral virtues like courage, prudence, temperance, and justice, but also with further developed imperial Christian virtues like magnanimity and generosity (*philanthrōpia*), kindness and mercy, meekness and gentleness (*praotēs*). The perfect ruler must be "noble, wise, brave, dignified, kind, merciful, just, devoted to his people, chaste in his private life, moderate, generous, truthful, prudent, self-restrained, modest. The prince should be a good soldier, show mercy to the enemy; he should provide for his people in peace; reward the deserving and help the needy; correct public morals, and check the royal expenditures. He should be a leader in mind and example, who is himself hardworking and good."[30]

Eusebius was familiar with Hellenistic concepts of divine kingship. He appropriated and adapted for Christians the idea that the ruler is a

---

26. Theodoret, *Church History* 1.22–24. Socrates and Sozomen report these events as well.

27. Socrates Scholasticus, *Church History* 4.33 (NPNF[2] 2:115); also in Sozomen, *Church History* 6.37 (NPNF[2] 2:373–74), noting that the Gothic Arians even experienced persecution and had their own martyrs.

28. Socrates Scholasticus, *Church History* 7.8, 20, 21, 30.

29. Plato, *Republic* 5.473.

30. Lester K. Born, "The Perfect Prince according to the Latin Panegyrists," *American Journal of Philology* 55 (1934): 23.

copy of God's perfection.[31] The *Life of Constantine* is suffused with Hellenistic monarchic ideals: Eusebius presented Constantine as a perfect copy of God's virtue, a leader whose reason, soul, character, and mind conformed to divine virtues. For Eusebius, the monarch should be wise, righteous and just, temperate and courageous, as well as pious and not oriented toward temporal things; rather, he maintains an otherworldly perspective.[32] In book 10 of the *Church History*, Eusebius presents Constantine and his son, Crispus, as ruling on earth just as the Father and his Son, Jesus, rule in heaven.[33]

While not all Christian historians adopted as overtly Hellenistic a theory as Eusebius did, they followed his lead by retaining and rehearsing the aspects most desirable in a Christian monarch, chiefly piety (*eusebeia*), understood as doctrinal orthodoxy. Through piety, the ruler remained personally close to God; but he was also expected to be a teacher of piety to his people by reflecting divine virtues to them. Through pious education of his subjects, the ruler could eliminate disorder caused by impious or heretical forces. Thus he retained the favor of God, a favor yielding victory over enemies of the state, as well as peace for his subjects.[34] The emperor was expected to be a Mosaic or Davidic-style ruler, one who was close to God, inspired his people to move toward God as well, and strove mightily for peace in both church and state.

The historians after Eusebius appraised all monarchs by this rubric of piety and Christian imperial virtues: virtuous Christian conduct in a ruler results in successful leadership defined by a peaceful reign. For example, even as Eusebius had concluded his *Church History* with the incredible boon of peace brought about by Constantine, his continuators also deemed peace a fitting goal for an emperor.[35] In fact, David Rohrbacher interprets both Socrates's and Sozomen's histories as celebrations of "the peace in both church and state in [their] time, and an exploration of the causes of disunity in the past."[36] Socrates's conclusion marveled that Theodosius's rule was so peaceful that, at that point, he had nothing else to write; he had run out of material![37]

---

31. Frances Dvornik, *Early Christian and Byzantine Political Philosophy: Origins and Backgrounds*, 2 vols., Dumbarton Oaks Studies 9 (Washington, DC: Dumbarton Oaks Center for Byzantine Studies, 1966), 2:616.

32. Ibid.

33. Eusebius, *Church History* 10.9 (Williamson, 332).

34. Eusebius, *Life of Constantine* 5.1–2, 4–5 (NPNF[2] 1:585–86).

35. Eusebius, *Church History* 10.9 (Williamson, 332).

36. Rohrbacher, *Historians of Late Antiquity*, 116.

37. Socrates Scholasticus, *Church History* 7.42, 7.48 (NPNF[2] 2:176, 178). "In such a flourishing condition were the affairs of the Church at this time. But we shall here close our history, praying that the churches everywhere, with the cities and nations, may live in peace; for as long

Sozomen wrote that Theodosius was so pious that he did not even have to really fight the barbarian incursions over the border; rather, God fought for him![38] In fact, his description of the imperial family and their acts of devotion made the palace sound more like a monastery. Even Theodoret concludes with peace as a desirable goal, although from his own vantage point, it was not to be.[39]

Biblical Influences

Eusebius followed the literary model of secular historiography and appropriated some of its ideological themes, but an equally powerful influence shaping his historical writing was the Bible and its theological outlook. These twin influences produced a historiographical model for Christian historians after him, especially for bishop-historians like Theodoret. Early Christian historians, therefore, were fusing a biblical doctrinal perspective and apologetic aims with a basically classical format.

In addressing standard historical topics from a providential, moral, and specifically Christian (confessional) standpoint, church histories are most like Joshua, Judges, Samuel, 1–2 Kings, and 1–2 Chronicles. These books narrate Israel's history by using the framework of the reigns of judges and kings in Israel and Judah. The Deuteronomistic Historian (and Chronicler) assessed each judge or ruler based on the theological fidelity shown to the prescriptions of torah. While obedience (monotheism) resulted in divine blessing, disobedience (idolatry) resulted in divine censure and retribution.

The Jewish historian Josephus, writing around AD 93 or 94, continued this historical-confessional trend in the *Antiquities of the Jews*, which in its first ten books retells Jewish history based on the Old Testament and therefore adopts its ethical assessment scheme. Josephus's history tied blessing and success to virtue, and it tied punishment to vice.[40] In the works of later Christian historians like Eusebius and his followers, adherence to Christian morality and kindness to Christ's

---

as peace continues, those who desire to write histories will find no materials for their purpose" (*Church History* 7.48 [*NPNF*[2] 2:178]).

38. Sozomen, *Church History* 9.3, 9.16 (*NPNF*[2] 2:421, 427). Concluding his description of the pious lifestyles of the royal princesses, Sozomen writes, "For this reason, the mercy of God is manifested and is conquering in behalf of their house; for He increases the emperor in years and government; every conspiracy and war concocted against him has been overthrown of itself" (*Church History* 9.3 [*NPNF*[2] 2:421]).

39. Theodoret, *Church History* 5.37. See also below.

40. See Sterling, *Historiography and Self-Definition*, 295–97.

people resulted in blessing (e.g., Constantine and his father, Constantius, before him);[41] whereas persecuting God's people resulted in abominable suffering (e.g., the third-century persecuting emperor Galerius), consistent with the outlook of Josephus concerning the villainous Herod, an outlook adopted and quoted by Eusebius in book 1 of his *Church History*.[42] Similarly among the church historians, maintaining orthodoxy resulted in peace, prosperity, and military victories, while heresy led to shame, misfortune, and military defeats.

Church historians appropriated from the Old Testament historians two additional elements: one conceptual and the other methodological. The conceptual similarity between the church historians and the Old Testament concerns spheres of action. While much of the action in the Historical Books focuses on the royal court, nonetheless there exists a kind of parallel universe away from the court, the world of the prophets. Men like Elijah and Elisha ministered in the wilderness, away from the hustle and bustle of the capital cities, appearing at critical points to speak a divine word. Similarly, the famous figures of the monastic movement, whose abode of *askēsis* was the desert, received attention from the church historians, reflecting the interest and curiosity of the audience about these remote, venerated, and sometimes eccentric figures. Sozomen is especially generous in his descriptions of the monks of Egypt, Palestine, Syria, and Persia in a sizable portion of book 6, even referring to these holy men as "ecclesiastical philosophers" in the tradition of Athanasius's descriptions of Antony and the deep wisdom produced by his holiness, a wisdom that trumps worldly philosophy.[43]

In terms of methodology, Eusebius appropriated from the Old Testament something new and quite different from the classical historiographical tradition: the use of copious documentation. On this, we may compare the relatively neglected books of Ezra and Nehemiah, in which the authors inserted a number of documents, some overlapping between the two books. The point of the documentation in those books was to prove the legitimacy of Judah's actions in returning to their patrimony and reclaiming their land. In a time of acute vulnerability for the Jews, when the reconstitution of their nation seemed tenuous at best, in spite of glorious prophetic promises, the documents were intended to prove that the Persian overlords had legitimately granted the Jews permission to reestablish themselves as a nation in their homeland. Eusebius had a rich library of sources at Caesarea, and these documents proved the

41. Eusebius, *Church History* 8.17, appendix (Williamson, 281).

42. Eusebius, *Church History* 1.8, 1.11 (Williamson, 24–28).

43. See Sozomen, *Church History* 6.28–6.29, regarding holy men of Egypt; 6.30–6.31, disciples of Antony; 6.32, monks of Palestine; and 6.33–6.34, monks of Syria, Persia, and Edessa.

historicity of his claims about the church and its relationship with the state—one of relative tolerance and friendship because it functioned as an unfolding of God's plan.[44]

What Do Our Sources Look Like?

The church historians composed narratives with particular goals and aims. Some goals reflected classical or Hellenistic historiography (like that of Josephus and his predecessors), while others were more in keeping with the historiographical style and concerns of the Old Testament. They pursued the thread of the overarching, divinely ordered plan and purpose (telos) of history. Not surprisingly, the vision of Daniel 7 highly influenced Christian understandings of divine influence over human history (as seen in the martyr documents of chap. 4), and the sweep of human history revealed in Daniel 9 had inspired chronographers to predict the end times.

Eusebius is the undisputed founder of ecclesiastical historiography, being the first to deal with difficulties passed down to him by classical predecessors such as Herodotus, Thucydides, Polybius, and others.[45] He wrote his opus in ten books, followed by three continuators of the Eusebian program: Socrates wrote a *Church History* in seven books, Sozomen after him left an incomplete *Church History* in nine books, while Theodoret composed a work in five books, an extremely compact history as histories go.[46] Each historian demonstrates unique emphases, but in the main, the focus of this chapter will rest upon Eusebius and Theodoret, two bishop-historians. While they shared many thematic and literary similarities with the two laymen, their understanding and expression of historical causation differed markedly. It also bears saying that aside from this group of historians, there were in fact other contemporaries (pagan, Christian, and heretical) writing history at the time.

As far as we can tell, Socrates and Sozomen were both Christian laymen and lawyers from or in Constantinople. Socrates wrote his

---

44. This habit of Eusebius has also helped enormously in preserving (ironically) a sizable cache of pagan literature in his apologetic works, *Preparation for the Gospel* and *Demonstration of the Gospel*. He cites large portions from Porphyry (whose writings had been destroyed by Constantine, and later by Theodosius I), largely with the goal of showing how Porphyry contradicts himself.

45. See Eusebius, *Church History*, preface.

46. David Rohrbacher calls it "a stripped down version of the genre, lacking many of the digressions and secular details which Socrates and Sozomen had experimented with in different ways" (*Historians of Late Antiquity*, 132).

Church History first, and Sozomen apparently felt free to plagiarize and adapt portions of his material. Each had planned to cover the period from the reign of Constantine to that of his current monarch, Theodosius the Younger.[47] Virtually all the information we have about these two writers comes from their historical works; all other biographical details are speculative. Sozomen had previously written a (now lost) two-book historical summary of the church, intending to cover its history "from the beginning," but he knew that other writers (like the chroniclers) had already done that. Therefore he wrote his work from Christ's resurrection to 324, the defeat of Constantine's opponent and co-ruler Licinius. Although these two were valiant continuators, they did not have—as Eusebius had—the theological and ecclesiastical concerns of a bishop, especially one who had a high-profile, personal involvement in doctrinal controversy. Theodoret, who *did* share such concerns, wrote about eighty years after Eusebius, who died around 339. Theodoret came to the episcopacy of Cyrus around 423, but he had also written before then, in his monastic period, mainly apologetic and exegetical works. His *Church History* also began with Constantine, his narrative opening with the upsurge of Arianism in the early fourth century, countered by the decisive response of the Council of Nicaea in 325. He closed his narrative at 428, avoiding the events of his own times in accordance with the dictates of wisdom or convention. His silence regarding contemporary events (namely, the Christological controversies of the 430s and 440s) was undoubtedly intentional.[48]

Theodoret therefore had professional churchmanship and its exigencies in common with Eusebius: both were active Nicene bishops interested in history, exegesis, and apologetics. In fact, Theodoret seems to have drawn on Eusebius's double apologetic project, *Demonstration of the Gospel* and *Preparation for the Gospel*, for his own apologetic work, *Cure for Pagan Maladies*.[49] All of these works illumine our understanding of these two bishops' historiographic concerns, setting them

47. Socrates covers the period from Constantine's accession (306) to Theodosius II (439), while Sozomen begins at 323 (Licinius's defeat) and ends his narrative at 423, falling sixteen years short of his goal for inexplicable reasons.

48. Theodoret had personal reasons to voice—via his *Church History*—his protest at his treatment at the time of writing (probably the late 440s, as his emphases throughout suggest). He was most likely under house arrest at Cyrus (or Apamea), having been deposed by the "Robber Council" of Ephesus in 449, and he awaited the imminent, dreaded notice of what he was certain would be his end: physical removal from his see and banishment to some remote and savage corner of the empire (Stefana Dan Laing, "Theodoret of Cyrus and the Ideal Monarch" (PhD diss., Southern Baptist Theological Seminary, 2004). The last verifiable document we have from Theodoret dates from 453, but he may have died later, in 457 or 460.

49. Eusebius, *Demonstration of the Gospel*, 2 vols., trans. W. J. Ferrar (London: Macmillan, 1920); Eusebius, *Preparation for the Gospel*, trans. Edwin Hamilton Gifford, 2 vols. (Grand

apart from the laymen historians, whose concerns were more political, social, and religious than theological. Unlike the bishops, Socrates and Sozomen did not seem to feel the effects of doctrinal upheaval in a personal way in their own lives and did not feel burdened by pastoral obligations.

Historiographical Features in Church History

Narrative

Writing primarily for a Christian audience, Eusebius covers the first three centuries of the church's story, from the birth of Jesus to the emperorship of Constantine in his own time (ca. 324). He interprets the church's history theologically and in biblical terms for the Christian reader, making sense of "what happened" in a way that expressed his biblical-historical worldview. Throughout the work he pursues a clear thesis that unifies the story and builds Christian identity. Eusebius depicts the church as a nation of ancient and divine origin, and history as unfolding on the timetable of Providence. He outlines God's ancient plan for the church and indicates its fruition in his own day, facilitated by the Roman Empire and the Pax Romana (Roman peace) established by Emperor Augustus across the Mediterranean. In order to more clearly show the unfolding of this plan from eternity, Eusebius actually goes further back than Jesus's birth, even beyond the Old Testament and into the cosmic realm of the time of the preincarnate Logos. Beginning at the origins of the world puts Eusebius's work in close relation to the chronicle genre (his continuators do not begin at the same point), thus indicating some measure of apologetic concerns in the work to follow. He explains that Christianity, as humanity's primeval and true religion, had expressed itself across the ages through God's covenant dealings with the Hebrews and their righteous fathers, beginning with Abraham. The Mosaic law given to the people became known worldwide, so that "by the time the Roman Empire appeared, all nations . . . were ready to receive knowledge of the Father."[50] At that time, therefore, the "Word became flesh," coming to earth as the Savior of all, foretold by the law and the prophets. Constantine's conversion and reign fulfilled these promises completely: his empire extended God's kingdom on earth as history's

Rapids: Baker, 1981); Theodoret, *Cure for Pagan Maladies*, trans. Thomas Halton, ACW 67 (New York: Newman, 2013).

50. John R. Franke, "Eusebius of Caesarea," in *Historians of the Christian Tradition: Their Methodology and Influence on Western Thought*, ed. Michael Bauman and Martin I. Klauber (Nashville: Broadman & Holman, 1996), 65.

consummation.[51] In fact Eusebius ends his church history with the image of God the Father and his Son, Jesus Christ, reigning on high, mirrored by the (Christian) emperor Constantine and his own son Crispus ruling on earth. The enemies of God are also the enemies of Constantine, and God thwarts them, giving the emperor and his son victory and bringing about a reign of blessed peace, humanity, and "true piety."[52]

His history, not unlike classic histories, consists of two main sections: a *prologue* and the *body* of the work. The prologue lists the main points he planned to cover (sometimes called "programmatic statements"). Prologues varied in length: some were very brief—like Theodoret's, barely a paragraph—while others were quite long and elaborate, especially if they were dedications to significant people or official parties: Sozomen's history is dedicated to Emperor Theodosius the Younger and is expansive, ornate, and flattering. In one variation on the prologue, Socrates realized he had not written an adequate prologue that laid out his points for the reader, so he offered a set of programmatic statements in book 3. Eusebius's prologue can be considered more expansive than most: it actually extended to the end of book 1. In fact, in book 2 he refers to book 1 as a "preface."

In his programmatic statements, then, Eusebius wrote that he intended to lay out five main points. First, he aimed to trace the "lines of succession from the holy apostles," what he deemed to be the most "important events . . . in the story of the Church," and those men and women who distinguished themselves, "the outstanding leaders and heroes of that story."[53] Second, Eusebius intended to relate the opposing work of heretics within the church, whose program ran counter to God's divine mission for the church, and who polluted the church with their false doctrine and created havoc within the flock. Third, Eusebius narrated the tragic fate of the Jews as a result of their rejection of the Messiah. His fourth aim was to highlight opposition to "the divine message" from "unbelievers" outside the church and to display the heroism of Christians (martyrs) who were prepared to give their lives to defend that message. Finally, Eusebius intended to narrate the martyrdoms of his own time during a particularly extensive, empire-wide persecution at the turn of the fourth century, and to emphasize to the reader the "kind and gracious deliverance accorded by our Saviour."[54]

By providing an introduction such as this, a historian indicates to the reader which points he intends to elaborate so that the reader can

51. Ibid., 71.
52. Eusebius, *Church History* 10.9 (Williamson, 332).
53. Eusebius, *Church History* 1.1 (Williamson, 1).
54. Eusebius, *Church History* 1.1 (Williamson, 1).

follow the writer's argument or *hypothesis*. It frames the rest of the narrative so the reader knows what to look for (or listen for, if it is read aloud). This introductory material is similar to prologues found in the Gospels, a genre that is a special kind of historical biography. In Luke, the prologue indicates that the following narrative has been passed down through eyewitness accounts and "servants of the word," and is intended to bolster the faith in which Theophilus has been trained (Luke 1:1–4 HCSB). In John's Gospel, the prologue of 1:1–18 indicates that the Gospel's focus will be on the divine origin of Christ and the signs of his deity, and the following verses (1:19–51) set up various themes that will be treated in expanded ways throughout the Gospel. Indeed virtually every chapter of John's Gospel is in some way connected thematically and lexically to the prologue. Like John the Evangelist, then, Eusebius too commences his account with "a conception too sublime and overwhelming for man to grasp—the dispensation [*oikonomias*] and divinity [*theologias*] of our Saviour Christ."[55]

The body of the work is organized in classical, annalistic fashion, by the reigns of Roman emperors, a scheme followed by his continuators. Under each reign, Eusebius placed materials he accessed from his library in Caesarea regarding the teachers, bishops, martyrs, and heretics active during that period. His materials included letters, martyr accounts, and biographical information of famous teachers like Origen, whose life and ministry occupy the bulk of book 6. As he had need in the narrative, Eusebius also included sermons, like that for the dedication of a new church at Tyre (book 10); references to rescripts (an official legal response to an appeal) like Trajan's and Hadrian's (actually appended), prohibiting governors from hunting out Christians indiscriminately (book 4); Maximinus's rescript with charges against the Christians, posted publicly at Tyre (book 9); and legal ordinances or proclamations like the "Edict of Milan," legalizing Christianity and declaring a general religious toleration (book 10). By organizing his sections this way, he was both following convention and making a point. In good apologetic form and consistent with prior apologists, Eusebius intentionally gave the impression, "proved" by his history, that only the bad emperors persecuted the church. Usually these rulers came to an ignominious end, while the good emperors showed favor to the church, and the whole empire benefited thereby.

Throughout the initial portion of the prologue, Eusebius clearly emphasizes Christ as the head of the church, as its inspiration and fount of strength, and as its rightful Lord. His history must necessarily tie back to Christ. His book is not just a research piece nor a completely

---

55. Eusebius, *Church History* 1.1 (Williamson, 2).

objective history: it is factually and historically true and document based, but its origin and end are soteriological (*oikonomias*) and theological (*theologias*).[56] By his use of the first term, he indicates his intent to narrate the earthly/incarnate life of Jesus and the church's beginning in time as the medium of God's salvific plan for the world; and by the second term, he indicates that the church's beginning, like Christ's, was divine and not human. Indeed, Eusebius proceeds to explain Christ's preexistence, his theophanies or appearances to the Jews, and the true teachings and ethics imparted to the Hebrews through the torah. The prophets predicted the Messiah's coming, and he did eventually appear in time and space, in human flesh, as the historical Jesus of Nazareth, under the reigns of Caesar Augustus and Herod the Great.

In their selection and arrangement of historical material, many classical histories featured digressions, anecdotes, and speeches. While Eusebius included several digressions, he did not make up speeches; instead, he relied on documents, copious writings quoted at length. Eusebius's great advantage over classical predecessors, who had to rely mainly on the spoken word and oral transmission, was his access to the document-rich library at Caesarea. Sometimes Eusebius felt he did not need to write narrative; rather, he allowed the documents to narrate for him. While Theodoret did use speeches in his *Church History*—for example, in Theodosius's confrontation with Ambrose for murders at Thessalonika—he also cited plenty of documents. Socrates cited documents more sparingly at the beginning of his narrative, since he had a particular idea about how to write history—an idea that serves as something of a critique of Eusebius: the narrative should be smooth and readable. Citing whole documents (or large portions thereof) tends to interrupt the flow of the narrative and contributes to digressions. In fact, whenever Eusebius digressed, he usually cut the section off at some point, indicating to the reader that he needed to leave the narrative there and move on to his next point.[57] Socrates did increase his use of documents noticeably toward the middle and end of his narrative so that readers would have a fuller account of the events. Writing after Socrates, Sozomen also cited numerous documents (like Eusebius), some of them lifted directly from Socrates. Sozomen did not write in the reserved style of Socrates, but rather in a more florid style, characteristic perhaps of those who entered the kinds of writing or rhetorical competitions sponsored by Emperor Theodosius II.

---

56. Eusebius, *Church History* 1.1.7, in *Eusèbe de Césarée: Histoire Ecclésiastique* [*History of the Church*], 4 vols., trans. Gustave Bardy, SC 31 (Paris: Cerf, 2001), 4.

57. See, for example, Eusebius, *Church History* 3.4, 3.10 (Williamson, 68, 79).

How did the historians treat the audience through the narrative? How did they bring the audience into the action? Sometimes they tied past events to current situations or tried to flesh out the significance of past events for contemporary audiences. Eusebius did this at several junctures in his *Church History*. The historians offered personal comments and opinions, showing their research process or weighing the credibility of their sources. These comments persuaded and reassured the readers that the historian had pursued avenues into truthfulness by giving multiple points of view.

Remembrance

In prologues, it was a *topos* to tip one's hat literarily to the value of commemorating the past and preserving it for future generations. The historian also knew that a case for whatever overarching *hypothesis* he was proposing would need to be made to his contemporaries. It remains an unassailable truth that gaining a historical understanding of events and institutions can bequeath wisdom in thought and action and create a mind-set of decision making that looks to the long view, not to decisions necessarily driven by the political, social, or economic exigencies of the moment. Still, keeping alive the memory of past greatness is valuable and right *in itself*, and noble deeds and great people should be celebrated for posterity. Eusebius and Theodoret both state this principle directly.

Eusebius conceives the church and tradition both vertically and horizontally. He does tie his history to Christ the Savior (vertically), as he must. However, he also highly values the work of many generations of faithful women and men who have invested their very lives in witnessing for Christ and building up the church. They have lived and died to preserve and pass on the truth of the gospel, the "deposit" that must be guarded (1 Tim. 6:20). This horizontal view describes, in its very best and theologically true sense, the process of building Christian tradition, and it must be seen as valuable and worth remembering, not as baggage to be discarded or overcome.

In his project, he plans to pass before his reader(s) those faithful from a bygone age in the church and to preserve their memory. "If I can save from oblivion the successors, not perhaps of all our Saviour's apostles but at least of the most distinguished, in the most famous and still pre-eminent churches, I shall be content."[58] The term translated as "save from oblivion" (*anasōsaimetha*) carries the meaning of saving what could be lost or preserving something in the memory. He

---

58. Eusebius, *Church History* 1.1 (Williamson, 2).

wishes to preserve the memories of his narrative's heroes, the Christian leaders who guided the church after the apostles, and also to bring honor to the results of their work and life's investment as manifested and embodied in the "most famous and still pre-eminent churches" (*mnēmoneuomenas ekklēsias*, "celebrated/commemorated churches"). Evidently he intended to preserve the names and lines of succession of leadership at these churches for posterity, not merely to prove a point in his own time. What these heroes achieved was formidable because, as Eusebius relates in various places in his narrative, after the demise of the "living voice" of the apostles and others who had seen, heard, and spoken with the Lord Jesus, the devil's attacks on the church increased.[59] Aside from commemorating the martyrs as Christian heroes, Eusebius also remembers great Christian teachers who combated heresy and were therefore doctrinal heroes. These figures trained disciples in sound doctrine and produced ministers with moral character and Christian maturity for the church, and some became martyrs themselves. One particular hero who draws Eusebius's ardent admiration was the teacher Origen, a giant of scriptural interpretation, biblical translation, and creative theology. Book 6 mainly occupies itself with Origen's life, fame, ascetic spirituality, and death.

While seeing himself horizontally in a succession of disciples, witnesses, and bishops, Eusebius also saw himself as part of a historical community of ecclesiastical writers and acknowledges those who went before him in composing accounts (albeit partial) of their own times. He hails them as beacons, flaming torches somehow guiding him on the way to reach his goal (the conclusion of his project), even though their own projects were not of the same nature, that is, complete historical narratives from the beginning until their own time. Socrates also wrote with prior historians in mind—specifically Eusebius, whose name is the first word in his book. "Eusebius, surnamed Pamphilus, writing the History of the Church in ten books, closed it with that period of the emperor Constantine," when the Great Persecution launched by Diocletian had ended.[60] He was aware of other works by Eusebius, and remarks that he will supply "what [Eusebius] has left out."[61]

In his prologue Theodoret demonstrates a keen sense of what he was leaving behind for posterity through his writing: "When artists paint on panels and on walls the events of ancient history, they alike delight the eye, and keep bright for many a year the memory of the past. Historians substitute books for panels, bright description for pigments, and thus

---

59. Eusebius, *Church History* 3.32 (Williamson, 96).
60. Socrates Scholasticus, *Church History* 1.1 (NPNF[2] 2:1).
61. Socrates Scholasticus, *Church History* 1.1 (NPNF[2] 2:1).

render the memory of past events both stronger and more permanent, for the painter's art is ruined by time."[62] Preserving the memory of the past is one of the greatest and most enduring accomplishments of the historian's "art." He also indicates that he will intentionally pick up the church's story where Eusebius has left off, with Constantine, "the prince beloved of God."[63] Like Eusebius, Theodoret commemorates as heroes great Christian bishops who fought for sound doctrine in the church and often endured opposition, false accusations, compulsion to compromise, and sometimes physical violence or even death. These bishops provide an example of uncompromising orthodoxy for readers to emulate.

Mimēsis

Historians most often had a pedagogical intent and used historical examples to teach lessons and form character; this intention is clear in both secular and Christian sources. Eusebius was confident that "those who are eager to learn the lessons of history" will find his account "most valuable."[64] As in the biblical historical literature and also the historical material of classical antiquity, the monarchs as well as high-profile bishops received attention in terms of character assessment. Eusebius especially focused upon Constantine as a pious monarch. After Constantine, the empire was frequently divided among his heirs or along East/West lines. The monarchs (and bishops) are also distinguished in terms of their adherence to orthodoxy and piety or their fomentation of heresy or impiety. Within this rubric of piety/orthodoxy and impiety/heresy, the historians interweave the perennial character assessments of the classic historians: possession of the chief virtues (prudence/wisdom [*phronēsis*]; temperance/moderation [*sōphrosynē*], which can mean self-control in many respects; justice [*dikē*]; and fortitude/courage [*andreia*]); or victim of the chief vices (hedonism/pleasure [*hēdonē*], grief/distress [*lypē*], fear [*phobos*], or desire [*epithymia*], which sometimes refers to vices in general).

Virtually all historians in their presentation and assessments of various people on the historical stage paint them in terms of virtue and vice. For classical historians this meant political virtues and vices, while for Christian historians this included a combination of philosophical/political virtues and Christian virtues: for example, in Theodoret's account, the emperor Jovian was virtuous and orthodox (book 4),

---

62. Theodoret, *Church History* 1.1 (*NPNF*² 3:33).
63. Theodoret, *Church History* 1.1 (*NPNF*² 3:33).
64. Eusebius, *Church History* 1.2 (Williamson, 2).

while Julian was vicious, impious, uncontrolled, and heretical/pagan (book 3); Constantine was pious and orthodox (book 1), while his sons and heirs were impious and heretical (Arians; book 2); Theodosius I was virtuous and devout, orthodox, and a destroyer of paganism, and importantly for bishops like Eusebius and Theodoret, he was devout and respectful of ecclesiastical authority (book 5).[65] Theodoret even seems to offer mimetic examples to the monarch, possibly as a kind of "mirror of princes" (*specula princeps*), a political, historical, or panegyrical type of work that paints an idealized portrait of a monarch, sometimes in acute contrast to the ruler actually in power; in this latter case, a "mirror of princes" functions as a critique.

Causation

In his monograph *The First Christian Histories*, Glenn Chesnut explains, "History writing in the early Christian period was dominated by the pagan Greco-Roman historiographical tradition that went back to Herodotus. Within that tradition various historians held that the historical process was controlled by acts of Fortune, that human free will was under the rule of Fate, and that the gods intervened in history with omens, retribution, and vindictive acts of jealousy."[66] The Christian historians' literary context was the pagan historiographical tradition, still very much admired and followed in their own day. Aside from the previous three features that applied to the composition of history generally, there is a dramatic difference between the Christian and pagan perspectives regarding the specific issue of causation and historical progress. Early Christian historians explained causation in a way that acknowledged pagan, classical conventions but saw them as

65. See throughout Theodoret, *Church History*.

66. Glenn Chesnut, *The First Christian Histories: Eusebius, Socrates, Sozomen, Theodoret, and Evagrius*, 2nd ed. (Macon, GA: Mercer University Press, 1986), 7. It seems that Chesnut may be contradicted by Thucydides, Tacitus, and possibly others who strongly and explicitly suggest otherwise, although they do reflect the breadth of Chesnut's view. Whether or not they were in the majority is unclear. For example, Tacitus writes, "Or perhaps not only the seasons but everything else, social history included, moves in cycles. Not, however, that earlier times were better than ours in every way—our own epoch too has produced moral and intellectual achievements for our descendants to copy. And such honourable rivalry with the past is a fine thing" (*Annals of Imperial Rome* 3.55, trans. Michael Grant [London: Penguin, 1971], 146). A stronger passage might be the following, in which Tacitus muses on causation stemming from human free will: he remarks that Marcus Lepidus "played a wise and noble part in events. . . . This compels me to doubt whether, like other things, the friendships and enmities of rulers depend on destiny and the luck of a man's birth. Instead, may not our own decisions play some part, enabling us to steer a way, safe from intrigues and hazards, between perilous insubordination and degrading servility?" (*Annals of Imperial Rome* 4.19 [Grant, 167]).

problematic, and thus transformed them in accordance with Christian theological convictions.

"O, Fortuna . . ."

Classical historiography tended to explain causation as cyclic (recurrent) or unpredictable, and in terms of Fate (*Fatum/Moira/Heimarmenē*) or Fortune (*Fortuna/Tychē*). The idea of causation had several different aspects. It could be defined on the human plane as the explanation for historical progress, moving actions along and producing outcomes through human events. A further element in causation is Fate, which involved a deterministic aspect as well as a retributive one. Another element is Fortune, which expressed the mystery, inscrutability, and uncertainty of human events. Fortune could be viewed as beneficent or ominous (even retributive) and was sometimes depicted holding a rudder, indicating her "power to influence the direction of events."[67] Some development within these categories occurred from the pre-Socratics to the writers of late antiquity, but the elements of causation remained virtually the same.

Fortune was increasingly personified as a goddess with a geographically broad cultic sway. References to *Fortuna* and *Tychē* functioned for most Greco-Romans as a part of their vocabulary of uncertainty in human life, expressing the unknown, paradoxical, or unpredictable elements in the web of human events (as briefly noted in chap. 2). Esther Eidinow explains that in the Hellenistic age, anxiety about changing fortunes in light of Macedonia's soaring conquests under Philip and his son, Alexander the Great, became very acute, to the point that "its personified force, Fortune (Tyche), became an obsession," so that her statues were widely distributed.[68] By the third century AD, her cult statues and altars flourished throughout the ancient Near East, so use of the term *tychē* carried idolatrous baggage. Thus Christian historians consciously eschewed that terminology, appealing instead to the biblical concept of Providence (*pronoia*) to explain causal agency.

Both Eusebius and Theodoret were well aware of the philosophical issues and even addressed them in their own apologetic works. In the *Preparation for the Gospel*, Eusebius challenged the idea of Fate head-on, devoting book 6 to refuting the validity of Fate, which destroys free will; he even adduced pagan arguments against it. This book is

---

67. Esther Eidinow, *Luck, Fate and Fortune: Antiquity and Its Legacy* (Oxford: Oxford University Press, 2011), 50.

68. Ibid., 51.

flanked on one side by books 4 and 5, which refute idolatry and oracles as being of demonic origin and ongoing demonic, deceitful activity; and on the other side by books 7 and 8, which extol God's providence over the universe, drawing on predecessors like the Jewish philosopher Philo of Alexandria.

Theodoret wrote in his apologetic work *Cure for Pagan Maladies* that he knows that some people deify and revere *Tychē*, Fate, and Destiny, rejecting the "controls of providence . . . insofar as they can," and appeal rather to the "three Sisters" (the Fates) to explain life outcomes. He also repudiates the idea of enslavement to Fate or "compulsive necessity."[69] He explains the significance of the names of the Fates, adding that their number indicates "the three stages of time in which all things proceed in a circular motion and through which they are accomplished."[70] Throughout his *Cure* he interacts with various philosophers and their ideas of causation. Examining Stoics, Pythagoreans, Cynics, Epicureans, Plato, and Aristotle, Theodoret identifies points of convergence and divergence with respect to Christianity.[71] Both bishops believed firmly in human freedom and a beneficent, providential God, the Ruler of the Ages, the one who steers the "rudder" of the ship of the universe, and the "All-seeing Eye."[72]

Not surprisingly, in their historical projects the Christian historians displaced Fate entirely, replacing its deterministic aspect with the biblically informed idea of Providence, by which they meant the personal being of the Triune God of Christianity. He is God over the universe and lovingly controls all its aspects, including the harmonious workings of the cosmos (just as a captain pilots a ship by its rudder) and the created world's benefits to human well-being and prosperity. As had apologists before them, they recognized that the validity of Fate would mean the denial of God's omnipotence and freedom to act, as well as undermining the free will of humans as active agents in the cosmos who have control over their own lives.[73] Christian historians focused the source of universal control squarely on the biblical God, and the bishop-historians were especially careful to sidestep even conventional terms for *Tychē*; the laymen Sozomen and Socrates did not always exercise such scruples.

Writers identified retribution as one aspect of the pagan understanding of Fate. Sometimes historians referred to the "jealousy (*phthonos*) of the gods" as a cause of trouble for humans, brought about by representatives

69. Theodoret, *Cure for Pagan Maladies* 6.3, 6.15 (ACW 67:134–37).

70. Theodoret, *Cure for Pagan Maladies* 6.12 (ACW 67:136–37).

71. Theodoret, *Cure for Pagan Maladies* 6.13–92 (ACW 67:137–58).

72. Theodoret, *Cure for Pagan Maladies* 6.22–24 (ACW 67:139–40).

73. Nicola Denzey Lewis, *Cosmology and Fate in Gnosticism and Graeco-Roman Antiquity: Under Pitiless Skies* (Leiden: Brill, 2013), 181.

called *daimones*, which could be acting on an unnamed god's behalf or as free agents (as described by Herodotus).[74] *Tychē* could also become unpredictably jealous, being "apt to envy men . . . particularly where one thinks one is especially fortunate and successful in his life."[75] Envy (*Phthonos*) could manifest itself as a personified force in the universe, who could not tolerate mortal prosperity and happiness and therefore threw human events into upheaval and chaos. Christian historiography incorporated (as had hagiography before it) multiple facets of this concept of the jealousy or envy of the gods, using the biblical figure of the devil (together with his demons), the enemy of God and his people, the church. This agent (although subordinate) actively defied and attacked the church through persecution, heresy, or some combination of the two. The Christian understanding of causation and circumvention of its pagan overtones are nicely illustrated through a brief examination of Eusebius's and Theodoret's histories.[76]

Eusebius

Eusebius often mentions the guidance and protection of God, who is solicitous for the church's growth and spread. God granted the church favor with rulers like Tiberius, who found no reason to persecute Christians: "Heavenly providence [*tēs ouraniou pronoias*] had purposefully put this into the emperor's mind in order that the gospel message should get off to a good start and speed to every part of the world."[77] "Thus," he writes, "with the powerful co-operation of Heaven [*ouraniō*] the whole world was suddenly lit by the sunshine of the saving word."[78] Eusebius also includes, as he must, the intrusive agent of evil, the devil, using various stock terms for him throughout his narrative from book 2 to the end: "the evil demon," "envy," "hater of the good," "enemy of God's church," and "adversary"—in general, one who acts against humanity's interests out of envy and jealousy. In Eusebius's narrative, the devil functions as a malignant and jealous demon, an intrusive figure who can work through pagans, unbelievers, and idolaters to harm the church and dislodge it from its intended divine mission. The church's

74. Eidinow, *Luck, Fate and Fortune*, 100–102.

75. Ibid., 52, citing Polybius, *The Histories* 39, in *Polybius: The Rise of the Roman Empire*, trans. Ian Scott-Kilvert (London: Penguin, 1979), 540.

76. For a recent and detailed account of the devil's appearance in Eusebius, Rufinus, Socrates, Sozomen, and Evagrius, see Sophie Lunn-Rockliffe, "Diabolical Motivations: The Devil in Ecclesiastical Histories from Eusebius to Evagrius," in *Shifting Genres in Late Antiquity*, ed. Geoffrey Greatrex and Hugh Elton, with Lucas McMahon (Farnham, UK: Routledge, 2016), 119–31.

77. Eusebius, *Church History* 2.2 (Williamson, 39).

78. Eusebius, *Church History* 2.3 (Williamson, 39).

progress infuriates him, and since God has providentially removed or punished the devil's agents—persecutors like Pilate, Herod Agrippa, Herod the Great, and Herod Antipas—the devil decides to pollute the church with heresy: "As faith in our Savior and Lord Jesus Christ was now spreading in all directions, the enemy [*polemios*] of man's salvation . . . brought Simon . . . and led them [many people in Rome] astray."[79] Here he refers to Simon Magus as the human agent of heresy in the church. For Eusebius, idol worship is a disease and polytheism is demonic.[80] "The demons" (*daimones*) led people astray through Simon and his magical sorceries. Simon was "raised up . . . by the evil power which hates all that is good and plots against the salvation of [hu]man-kind." But "divine and celestial grace" put out "the flames of the Evil One before they could spread."[81] As Simon's influence grew in other places, including Rome, the "all-gracious and kindly providence of the universe" brought Peter (another Simon, incidentally) to Rome, through whose gospel proclamation "Simon's power was extinguished."[82] Si-mon's successor, Menander, is described in a similar way, as "a second tool of the devil's ingenuity,"[83] and thus are many subsequent heretics introduced and dispatched, including the Gnostics, Montanists, and Manichaeans.[84] The jealous and "evil demon" also launched persecu-tion against Origen, Polycarp, and the martyrs of Lyons.[85] Toward the very end of his narrative, Eusebius wrote in very explicit terms about demonic influence in the life of Constantine's co-ruler Licinius and its impact in terms of the persecution of the church. Once Christianity had become tolerated and the churches settled down once more, he writes, "In the eyes of the evil-minded envy and of the malignant demon the sight of what was going on was beyond endurance," and Licinius em-bodied the devil's hostility against the church, thereby "rushing into conflict with the God of the universe."[86] In short, Eusebius perceived the cause of heresy and persecution as the work of the devil and an aberration to orthodoxy, and he illustrates amply his adaptation and transformation of this traditional historiographical feature.[87]

79. Eusebius, *Church History* 2.13 (Williamson, 47).
80. Eusebius, *Church History* 1.3.
81. Eusebius, *Church History* 2.14 (Williamson, 48).
82. Eusebius, *Church History* 2.14–15 (Williamson, 49).
83. Eusebius, *Church History* 3.26 (Williamson, 89).
84. Eusebius, *Church History* 4.7, 5.14, 7.31.
85. Eusebius, *Church History* 6.39, 4.15, and 5.1–2, respectively.
86. Eusebius, *Church History* 10.8 (Williamson, 328–29).
87. Incidentally, Eusebius does not blame the devil alone for persecution or trouble in the church. Book 8 of the *Church History* opens with a lament regarding the Great Persecution of Diocletian beginning in AD 303, and he attributes its cause to God's righteous punishment of his people for their spiritual laxity and disunity, calling them "a lot of atheists," going from

Theodoret

Theodoret's *Church History* is much more limited in both its scope and size, and its repeated emphases actually provide clues as to his situation and the difficulties in which he was embroiled at the time of writing, clues that are bolstered by examining his letters written around the same time. The Arian controversy and its aftermath occupy four of the five books of Theodoret's *History*. His constant emphasis on piety versus impiety leads one to think that Theodoret may have been on the defensive regarding his own piety (which he was, as it happens). In Theodoret's historical program, the church is a ship, providentially steered by the Lord as its captain, but buffeted by storms of heretics and persecutors. In this case, the heretics and persecutors (for the most part) are one and the same: the Arians. The way in which Theodoret describes the course of Arianism is both traditional and Christian, as is well illustrated in the first chapter of book 1.

After a brief prologue, Theodoret describes how the church's persecutors (before Constantine) were like hurricanes that were eventually hushed so that the church could "enjoy a settled calm."[88] This settlement came via Constantine's divine "apostolic" calling. But "the devil, full of all envy and wickedness [*pamponēros kai baskanos daimōn*], the destroyer [*alastōr*] of [hu]mankind, unable to bear the sight of the church, . . . stirred up plans of evil counsel, eager to sink the vessel steered by the Creator and Lord of the universe."[89] Finding that idolatry ("the error of the Greeks") had been exposed and was no longer practiced (i.e., no longer a threat to the church), the devil pursued an alternate strategy. "He did not dare to declare open war against our God and Saviour," but he found some men who were morally weak and "slaves to ambition and vainglory [and] made them fit instruments for the execution of his designs."[90] The devil drew people back into a reverse idolatry—no longer the worship of idols or creatures, but the reduction of "the Creator and Maker of all . . . to a level with the creature."[91] Arius was "stung by this passion" (i.e., jealousy, *phthonos*), and "envy [*phthonos*] would not let him rest." Thus he became "an

"wickedness to wickedness," and stirring up "divine judgment" (*Church History* 8.1 [Williamson, 257–58]). In this attribution, he is followed by Socrates, who holds to an idea dubbed "cosmic sympathy," in which events in the state influence events in the church and vice versa. Socrates also believed that disturbances in the church sometimes proceed "from our iniquities" (Socrates Scholasticus, *Church History* 5, preface [*NPNF*² 2:118]).

88. Theodoret, *Church History* 1.1 (*NPNF*² 3:33).
89. Theodoret, *Church History* 1.1 (*NPNF*² 3:33).
90. Theodoret, *Church History* 1.1 (*NPNF*² 3:33–34).
91. Theodoret, *Church History* 1.1 (*NPNF*² 3:34).

instrument" used by "the enemy of the church."[92] By these descriptions as well as the use of the image of the enemy coming at night to sow tares among the wheat (Matt. 13:24–30), Theodoret set the stage for the entire history. The net effect of Arius's instigation of his heresy evokes a lament from Theodoret: "These were indeed scenes fit for the tragic stage. For it was not as in bygone days when the church was attacked by strangers and by enemies," but now it was attacked by those who are "members of one another, and belonged to one body."[93]

Theodoret (and Eusebius as well) sees the church's history as occurring on two planes, the divine and human, with conflicts both visible and invisible. Through the Arian party, the devil is in combat with God and his church. Since the devil is so prominent right at the outset of the work, one translator even remarks that the devil is "the principal agent of this history, after God!"[94] Theodoret uses the term *baskanos* for the devil, a strong word with multiple connotations appropriate to a malevolent agent.[95] It derives from *baskainō*, meaning "to bewitch" or "to give the evil eye" to someone. In the fourth century BC, it had associated meanings of "magic, sorcery, and witchcraft." By the fifth century AD, *baskanos* meant "a deceiver, evil one, envious or jealous one, or malignant power." It entailed not merely the idea of error but also demonic deceit and seduction.[96]

Throughout the *History*, the demonic and deceitful nature of the *baskanos* is manifest in the Arians' outrageous actions. They were morally corrupt and so perverse in their heresy that they were outdone in piety by the emperor Constantine, who was a recent convert, while the Arians were bishops! While Constantine was pious in advocating orthodoxy and concord within the church, and was its generous and kind protector and patron, the Arians advocated their heresy, returning

92. Theodoret, *Church History* 1.1 (NPNF[2] 3:34).

93. Theodoret, *Church History* 1.5 (NPNF[2] 3:43). This portion explaining the inception of the Arian controversy is markedly similar to Eusebius's explanation of the cause of Licinius's sudden reneging on the terms of toleration in the Edict of Milan, and his beginning to persecute the church once more, thereby running headlong into open conflict with Constantine (Eusebius, *Church History* 10.8).

94. Annick Martin, introduction to *Théodoret de Cyr: Histoire ecclésiastique, Livres I–II*, trans. L. Parmentier and G. C. Hansen, SC 501 (Paris: Cerf, 2006), 51, my translation; part of a longer section on combat between God and Satan in Theodoret's text (50–55).

95. This term appears in hagiography and martyrology as well (see the section "Causation" in chap. 4).

96. Martin Hinterberger, "Phthonos: A Pagan Relic in Byzantine Imperial Acclamations," in *Court Ceremonies and Rituals of Power in Byzantium and the Medieval Mediterranean: Comparative Perspectives*, ed. Alexander Beihammer, Stavroula Constantinou, and Maria Parani (Boston: Brill, 2013), 51–65. See further Matthew W. Dickie, "The Fathers of the Church and the Evil Eye," in *Byzantine Magic*, ed. Henry Maguire (Washington, DC: Dumbarton Oaks, 1995), 9–34.

the world to the error of idolatry and the way of deceiving demons. The Arians constantly stirred up strife and behaved abominably: they committed illegalities with respect to canon law; they were verbally abusive through slander and multiple calumnies of innocent bishops whom they wanted to destroy, framing them in various situations; they acted violently via exile (against Athanasius, John Chrysostom, and many others), physical force (against Hosius of Cordova), and occasionally murder (against Paulinus of Constantinople). Arius himself perished in an excruciatingly humiliating manner, still excommunicated. The persecution by the Arians showed no abating, however, because they were working vigorously to influence the rulers of the empire, to sway their theology and therefore their ecclesiastical politics. The Arian-influenced emperors Constantius II and Valens continued to persecute the orthodox, while a respite was obtained in the reigns of the orthodox emperors Constans, Gratian, Jovian, and especially Theodosius I. Julian the Apostate made a complete and utter shipwreck of himself but did not conquer the church, and his reign only lasted a few brief years.

Theodoret did not really give a happy ending like the other historians who concluded with the realized ideal of empire-wide peace. Rather, Theodoret issued a challenge in which he illustrates his understanding of Providence, and possibly his critique of the contemporary administration. Although brutalities and impieties came against the church in the past as well, the church had risen up again and flourished after only a few years, while its impious persecutors disappeared. Times of peace often lead to "softening," complacency, and cowardliness; but war and conflict are sometimes more profitable than peace, since they build up our courage and teach us to hold the things of this world lightly.[97]

History, Continuity, and the Construction of Christian Identity

Throughout our study of Christian histories, there is a clear sense in which the historians are facilitating the construction of a distinct identity for the church by telling its story. A time of radical change and upheaval in the empire such as Eusebius experienced called for a new

---

97. Theodoret, *Church History* 5.41 (NPNF[2] 3:158–59). This idea accords with his explanation of various aspects of Providence in *De Providentia*, an expanded version of chap. 6 in the *Cure for Pagan Maladies*. He writes there that what we might conventionally consider "bad" or "evil," like poverty or illness, has benefits that might outweigh the "good" situations of wealth or health. One must trust Providence for the results of one's situation.

kind of history.[98] In his view, the church is an institution of ancient and divine origins, much as the Romans liked to think of themselves and their national history, and as they also perceived the Jewish nation. In his preface, Eusebius ties the church to Christ, its divine founder, writing, "My book will start with a conception too sublime and overwhelming for man to grasp—the dispensation and divinity of our Saviour Christ. Any man who intends to commit to writing the record of the Church's history is bound to go right back to Christ Himself, whose name we are privileged to share, and to start with the beginning of a dispensation more divine than the world realizes."[99] However, he insists that the faithful people of God did not originate at the time of the incarnation, but rather existed as far back as Abraham and Jacob, as God had appeared in theophanies and visions to those in every generation who "were distinguished for righteousness and the purity of their religion."[100]

Because of its "antiquity and divine character," Christianity ought not to be perceived as a new cult or mystery religion, "appearing yesterday for the first time"—this was the message of the apologists, which Eusebius picks up in his introduction.[101] Moreover, because Christianity springs from a divine origin, not just the incarnate Christ but the preincarnate Logos, it therefore can never be conquered and must necessarily triumph. Thus Eusebius explains the Constantinian achievement and the position of strength in which the church in his day found itself as a fulfillment of prophecy (Pss. 98:1–2; 46:8–9; 37:33–36).[102] Eusebius's project was to show how the divine plan had been in operation before the great empires of the world ever existed, and how this plan was intended to culminate providentially in what the Roman Empire had wrought. A proper biblical and theological understanding of the church's struggles for legitimacy vis-à-vis the empire led Eusebius to the conclusion that the empire itself was not Christianity's enemy; instead, a malevolent agent, the devil, was responsible for persecutions from without (an idea squarely in line with the apologetic and martyrological literature) as well as heresies from within once persecutions had subsided. Theodoret followed this causal explanation much more closely than the laymen historians Socrates and Sozomen. The latter were more likely to attribute causation to human decision making and the personal

---

98. Eusebius, *Church History* 10.1 (Williamson, 303–4: "After those terrifying darksome sights and stories I was now privileged to celebrate such things as in truth many righteous men and martyrs of God before us desired to see on earth and did not see, and to hear and did not hear").

99. Eusebius, *Church History* 1.1 (Williamson, 2).

100. Eusebius, *Church History* 1.2 (Williamson, 4).

101. Eusebius, *Church History* 1.2 (Williamson, 3).

102. Eusebius, *Church History* 10.1 (trans. Williamson, 303–4).

characteristics of those involved (e.g., whether they were motivated by a virtuous desire for peace or inclined toward fractiousness), although they also wrote in more muted tones of Divine Providence aiding the godly. In addition, these two historians show a greater indebtedness to classical historical understandings of causation than to the Eusebian providential model.[103] Theodoret, however, returned more faithfully to the Eusebian style, consistently presenting the devil as the underlying causal influence behind heresies and persecution of the orthodox (like himself). Both bishops continued in the historical causal tradition of the apologists and the martyrs' two-tiered understanding of history as having simultaneously an earthly and a heavenly dimension, similar to the descriptions of Daniel 7.

Eusebius and Theodoret evince a further common historical and apologetic interest, namely, a concern for continuity in the church through apostolic succession. The idea of historical continuity via apostolic succession and notable Christian teachers was critical both for the church's identity and for preserving doctrinal integrity. Throughout his narrative Eusebius especially notes the succession of bishops in various major sees of the empire; and he highlights renowned teachers like Origen, whose doctrines were consistent with the Rule of Truth, the encapsulation of the apostolic teaching. Eusebius's copious citations of sources over a three-hundred-year span shows "continuity of the church's traditions and teachings," carefully preserved and transmitted.[104] At the close of book 5 in his *Church History*, Theodoret reports the passing of notable bishop-teachers who were heroes to him, though not well regarded doctrinally by the time of Theodoret's writing. These included Theodore of Mopsuestia and Diodore of Tarsus, champions of orthodoxy who combated the "Arian madness" in their time. Theodoret follows this notice with an entire list of episcopal successions in various sees of the empire, including Rome, Antioch, Alexandria, Jerusalem, and Constantinople, carefully indicating which bishops were orthodox and which were various kinds of heretics: Arians, Eustathians, or, as Macedonius of Constantinople is labeled, "the enemy of the Holy Ghost."[105]

It is significant that Eusebius, the pioneering church historian, decided that his history would highlight men and women who made contributions to the kingdom of God: those who led, taught, suffered, pastored, preached, and wrote, thereby serving as agents to make the church of his time the grand institution that it was. However, he recognized

103. Sophie Lunn-Rockliffe ("Diabolical Motivations," 125–28) explores this idea in more depth.
104. Adler, "Early Christian Historians and Historiography," 593.
105. Theodoret, *Church History* 5.39 (NPNF[2] 3:159).

that these people in and of themselves did not make the church great, but rather the One who empowered them did. He calls these people "ambassadors of the divine word," by which he likely refers to Christ, not merely to the Scriptures. His view of the church's story, then, is that Christ's mission in the world had extended down to his time, and it would continue into the future via the medium of Christ's followers who continued his work in various ways. This is a healthy view for believers even today, a reminder to value not only the great teachers of sound doctrine who strengthen and nurture the church now, but also those in the past to whom we are connected because of Christ, the sure foundation, and the era-transcending nature of his church. It is critical that this generation commemorate the "ambassadors of the divine word" in previous generations, for they have truly built on the foundation of Christ and of the apostles and martyrs, and we too continue to build the church based on their contributions.

Conclusions and Trajectories

Simply stated, . . . my job is to transmit to you all the memories I have within me. Memories of the past. . . . It is how wisdom comes. And how we shape our future.

—Lois Lowry, *The Giver* (Boston: Houghton Mifflin, 1993), 97–98

In chapter 1 we began with a quote advising us to know "our pertinent history" and "where we've been" in order to move forward in life. This volume has been considering "where we've been" in faith, practice, and historical circumstance, and how Christian identity has been challenged, shaped, and strengthened by those circumstances in the first five centuries of the church.

The work of identity building in Christianity began in the Old Testament as God admonished his people to look back to his miraculous and gracious deeds on their behalf. Israel was God's chosen nation, a people called to be faithful to a gracious and faithful God. They were also called to be holy like God, reflecting that holiness to others (an evangelistic characteristic) to draw them to God's goodness. In the New Testament, that identity carried forward, although the incarnation both continued and changed everything. God's self-revelation in Christ called believers to faith, holiness, and self-sacrificial discipleship and gave them a mission to carry the gospel forward globally.

Opposition was not slow in coming, but the church had been fore-warned of persecution by its founder, who not only had encountered rejection and persecution by "his own" who "did not receive him" (John 1:11), but who also was in fact the Suffering Servant of Isaiah's prophecy. In its gradual estrangement from Judaism, and also in its frequent encounters with Greco-Roman pagan culture, the church developed arguments in self-defense that were at times rational and persuasive (and sometimes inviting), and at other times polemical and accusing. As Paul reasoned philosophically with Jews, Stoics, and Epicureans, seeking a congenial, hospitable, and reasonable hearing for the gospel (Acts 17), Peter advised the churches of the diaspora not to give offense in their various settings (1 Pet. 2). Nonetheless, they were to be clear about their identity: in the world but not of it. They were sojourners and exiles, living in a world to which they should not conform. They were to be a holy, chosen race, and living stones being built into a holy temple and living as a holy priesthood. They were also called to *imitatio Christi*, conformity to the image of the Suffering Servant as a global, suffering brotherhood (1 Pet. 2–5). Significantly, all the images for the church are collective, emphasizing a corporate, not an individual identity.

To assess "where we've been," let us review the legacy bequeathed to us by the ancient church. The apologists presented the church as holding a truthful, intelligent, and reasonable faith, one that is credible and historical, grounded in facts and provable data, not in mythical fables. Jesus's life, death, and resurrection are historical and located by apologetic literature in the context of the Roman Empire. Christians are honorable and truly virtuous, even by the standards of nonbelievers and their respected philosophers. Their faith is ancient and venerable, the apologists argued, having a more ancient pedigree than the Greeks and Romans themselves. In fact, in their continuity with Judaism, Christians are heirs of the Old Testament covenant promises fulfilled in Jesus, the promised Messiah. Judaism is superseded but not rejected by the Christians, as Jews and Christians hold a shared revelation. In fact, teachers of dubious virtue like Marcion (who advocated a very different God, rejecting the One revealed in the Scriptures) were considered agents of the devil, spreading lies and deception, heresies that divide and splinter the church and violate a correct understanding of the Scriptures.

Responsibility for correct worship lies in the free will of every person, but truth and true worship are counterfeited at every turn by the devil and demonic agents who are behind heresies, persecution, and idolatry. These malicious agents cannot stand to see the progress of God's people, growing numerically and handing down the apostolic teaching with integrity and accuracy in sound doctrine; therefore they entice, deceive, and manipulate men and women to lead others astray with false doctrine. The pastoral note sounded by Irenaeus offers a healthy perspective for Christians as we engage false teachers: these teachings need to be exposed and understood in order to be overthrown. But we should remember the real agents of heresy and discord by whom these teachers are deceived. Therefore, as much as possible, engage false teachers with wisdom and love, hoping that some may return to the truth. Further, the heresiologists alert us to the great danger of teachers who twist the Scriptures and who interpret it apart from its theological and historical foundations in the apostolic teaching and creedal commitments.

Drawing upon the biblical imagery of sojourn and exile, Christians know they are transient in this world, temporary dwellers in the Earthly City, but citizens of the Heavenly City. Augustine's historical apologetic offers timely political wisdom, as he warns strongly against equating any earthly, worldly institution with the kingdom of God. Through his historical analysis he demonstrates that just because tragedy befalls a nation, that is not a certain indication of God's abandonment. Conversely, just because a nation grows into a prosperous empire, that is not a certain indication of its moral superiority or of divine sanction. There have always been victories and tragedies in human history, but ultimately one must wait to see what Providence (not Fate) seeks to accomplish.

The martyrs help Christians understand themselves through several powerful images. Christians are overcomers (Rev. 1–3), victims neither of the state machinery nor of demonic forces manipulating idol-worshiping pagans. They are victors against the devil and his agents, as they war "against the authorities, against the cosmic powers," not merely "flesh and blood" (Eph. 6:12). The martyrs saw themselves in collective terms as a family, a fellowship of suffering bound together in their call to *imitatio Christi*. They had taken on the name of Christ and therefore a new identity, to the point that when they were asked their name under interrogation, they answered simply "Christian." For them, this new identity superseded all earthly loyalties to family or allegiance to country. No matter who or what else they were in daily life, they were Christian first. This identity then carried forward to the generations after Constantine's establishment, generations who looked back to the time of the martyrs for encouragement, inspiration, and instruction in living and witnessing.

Reading and encountering Christian lives through biographies confronts us with our own worldliness and the ease and comfortability of our Christianity. We are struck by their otherworldliness and are inspired to strive for holiness, which breeds a host of spiritual virtues. We can also be challenged by the intense level of discipleship apparent in the stories of Antony, Macrina, and Melania. The commitment to deny oneself and die daily to one's own desires remains constant, whether in times of freedom or persecution. Early Christians show us that overcoming the devil's temptations to sin was possible through a fervent, loving attachment to Jesus and through the faithful, obedient, and free exercise of the will and involvement, under Jesus's lordship, in the Christian disciplines: intense prayer, fasting, immersion in the Scriptures, and times of withdrawal and contemplation, balanced by active service and lavish generosity. This *attachment* to Jesus along with its host of fruits is only possible when we are *detached* from the world and its snares of money, possessions, and the lure of self-indulgence at every turn; not that we must necessarily follow the monastic route, but we must recognize and rid ourselves of the idols that easily creep into our hearts and divert us from our true loyalty to Jesus. Only thus can we serve him freely, sacrificially, and unstintingly.

Finally, from the study of church history proper, we gather that the God of history guides all human events providentially toward his own telos. Fate and chance (fortune) are categorically excluded as driving forces of history. In their insistence on providential guidance, the ancient Christian historians exemplified the idea of historian Hayden White that "there can be no proper history without the presupposition of a full-blown metahistory by which to justify those interpretive strategies necessary" to explain historical events and the facts that comprise one's historical narrative.[1] The late antique historians' metanarrative was salvation history, the memory of God's dealings with his people, Israel.

A further task of the historical writer (whether professional or occasional) involves maintaining social and collective memory, for it is this memory that creates identity for persons, nations (like China and Romania in our opening examples in the preface), and institutions like the church. Jay Green avers that

> these social entities might display an outward appearance of functionality and strength, but if they proceed in a state of willful amnesia, . . . they will be no more capable of sustaining long-term civic health than the advanced Alzheimer's patient is of carrying on a meaningful conversation with an old friend. Social organisms must have within them historically minded individuals who will help cultivate an honest, open, sometimes uncomfortable relationship with their pasts if they ever hope to develop in responsible ways. . . . The demands of active remembrance should be borne by us all.[2]

1. Eric Miller, John Fea, and Jay Green, "So What Is the Historian's Vocation?," *Books & Culture: A Christian Review* 18, no. 1 (2012): 21 (Eric Miller).
2. Ibid., 23 (Jay Green).

Remembrance is a command from God to his people in the Old Testament, a mandate from Jesus to his disciples in the Gospels, an urgent exhortation from the apologists and martyrs, a task carried out by biographers and historians, and still an ongoing work in the service of the church to be fulfilled by Jesus's disciples. Noble people and notable events should be commemorated and not forgotten, and great examples of virtuous character and steadfastness of sound doctrine ought to be remembered, praised, emulated, and passed to the next generation, so that they will "set their hope in God and not forget the works of God" (Ps. 78:7). As we remember our forebears, we ought always to look to their God, the God of history, of whom they bore witness, our great God who has accomplished his work through women and men in every era to build up the church.

BIBLIOGRAPHY

Primary Sources

Ammianus Marcellinus. *The Later Roman Empire (AD 354–378)*. Translated by Walter Hamilton. Introduction and notes by Andrew Wallace-Hadrill. New York: Penguin, 1986.

Athanasius. *Athanase d'Alexandrie: Vie d'Antoine [Life of Antony]*. Translated by G. J. M. Bartelink. SC 400. Paris: Cerf, 1994.

———. *Four Discourses against the Arians*. Translated by Philip Schaff and Henry Wace, 303–447. NPNF² 4. Peabody, MA: Hendrickson, 1994.

———. *Life of Antony*. In *Early Christian Lives*. Translated and edited by Carolinne White. New York: Penguin, 1998.

———. *St. Antony of the Desert by Athanasius*. Translated by J. B. McLaughlin. Rockford, IL: TAN Books, 1995.

Augustine. *City of God*. Edited by G. R. Evans. Translated by Henry Bettenson. London: Penguin, 1972.

———. *Confessions*. Translated by R. S. Pine-Coffin. London: Penguin, 1961.

———. *On the Morals of the Manichaeans*. Translated by Richard Stothert, 65–89. NPNF¹ 4. Peabody, MA: Hendrickson, 1994.

Clement of Alexandria. *Miscellanies*. Edited by Alexander Roberts and James Donaldson, 299–567. ANF 2. Peabody, MA: Hendrickson, 1994.

deFerrari, Roy J., ed. *Early Christian Biographies*. FC 15. Washington, DC: Catholic University of America Press, 1952.

Egeria. *Diary of a Pilgrimage*. Edited by George E. Gingras. ACW 38. New York: Newman, 1970.

Eusebius of Caesarea. *Demonstration of the Gospel*. 2 vols. Translated by W. J. Ferrar. London: SPCK, 1920.

————. *Eusèbe de Césarée: Histoire Ecclésiastique* [*History of the Church*]. 4 vols. Translation and annotation by Gustave Bardy. SC 31. Paris: Cerf, 2001.

————. *The History of the Church*. Translated by G. A. Williamson. Revised and edited by Andrew Louth. New York: Penguin, 1989.

————. *Life of Constantine*. Translated by Ernest Cushing Richardson, 405–610. *NPNF*² 1. Peabody, MA: Hendrickson, 1994.

————. *Preparation for the Gospel*. 2 vols. Translated by Edwin Hamilton Gifford. Grand Rapids: Baker, 1981.

Evagrius Ponticus. *Evagrius Ponticus: Praktikos and Chapters on Prayer*. Translated by John E. Bamberger. Kalamazoo, MI: Cistercian, 1981.

Gerontius. *Life of Saint Melania*. In *Handmaids of the Lord: Holy Women in Late Antiquity and the Early Middle Ages*. Translated by Joan M. Petersen, 311–61. Kalamazoo, MI: Cistercian, 1996.

————. *The Life of Melania the Younger: Introduction, Translation, and Commentary*. Translated by Elizabeth A. Clark. Studies in Women and Religion 14. New York: Edwin Mellen Press, 1985.

————. *Vie de sainte Mélanie* [*Life of Saint Melania*]. Edited and translated by Denys Gorce. SC 90. Paris: Cerf, 1962.

Gregory of Nazianzus. *Orations*. Translated by Charles Gordon Browne and James Edward Swallow, 185–434. *NPNF*² 7. Peabody, MA: Hendrickson, 1994.

Gregory of Nyssa. *Grégoire de Nysse: Vie de sainte Macrine* [*Life of Saint Macrina*]. Translated by Pierre Maraval. SC 178. Paris: Cerf, 1971.

————. *Life of Macrina*. In *Handmaids of the Lord: Holy Women in Late Antiquity and the Early Middle Ages*. Translated by Joan M. Petersen, 41–86. Kalamazoo, MI: Cistercian, 1996.

Herodotus. *The Histories*. Translated by Robin Waterfield. Oxford: Oxford University Press, 2008.

Hippolytus. *Refutation of All Heresies*. Translated by J. H. McMahon, 9–153. *ANF* 5. Peabody, MA: Hendrickson, 1994.

Irenaeus. *St. Irenaeus of Lyons: Against the Heresies*. Translated by Dominic J. Unger. ACW 55. New York: Paulist Press, 1992.

John Chrysostom. "Homily Delivered after the Remains of Martyrs Etc."; and "A Homily on Martyrs." In *John Chrysostom*, edited and translated by Wendy Mayer and Pauline Allen, 85–97. London: Routledge, 2000.

Justin Martyr. *1 Apology*. Edited by Alexander Roberts and James Donaldson, 163–87. *ANF* 1. Peabody, MA: Hendrickson, 1994.

Lucian. *How to Write History*. In *Ancient Literary Criticism: The Principal Texts in New Translations*, edited and translated by D. A. Russell and Michael Winterbottom, 536–47. Oxford: Clarendon, 1972.

Musurillo, Herbert, ed. and trans. *The Acts of the Christian Martyrs*. Oxford: Clarendon, 1972.

Peter Chrysologus. "Saint Peter Chrysologus: Selected Sermons and Letter to Eutyches." In *Saint Peter Chrysologus: Selected Sermons; and Saint Valerian; Homilies*, 25–287. Translated by George E. Ganss. FC 17. New York: Fathers of the Church, 1953.

Plato. *Apology*. Edited by Louis Dyer. Revised by Thomas Day Seymour. New Rochelle, NY: Cartazas, 1981.

———. *Republic*. In *Dialogues of Plato*. Translated by Benjamin Jowett. In *Great Books of the Western World*, vol. 6, edited by Mortimer Adler, 295–441. 2nd ed. Chicago: Encyclopedia Britannica, 1990.

Plutarch. *Fall of the Roman Republic*. Translated by Rex Warner. London: Penguin, 1972.

———. *Life of Coriolanus*. In *Makers of Rome*. Translated by Ian Scott-Kilvert, 15–52. London: Penguin, 1965.

———. *The Rise and Fall of Athens*. Translated by Ian Scott-Kilvert. London: Penguin, 1960.

Prudentius. *Prudentius: Peristephanon*. Translated by Sister M. Clement Eagan. FC 43. Washington, DC: Catholic University of America Press, 1962.

Socrates Scholasticus. *Church (Ecclesiastical) History*. Translated by A. C. Zenos, 1–178. NPNF² 2. Peabody, MA: Hendrickson, 1994.

———. *Histoire Ecclésiastique*. Edited and translated by P. Maraval and P. Peridon. Sources chrétiennes 477, 493, 505, 506. Paris: Cerf, 2004–2007.

Sozomen. *Ecclesiastical History*. Translated by Chester Hartranft, 179–427. NPNF² 2. Peabody, MA: Hendrickson, 1994.

———. *Histoire Ecclésiastique*. Edited and translated by A.-J. Festugiere, B. Grillet, and G. Sabbah. Sources chrétiennes 306, 418, 495, 516. Paris: Cerf, 1983–2008.

Suetonius. *Lives of the Twelve Caesars*. Translated by Robert Graves and Michael Grant. London: Penguin, 1979.

Tacitus. *Annals of Imperial Rome*. Rev. ed. Translated by Michael Grant. London: Penguin, 1971.

———. *Histories*. In *Complete Works of Tacitus*, edited by Moses Hadas, translated by Alfred John Church and William Jackson Broadribb, 419–673. New York: Modern Library, 1942.

Tertullian. *Ad Martyras (To the Martyrs)*. Translated by S. Thelwall, 693–96. ANF 3. Peabody, MA: Hendrickson, 1994.

———. *Apology*. Translated by S. Thelwall, 17–55. ANF 3. Peabody, MA: Hendrickson, 1994.

———. *The Passion of the Holy Martyrs Perpetua and Felicitas*. Translated by R. E. Wallis, 699–706. ANF 3. Peabody, MA: Hendrickson, 1994.

————. *Prescription against Heretics*. Translated by Peter Holmes, 243–65. *ANF* 3. Peabody, MA: Hendrickson, 1994.

————. *To the Nations*. Translated by Peter Holmes, 109–47. *ANF* 3. Peabody, MA: Hendrickson, 1994.

————. *A Treatise on the Soul*. Translated by Peter Holmes, 181–235. *ANF* 3. Peabody, MA: Hendrickson, 1994.

Theodoret of Cyrus. *Church History*. Edited by Philip Schaff and Henry Wace, 33–159. *NPNF*² 3. Peabody, MA: Hendrickson, 1994.

————. *Cure for Pagan Maladies*. Translated by Thomas Halton. ACW 67. New York: Newman, 2013.

————. *Théodoret de Cyr: Histoire ecclésiastique, Livres I–II* [*Ecclesiastical History, Books 1–2*]. Based on the Greek text by L. Parmentier and G. C. Hansen. Translated and annotated by P. Canivet, J. Bouffartigue, L. Pietri, F. Thelamon. Introduction by Annick Martin. SC 501. Paris: Cerf, 2006.

————. *Théodoret de Cyr: Histoire ecclésiastique, Livres III–V* [*Ecclesiastical History, Books 3–5*]. Based on the Greek text by L. Parmentier and G. C. Hansen. Translated and annotated by P. Canivet, J. Bouffartigue, L. Pietri, and F. Thelamon. Introduction by Annick Martin. SC 530. Paris: Cerf, 2009.

Theophilus of Antioch. *To Autolycus*. Translated by Marcus Dods, 89–121. *ANF* 2. Peabody, MA: Hendrickson, 1995.

Thucydides. *History of the Peloponnesian War*. Translated by Richard Crawley. Edited by W. Robert Connor. London: Everyman, 1993.

Valerian. "Saint Valerian, Homilies and Letter to the Monks." In *Saint Peter Chrysologus: Selected Sermons; and Saint Valerian; Homilies*, 291–440. Translated by George E. Ganss. FC 17. New York: Fathers of the Church, 1953.

Secondary Sources

Bamberger, John E., trans. *Evagrius Ponticus: Praktikos and Chapters on Prayer*. Kalamazoo, MI: Cistercian, 1981.

Barnes, Timothy D. *Early Christian Hagiography and Roman History*. Tübingen: Mohr Siebeck, 2010.

Bauman, Michael, and Martin Klauber. *Historians of the Christian Tradition*. Nashville: B&H, 1995.

Born, Lester K. "The Perfect Prince according to the Latin Panegyrists." *American Journal of Philology* 55 (1934): 20–35.

Bovon, François. *Studies in Early Christianity*. Grand Rapids: Baker, 2005.

Bowersock, G. W. *Martyrdom and Rome*. Cambridge: Cambridge University Press, 2002.

Boyarin, Daniel. *Dying for God: Martyrdom and the Making of Christianity and Judaism*. Stanford, CA: Stanford University Press, 1999.

Brook, Eric. "Hagiography, Modern Historiography, and Historical Representation." *Fides et Historia* 42, no. 2 (2010): 1–26.

Bruce, F. F. *The Book of the Acts*. NICNT. Grand Rapids: Eerdmans, 1988.

Burrows, Mark S. "Christianity in the Roman Forum: Tertullian and the Apologetic Use of History." In *The Christian and Judaic Invention of History*, edited by Jacob Neusner, 51–75. AAR Studies in Religion 55. Atlanta: Scholars Press, 1990.

Cameron, Averil. "How to Read Heresiology." *Journal of Medieval and Early Modern Studies* 33, no. 3 (2003): 471–92.

Castelli, Elizabeth. *Martyrdom and Memory: Early Christian Culture Making*. New York: Columbia University Press, 2005.

———. *Visions and Voyeurism: Holy Women and the Politics of Sight in Early Christianity*. Vol. 2 of *Protocol of the Colloquy of the Center for Hermeneutical Studies*. New Series. Edited by Christopher Ocker. Berkeley, CA: Center for Hermeneutical Studies, 1995.

Chesnut, Glenn F. *The First Christian Histories: Eusebius, Socrates, Sozomen, Theodoret, and Evagrius*. Macon, GA: Mercer University Press, 1986.

Chin, Catherine M., and Caroline T. Schroeder, eds. *Melania: Early Christianity through the Life of One Family*. Oakland: University of California Press, 2017.

Collingwood, R. G. *The Idea of History*. Rev. ed. Edited by Jan van der Dussen. New York: Oxford University Press, 1993.

Cope, Glenn Melvin. "An Analysis of the Heresiological Method of Theodoret of Cyrus in the *Haereticarum Fabularum Compendium*." PhD diss., Catholic University of America, 1990.

Croke, Brian, "The Origins of the Christian World Chronicle." In *History and Historians in Late Antiquity*, ed. Brian Croke and Alanna M. Emmett, 116–31. Sydney: Pergamon Press, 1983.

Daley, Brian E. *The Hope of the Early Church: A Handbook of Patristic Eschatology*. Cambridge: Cambridge University Press, 1991; repr., Peabody, MA: Hendrickson, 2003. Page references are to the 2003 edition.

Danto, A. C. "Mere Chronicle and History Proper." *Journal of Philosophy* 50, no. 6 (1953): 173–82.

Davis, Stephen. *The Cult of St. Thecla*. Oxford: Oxford University Press, 2001.

Di Berardino, Angelo, and Basil Studer, eds. *The Patristic Period*. Vol. 1 of *History of Theology*. Translated by Matthew J. O'Connell. Collegeville, MN: Liturgical Press, 1997.

Dickie, Matthew W. "The Fathers of the Church and the Evil Eye." In *Byzantine Magic*, edited by Henry Maguire, 9–34. Washington, DC: Dumbarton Oaks, 1995.

Droge, Arthur J., and James D. Tabor. *A Noble Death: Suicide and Martyrdom among Christians and Jews in Antiquity*. San Francisco: HarperSanFrancisco, 1992.

Dulles, Avery. *A History of Apologetics*. Eugene, OR: Wipf & Stock, 1999.

Dvornik, Frances. *Early Christian and Byzantine Political Philosophy: Origins and Backgrounds*. 2 vols. Dumbarton Oaks Studies 9. Washington, DC: Dumbarton Oaks Center for Byzantine Studies, 1966.

Edwards, Mark J., Martin Goodman, Simon Price, and Christopher Rowland, eds. *Apologetics in the Roman Empire: Pagans, Jews, and Christians*. Oxford: Oxford University Press, 1999.

Eidinow, Esther. *Luck, Fate and Fortune: Antiquity and Its Legacy*. Oxford: Oxford University Press, 2011.

Fea, John. *Why Study History? Reflecting on the Importance of the Past*. Grand Rapids: Baker Academic, 2013.

Foster, Richard. *Celebration of Discipline*. San Francisco: HarperCollins, 1998.

Fox, Robin Lane. *Pagans and Christians in the Mediterranean World from the Second Century AD to the Conversion of Constantine*. London: Penguin, 1986.

Garbarino, Collin S. "Reclaiming Martyrdom: Augustine's Reconstruction of Martyrdom in Late Antique North Africa." MA thesis, Louisiana State University and A&M College, 2007.

George, Timothy. *Reading Scripture with the Reformers*. Downers Grove, IL: IVP Academic, 2011.

Grant, Michael. *Greek and Roman Historians: Information and Misinformation*. London, New York: Routledge, 1995.

———, ed. *Readings in the Classical Historians*. New York: Scribners, 1992.

Grant, Robert M. "The Uses of History in the Church before Nicaea." *Studia Patristica* 11 (1972): 166–84.

Harvey, Susan Ashbrook, and David Hunter, eds. *The Oxford Handbook of Early Christian Studies*. Oxford: Oxford University Press, 2008.

Hinterberger, Martin. "Envy and Nemesis in the *Vita Basilii* and Leo the Deacon: Literary Mimesis or Something More?," in *History as Literature in Byzantium: Papers from the Fortieth Spring Symposium of Byzantine Studies, University of Birmingham, April 2007*, edited by Ruth J. Macrides, 187–203. Burlington, VT: Ashgate, 2010.

———. "Phthonos: A Pagan Relic in Byzantine Imperial Acclamations." In *Court Ceremonies and Rituals of Power in Byzantium and the Medieval Mediterranean: Comparative Perspectives*, edited by Alexander Beihammer, Stavroula Constantinou, and Maria Parani, 51–65. Boston: Brill, 2013.

Holmes, Stephen. *Listening to the Past: The Place of Tradition in Theology*. Grand Rapids: Baker Academic, 2002.

Hurtado, Larry. *At the Origins of Christian Worship*. Grand Rapids: Eerdmans, 1999.

Husbands, Mark, and Jeffrey Greenman, eds. *Ancient Faith for the Church's Future*. Downers Grove, IL: IVP Academic, 2008.

Kim, Young Richard. "The Transformation of Heresiology in the *Panarion* of Epiphanius of Cyprus." In *Shifting Genres in Late Antiquity*, edited by Geoffrey Greatrex and Hugh Elton, with the assistance of Lucas McMahon, 53–65. Farnham, UK: Routledge, 2016.

Laing, Stefana Dan. "Theodoret of Cyrus and the Ideal Monarch." PhD diss., Southern Baptist Theological Seminary, 2004.

Leemans, Johann, ed. *The Discourse of Martyrdom and the Construction of Christian Identity in the History of Christianity*. Leuven: Peeters, 2005.

LeGoff, Jacques. *History and Memory*. Translated by Steven Rendall and Elizabeth Claman. New York: Columbia University Press, 1992.

Lewis, Nicola Denzey. *Cosmology and Fate in Gnosticism and Greco-Roman Antiquity: Under Pitiless Skies*. Leiden: Brill, 2013.

Lunn-Rockliffe, Sophie. "Diabolical Motivations: The Devil in Ecclesiastical Histories from Eusebius to Evagrius." In *Shifting Genres in Late Antiquity*, edited by Geoffrey Greatrex and Hugh Elton, with the assistance of Lucas McMahon, 119–31. Farnham, UK: Routledge, 2016.

Markus, R. A. *Saeculum: History and Society in the Theology of St. Augustine*. Cambridge: Cambridge University Press, 1970.

McCarty, V. K. "Beauty for the Rest of Us: Re-considering Gregory of Nyssa's *On Virginity*." Paper presented at the Fourth Annual Conference of the Sophia Institute, Union Theological Seminary, New York, 2012.

McGrath, Alister. *Roots That Refresh*. London: Hodder & Stoughton, 1992.

McKenzie, Steven. *How to Read the Bible: History, Prophecy, Literature*. Oxford: Oxford University Press, 2005.

Milburn, R. L. P. *Early Christian Interpretations of History*. London: Black, 1954.

Mins, Dennis, and Paul Parvis. *Justin: Philosopher and Martyr*. Oxford: Oxford University Press, 2009.

Momigliano, Arnaldo. *The Classical Foundations of Modern Historiography*. Berkeley: University of California Press, 1990.

———. *Essays in Ancient and Modern Historiography*. Middletown, CT: Wesleyan University Press, 1982.

Moss, Candida R. *Ancient Christian Martyrdom: Diverse Practices, Theologies, and Traditions*. New Haven: Yale University Press, 2012.

Muehlberger, Ellen. "Salvage: Macrina and the Christian Project of Cultural Reclamation." *Church History* 82, no. 2 (2012): 273–97.

Neusner, Jacob. "The Birth of History in Christianity and Judaism." In *The Christian and Judaic Invention of History*, edited by Jacob Neusner, 3–15. AARSR 55. Atlanta: Scholars Press, 1990.

Parvis, Sara, and Paul Foster, eds. *Justin Martyr and His Worlds*. Minneapolis: Fortress, 2007.

Patterson, L. G. *God and History in Early Christian Thought: A Study of Themes from Justin Martyr to Gregory the Great*. New York: Seabury, 1967.

Pelikan, Jaroslav. *Christianity and Classical Culture: The Metamorphosis of Natural Theology in the Christian Encounter with Hellenism*. New Haven: Yale University Press, 1993.

Petersen, Joan, ed. and trans. *Handmaids of the Lord: Holy Women in Late Antiquity and the Early Middle Ages*. Kalamazoo, MI: Cistercian, 1996.

Prothero, Stephen. *Religious Literacy: What Every American Needs to Know—and Doesn't*. New York: Harper Collins, 2007.

Quasten, Johannes. *The Golden Age of Greek Patristic Literature*. Vol. 3 of *Patrology*. Utrecht: Spectrum, 1966.

Rohrbacher, David. *The Historians of Late Antiquity*. London: Routledge, 2002.

Rousseau, Philip. "Christian Asceticism and the Early Monks." In *Early Christianity: Origins and Evolution to A.D. 600*, edited by Ian Hazlett, 112–22. Nashville: Abingdon, 1991.

Russell, D. A., and Michael Winterbottom, eds. and trans. *Ancient Literary Criticism: The Principal Texts in New Translations*. Oxford: Clarendon, 1972.

Salisbury, Joyce. *Perpetua's Passion: The Death and Memory of a Young Roman Woman*. New York: Routledge, 1997.

Schauf, Scott. *The Divine in Acts and in Ancient Historiography*. Minneapolis: Fortress, 2015.

Schneemelcher, Wilhelm, ed. *Writings Related to the Apostles*. Vol. 2 of *New Testament Apocrypha*. Edited and translated by Robert McLachlan Wilson. Philadelphia: Westminster, 1964.

Schott, Jeremy. *Christianity, Empire, and the Making of Religion in Late Antiquity*. Philadelphia: University of Pennsylvania Press, 2008.

———. "Heresiology as Universal History in Epiphanius's *Panarion*." *Zeitschrift für Antikes Christentum* 10 (2007): 546–63.

Sittser, Gerald. *Water from a Deep Well*. Downers Grove, IL: InterVarsity, 2007.

Sterling, Gregory E. *Historiography and Self-Definition: Josephos, Luke-Acts and Apologetic Historiography*. NovTSup 64. Leiden: Brill, 1992. Reprint, Atlanta: SBL, 2005.

Stevenson, James, ed. *A New Eusebius: Documents Illustrating the History of the Church to AD 337*. Revised by W. H. C. Frend. London: SPCK, 1987.

Sulek, Marty. "On the Classical Meaning of *Philanthropia*." *Non-profit and Voluntary Sector Quarterly* 39, no. 3 (2010): 385–408.

Thomas, G. S. R. "Maximin Daia's Policy and the Edicts of Toleration." *L'Antiquité Classique* 37, no. 1 (1968): 172–85.

Trenkner, Sophie. *The Greek Novella in the Classical Period*. Cambridge: Cambridge University Press, 1958.

Trompf, G. W. *Early Christian Historiography: Narratives of Retribution*. London: Equinox, 2000.

Urbainczyk, Theresa. *Socrates of Constantinople*. Ann Arbor: University of Michigan Press, 1997.

———. *Theodoret of Cyrrhus: The Bishop and the Holy Man*. Ann Arbor: University of Michigan Press, 2002.

Volf, Miroslav. *The End of Memory: Remembering Rightly in a Violent World*. Grand Rapids: Eerdmans, 2006.

Wilken, Robert. *The Christians as the Romans Saw Them*. New Haven: Yale University Press, 1984.

———. *Remembering the Christian Past*. Grand Rapids: Eerdmans, 1995.

———. *The Spirit of Early Christian Thought*. New Haven: Yale University Press, 2003.

Willard, Dallas. *Spirit of the Disciplines*. San Francisco: HarperSanFrancisco, 1988.

Williams, Daniel H. *Retrieving the Tradition and Renewing Evangelicalism: A Primer for Suspicious Protestants*. Grand Rapids: Eerdmans, 1999.

———. "*Similis et Dissimilis*: Gauging Our Expectations of the Early Fathers." In *Ancient Faith for the Church's Future*, edited by Mark Husbands and Jeffrey Greenman, 69–89. Downers Grove, IL: IVP Academic, 2008.

Williams, Rowan. *Why Study the Past? The Quest for the Historical Church*. Grand Rapids: Eerdmans, 2005.

Wills, Lawrence Mitchell. *The Jewish Novel in the Ancient World*. Ithaca, NY: Cornell University Press, 1995.

Young, Frances, Lewis Ayres, and Andrew Louth, eds. *The Cambridge History of Early Christian Literature*. Cambridge: Cambridge University Press, 2004.

Young, Robin Darling. *In Procession before the World: Martyrdom as Public Liturgy in Early Christianity*. The Père Marquette Lecture in Theology. Milwaukee: Marquette University Press, 2001.

INDEX